MANAGEMENT SKILLS: PRACTICE AND EXPERIENCE

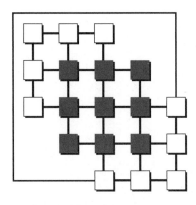

MANAGEMENT SKILLS:
PRACTICE AND EXPERIENCE

PATRICIA M. FANDT

University of Central Florida

with the cooperation of
Wilson Learning Corporation

WEST PUBLISHING COMPANY
Minneapolis/St. Paul   New York   Los Angeles   San Francisco

Copyediting: Julie Bach
Composition: Printing Arts, Inc.

WEST'S COMMITMENT TO THE ENVIRONMENT

Production, Prepress, Printing and Binding by West Publishing Company.

 PRINTED ON 10% POST CONSUMER RECYCLED PAPER

Library of Congress Cataloging-in-Publication Data

Fandt, Patricia M.
    Management skills: practice and experience/Patricia M. Fandt.
    p. cm.
    Includes index.

    ISBN 0-314-02810-2

    1. Executive ability.   2. Communication in management.
    3. Interpersonal relations.   4. Business communication.   I. Title.

HD38.2.F36 1994   IN PROCESS
658.4'09--dc20   93-6047
                                                              CIP

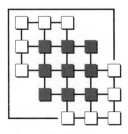

CONTENTS

Module 2

Leadership Skills: Providing Direction   *49*

Module 4

PART FOUR
ENABLING SKILLS:
RECOGNIZING THE NEED FOR
AND ADAPTING TO CHANGE   375

Module 8

Decisiveness Skills: Taking Action   *377*

INTRODUCTION   *377*

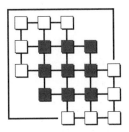

PREFACE

As men and women enter today's competitive business world, they need skills as well as knowledge of the material covered by courses in a business school curriculum. This book is designed to provide business students and future business professionals with the fundamental job-relevant skills and insights necessary for success. The book focuses on applying and practicing specific management skills: interactive skills, communication skills, problem-solving skills, and enabling skills. The learning model for the book is based on these identifiable skills, which are required for successful performance in managerial positions, regardless of the level or organizational setting.

The book can be used alone as the primary text in a course designed to develop competencies and managerial skills, or to supplement a more traditional text—either in organizational behavior, management principles, or general business courses—to accomplish the same objective.

PEDAGOGICAL FRAMEWORK

The text is based on learning through experience and is directed toward student involvement in developing and practicing job-relevant managerial skills. The text focuses on applying practical knowledge that is particularly relevant for present or prospective managers. The material is presented in the form of self-assessments, in-basket exercises, and skill-building exercises. Learners assume the role of a manager in various situations that require them to use the particular skill being taught.

Approach: Real World Management

The book contains in-basket exercises that are based on real-life situations and take place in a variety of settings. Whether or not the settings resemble a student's own organization or experience is unimportant. The problems presented are similar to those all managers face. The method of teaching in the text is based on practice. What students learn will be derived from a situational analysis and reinforced by practice and application. Learners can practice the skills over a range of situations and become aware of the importance of these skills to managerial success.

Before practicing a particular skill, learners have an opportunity to assess their level of competency by using assessment instruments in each module. Because the assessment instruments and the text material are closely related, students should find these tools especially helpful.

The in-basket exercises and the assessment instruments are based on materials developed by Wilson Learning Corporation (WLC). WLC is a human resources management consulting firm with more than twenty-five years of experience working with a wide variety of organizations across many industries and at all levels of management training and development. The in-basket exercises and the assessment instruments have been tested and used extensively in management training programs. The reliability ratings and validity of the assessment instruments are provided in the *Instructor's Resource Manual.* Additionally, the assessment instruments have been tested with a group of undergraduate and graduate business students; normative data is provided.

Content Focus

Studies examining the skills used by successful managers show that they need to work productively with others (using interpersonal and leadership skills), communicate effectively both in writing and orally, formulate and execute solutions to problems (using perception, organizing and planning, and decision-making skills), and recognize the need for and adapt to change (using decisiveness and flexibility skills). It is notable that these skills are behaviors. This is important because, unlike personality attributes, behaviors can be learned.

Evidence indicates that many managers have not learned these skills, and corporate America is aware of these shortcomings. A recent survey of Fortune 500 CEOs was conducted to determine their satisfaction with business school graduates. While many respondents were satisfied with the technical and analytical skills of business school graduates, most were not satisfied with graduates' management or interpersonal skills. Modern organizations need competent leaders. These are people who can help the organization prosper in a world of constant change and intense competition. Such leadership calls for technical, analytical, and interpersonal competence.

The text emphasizes how to learn these valuable managerial skills through the use of skill assessment instruments, practice, feedback, and role modeling. An intricate component of this text is a package of videos that allows the instructor to demonstrate successful managerial skills. Learning in all nine modules takes place through practice and experience guided by feedback from the instructor.

Skill Interrelationships

Managerial skills are interrelated and build upon one another in complex ways. For example, clarifying a goal and establishing a system to assure that necessary information is readily available (organizing and planning), combined with an ability to determine and understand essential factors (perception), should lead to heightened ability to evaluate facts in order to reach logical conclusions (decision making). Once the logical conclusions have been reached and courses of action have been selected based on the data, an individual is better able to assign tasks to others, following the requirements of the course of action (leadership). Getting others to follow the course of action requires an ability to pass those ideas on to them in a way they will accept (oral and written communication and interpersonal skills). Skills that facilitate the demonstration and development of all of the other behaviors are decisiveness and flexibility.

ORGANIZATION OF THE BOOK

Management Skills: Practice and Experience is organized into four parts—Interactive Skills, Communication Skills, Problem-Solving Skills, and Enabling Skills. **Interactive skills** are presented in Part I. These skills require face-to-face interaction with people and include interpersonal and leadership skills. **Communication skills,** including talking with and writing to others, are of critical importance for managers. Oral and written communication skills are covered in Part II. **Problem-solving skills** include formulating and executing solutions to problems. These skills are of critical importance when dealing with schedules, procedures, and other management issues. Part III covers the skills of perception, decision making, and organizing and planning. **Enabling skills,** covered in Part IV, are required both when working alone and when working closely with others. These skills always involve some type of action or reaction that helps tie the other three skills categories together. Flexibility and decisiveness fit in this category.

Each module is organized into six sections:

- **Introduction:** This section introduces the skill and provides a brief overview of how the skill is used in managerial work.
- **Skill Assessment:** This section provides a skill assessment instrument designed to test for the skills and behaviors presented in the module.
- **Skill Understanding:** This section defines and presents an overview of the skill, including conceptual foundations and basic principles.
- **Skill Practice:** This section asks learners to assume the role of a manager in an organization and then presents them with a number of related situations in the form of in-basket exercises. Exhibits and relevant materials are provided to make the situation realistic. Learners then have an opportunity to practice using the individual behavioral components of the skill. The videos are an important tool for use in this section since they provide specific actions that show learners how to improve their skills.
- **Assessment of Change:** This section provides a review of the skill and another opportunity for skill assessment. Once learners have completed the module, their behavior can be measured so that changes can be determined in their competency. Learners retake the first self-assessment instrument and then complete a second assessment instrument. Taken

together, the skill assessments provide a complete analysis of learners' progress and areas in which they can work to improve.

- **Skill-Building Exercises:** This final section provides several additional exercises that are focused on real-world application of skills. These exercises often ask learners to apply the new behavior outside of the classroom. The exercises can be completed individually or in a work group.

SUPPLEMENTAL RESOURCE MATERIALS

Supplemental resource materials include the *Instructor's Resource Manual,* a computerized test bank, and a distinct video package.

Instructor's Resource Manual

The resource manual includes an overview of content material and a detailed lecture outline. Specific guidelines on how to help students use the self-assessment instruments, including reliability and validity data for each assessment instrument, along with normative data, are provided. Suggested responses for the in-basket exercises are given along with teaching tips for helping students gain insight from their responses. Instructions are also included for each of the skill-building exercises at the end of each module. Transparency masters are included for all the figures in the module.

Videos

A distinct video package differentiates this text from others on the market. Each module has a separate video that is closely linked to the specific skills in the module and parallels the Practicing Skills section and the in-basket exercises. The videos have a contemporary focus, provide role-modeling behaviors, and are action-oriented to capture students' attention and provide them with an opportunity to see the day-to-day world of the manager. The videos help the instructor by supporting and extending the material in the module but are not required for the module to be fully utilized if audiovisual equipment is not available. The videos are based on material professionally produced and developed by Wilson Learning Corporation.

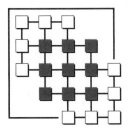

ACKNOWLEDGEMENTS

Many people have played critical roles in the development of this book. I greatly appreciate the contributions of several outstanding graduate students who worked with me. Mark Pregmon, Anita Young, and Julie McDavid were involved in the early stages of this project and provided insight and creativity; Sally Weber refined ideas and provided feedback for improvement; and Leslie Connelly assisted throughout the many revisions and helped keep the project on track with her dedication, talent, and willingness to share.

A special thank-you goes to Norm Stanton and Wilson Learning Corporation for the support and professionalism they provided. I would like to thank the entire publishing team at West. Executive editor Rick Leyh had a vision of this project and maintained his enthusiasm throughout. Jessica Evans, developmental editor, provided creative ideas and expert assistance.

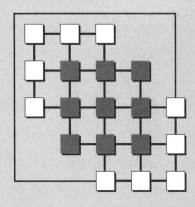

PART 1
INTERACTIVE SKILLS: WORKING PRODUCTIVELY WITH OTHERS

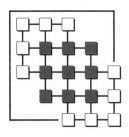

MODULE 1
INTERPERSONAL SKILLS:
INTERACTING WITH OTHERS

INTRODUCTION

Whenever people work together, especially if they have different backgrounds, successful interaction depends on effective interpersonal skills. For managers, interpersonal skills mean the ability to be a facilitator—to foster a collective effect; get along with peers, subordinates, and superiors; and manage interactions with others.

Modern corporations can no longer afford to hire people who cannot relate with others. They have come to see interpersonal skills not so much as desirable but as required. In a managerial setting, interpersonal skills include the ability to intervene if necessary, to develop and foster cohesion and morale, to obtain input and participation, and to effectively interact with others regardless of differences in status, opinion, and temperament. In addition, an ability to evaluate the feelings, strengths, and flaws of others and to respond appropriately is crucial to managerial success.

All managerial actions are facilitated by good interpersonal skills. In a managerial context, interpersonal skills include the following categories of behaviors: (1) developing and maintaining rapport, (2) listening to others, (3) displaying sensitivity to others, (4) eliciting ideas, feelings, and perceptions from others, and (5) presenting feedback.

The purpose of this module is to help you develop your interpersonal skills or to strengthen the skills you already have. You will assume the role of manager in a variety of situations. In each situation, you will be provided with information in the form of materials that typically find their way to the manager's desk. As a manager, you must use your interpersonal skills to solve a potential problem. By actually participating in situations, you will learn and practice interpersonal skills.

The module is organized so that you will develop a before-practice assessment of your interpersonal skills by completing the Interpersonal Skill Inventory (ISI). This questionnaire is an assessment instrument that measures your interpersonal skills at the present time. A brief discussion of interpersonal skills follows. Next, through in-basket exercises, you will practice various interpersonal skills. Feedback from your instructor will help you judge the quality of your responses and will provide guidance on improving specific behaviors.

After you have completed the exercises, you will retake the ISI and compare your after-practice results with your earlier results. You will also complete the Interpersonal Choices Questionnaire (ICQ). This assessment instrument examines how you actually behave in situations where interpersonal skills are needed. It will give you more insight into your behaviors in situations requiring interpersonal skills.

After completing this module, you may find that the exercises result in immediate improvement, or you may find that improvement is more noticeable after you have had opportunities to perform on the job or in a classroom group situation.

ASSESSING INTERPERSONAL SKILLS

Complete the ISI on the following pages before proceeding with the rest of the module. It is both a teaching tool and a means of evaluating your present interpersonal skills. Take time to complete the instrument carefully. Your answers should reflect your behaviors as they are now, not as you would like them to be. Be honest. This instrument is designed to help you discover where you are now so you can work to improve your interpersonal skills.

The Interpersonal Skill Inventory (ISI)

The Interpersonal Skill Inventory (ISI) is an assessment questionnaire designed to evaluate your current level of interpersonal skills. If you do not have experience in a management position, consider a group you have worked with either in the classroom or in an organization such as a fraternity, sorority, club, church, or service group. You will find the questions applicable to your own experience even if you are not yet a manager.

Use the following scale to rate the frequency with which you perform the behaviors described in each question. Place the corresponding number (1–7) in the blank space preceding the statement.

Rarely	Irregularly	Occasionally	Usually	Frequently	Almost Always	Consistently
1	2	3	4	5	6	7

_____ **1.**   I am available when others want to speak to me.

_____ **2.**   I greet others in a friendly manner.

_____ **3.**   I use humor to lighten tense situations.

_____ **4.**   I indicate my concern for others while speaking with them.

_____ 5. I am open to the views and opinions of others, even when they challenge my own views and opinions.

_____ 6. I face the person I am interacting with and maintain comfortable eye contact.

_____ 7. I lean toward the person who is speaking to me.

_____ 8. I rephrase what is said to me to make certain that I have understood.

_____ 9. I listen for messages underlying what is actually being said.

_____ 10. I note the body language of those with whom I interact (facial expressions, stance, vocal inflections, etc.).

_____ 11. I am comfortable with individual differences.

_____ 12. I respect the right to privacy.

_____ 13. I show that I understand the problems of others, though I avoid becoming personally involved in these problems.

_____ 14. I try to prevent others' personal problems from becoming job problems.

_____ 15. I let others know that I am concerned about their well-being.

_____ 16. I encourage others to express their ideas, feelings, and perceptions.

_____ 17. I create a nonthreatening environment in which ideas, feelings, and perceptions may be safely expressed.

_____ 18. I ask questions that will help others think through the matters under discussion.

_____ 19. To promote a free flow of information, I ask open-ended questions rather than questions that require specific responses.

_____ 20. I communicate to others that their ideas, feelings, and perceptions are of value.

_____ 21. I identify the positive aspects of another person's performance and accomplishments and reinforce these with compliments and encouragement.

_____ 22. I discuss negative behavior objectively by reviewing guidelines and current standards.

_____ 23. I present feedback in a helpful manner and with a workable plan for improvement if required.

_____ 24. I ask others to evaluate themselves.

_____ 25. When presenting feedback to others, I protect their self-esteem.

ISI Scoring

The scoring sheet in Figure 1 summarizes your responses for the ISI. It will help you identify your existing strengths and pinpoint areas that need improvement. Right now, fill in the before-practice assessment score column for each skill area by adding your scores for each item. Add the five category scores to obtain a total score. Enter that total score in the space indicated. After completing the module, you will take the ISI again and fill in the after-practice assessment column.

FIGURE 1
Interpersonal Skills Inventory (ISI)
Scoring

Skill Area	Items	Assessment	
		Before Practice	After Practice
Developing and maintaining rapport	1,2,3,4,5		
Listening to others	6,7,8,9,10		
Displaying sensitivity to others' needs	11,12,13,14,15		
Eliciting ideas, feelings, and perceptions from others	16,17,18,19,20		
Presenting feedback	21,22,23,24,25		
TOTAL SCORE			

ISI Evaluation

Figure 2 shows score lines for your total score and for each category measured on the ISI. Each line shows a continuum from the lowest possible score to the highest. Place the letter B (before-practice) where your personal score falls on each of these lines.

The score lines in Figure 2 show graphically where you stand with regard to five interpersonal behaviors. If you have been honest with yourself, you now have a better idea of your relative strengths and weaknesses in the categories of behavior that make up interpersonal skills.

Learning to Use the ISI Skills

You have now completed the initial evaluation of your interpersonal skills. In the ISI, you rated the frequency with which you demonstrate behaviors in the five categories of interpersonal skills. This questionnaire provides a baseline against which you will assess improvements that have taken place after you have completed this module.

Before moving on, think about what you have discovered about yourself in this evaluation. What areas of your interpersonal skills are least developed? These will require more of your attention during the remainder of this module. What categories of interpersonal behaviors are your strongest? Use this module to fine-tune these so that you may take full advantage of them. For these stronger areas, learning only one or two new things may be all you need for significant improvement in your interpersonal skills.

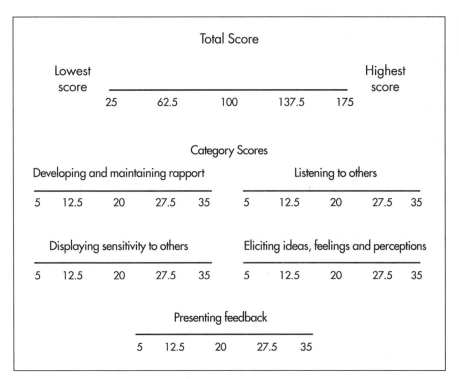

FIGURE 2
Interpersonal Skills Inventory (ISI)
Evaluation

The ISI will help you identify interpersonal behaviors that are appropriate for the management situations described in this module. After you have completed the module and have put into practice what you have learned, retake the ISI. Then, compare your after-practice scores with your before-practice scores. This comparison will show you where you have progressed and where further work is needed.

UNDERSTANDING INTERPERSONAL SKILLS

A large part of a manager's responsibility involves working with and through others. The manager's skills in interpersonal interactions can mean the difference between success and failure. A manager's lack of interpersonal skills can impede the performance of employees. For example, employees who are managed by someone who lacks interpersonal skills usually are passive, lack initiative, and depend too much on instructions and directions from others. Interpersonal problems between the employees and the manager often show in high turnover rates, decreased productivity, absenteeism, and increased grievances. Additional indications may be an increase in production errors and general indifference on the part of employees toward the quality or quantity of their output.

Employees have other problems besides those stemming from their jobs. Personal pressures such as illness, marital difficulties, family responsibilities, and financial burdens are just a few. Sometimes employees are unable to cope with these pressures. Managers may notice an increase in distraction, loss of efficiency, or even self-destructive behaviors such as alcohol or chemical dependencies. Both types of problems (personal and job-related) can have a major impact on job performance. A manager with good interpersonal skills will tune into these negative behaviors before they can affect job performance. By identifying and alleviating problems early the manager will help not only the employee but the company as well. Managers need strong interpersonal skills to deal successfully with these problems.

Interpersonal Skills Needed by Managers

Effective managers demonstrate competency in five categories of interpersonal skills: (1) developing and maintaining rapport, (2) listening to others, (3) displaying sensitivity to others, (4) eliciting ideas, feelings, and perceptions from others, and (5) presenting feedback. Let's take a brief look at each of these components.

Developing and Maintaining Rapport

Developing and maintaining rapport is the first category of behaviors in interpersonal skills. Rapport exists when there is a relationship of mutual trust. It is established when you appear open to others and their ideas, have a friendly manner, show interest in others, and use humor in a way that diminishes tensions but does not belittle the concerns of others. You can also develop rapport by demonstrating interest in what others have to say and showing sensitivity to their needs and feelings. Rapport helps build confidence and encourages the sharing of helpful suggestions.

A manager becomes aware of problems through observation, from an employee who is experiencing a difficulty, or from other employees. The manager who has established rapport with employees and is friendly and accessible is likely to learn of problems in time to help both the employee and the team.

Listening to Others

Of all the skills associated with good communication, perhaps the most important is listening. People usually hear messages but lose or distort their meaning. Most people fail to realize just how poorly they listen.

Listening is not the same as hearing. Listening is an intellectual and emotional process in which you use all resources at hand to understand the meaning of a message. In order to be an effective listener, you must be objective and understand the sender's viewpoint. This requires a conscious attempt to understand the speaker without letting personal opinions influence the content of the message. You must concentrate on understanding what is being said and not what you want to hear.

Listening is an active process. Good listening behaviors include maintaining eye contact, rephrasing what has been said, listening for the message underlying the overt meaning of the words that have been spoken, and observing the body language of the speaker, especially its congruence with the spoken words.

The listener responds through body language to the person who is speaking. By maintaining appropriate eye contact, leaning toward the speaker, occasionally nodding, and smiling or frowning at appropriate times, the listener sends signals that the speaker is being heard. By rephrasing what has been said and by asking questions about the matters under discussion, the listener demonstrates that the speaker is being understood.

Active listening requires attentiveness and concentration. It communicates acceptance of those with whom you are interacting and it also encourages the other person to continue the interaction. Active listening is time-consuming. It requires confidence in one's interpersonal skills and the courage to possibly hear things that are less than complimentary.

Displaying Sensitivity to Others

Interpersonal skills involve the ability to be empathic—to understand the needs and feelings of others and to deal with these feelings carefully and considerately. This includes accepting individual differences and the right to privacy in personal matters.

When interacting with others, the sensitive manager makes it clear that the other person's needs and feelings are a matter of concern and that, in meeting the needs of the job situation, that person will not be overlooked. There is a payoff for showing concern for others. Concern breeds reciprocal concern; employees who are dealt with in this way are likely to increase their efforts and their commitment to the job. Also, genuine sensitivity to employees' needs and feelings will help managers identify and resolve problems that affect job performance.

Eliciting Ideas, Feelings, and Perceptions from Others

An essential interpersonal skill is the ability to elicit employees' ideas, feelings, and perceptions. By creating a safe environment and skillfully encouraging others to express their thoughts, the manager can tap into information resources that would not otherwise be available.

Using open-ended questions is a good way to encourage employees to talk. For example, questions like "Can you tell me more?" or "How did you feel when that happened?" can help employees express their ideas, feelings, and perceptions. Evaluative, judgmental, and advising statements should be avoided, as well as factual, yes-or-no questions like "Do you realize that you have been late two days in a row?"

Statements that reflect back to the speaker what he or she said also help to keep the flow of communication open. For example, "Let me see if I understand what you are saying" is a reflective statement. Instead of telling the listener, the reflective statement helps the other person to discover. These reflective statements promote the flow of information to the manager. Trust and concern between managers and employees grows, and more effective and lasting problem solving takes place.

Presenting Feedback

This is the most important category of interpersonal skills needed by managers. It requires a fine balance of behaviors that permit the discussion of performance deficits while protecting the employee's self-esteem. Feedback is meant to improve, correct, and inspire others to greater achievement. For example, simple statements such as "I think you handled the customer complaints very professionally" and "I appreciate your error-free report" show employees that you recognize and appreciate what they are doing. This type of feedback prompts them to continue to perform well.

When an employee's behavior gets out of line, negative feedback can be given to correct the deviation. It is not wise to ignore an employee's deviant personal or work behavior. The employee may see silence as tacit approval. Comments to the employee like "I've avoided assigning you to the new project because of the work you have missed lately" or "I see that you didn't complete the job by the deadline" provide the employee with verbal feedback so he or she can correct the behavior.

The following guidelines will help you use feedback effectively.

- Before giving feedback, examine your motivation; make sure the receiver is ready and open to hear you.
- Do not assume that others understand your frame of reference. Establish common understanding of words and phrases that could be misunderstood.
- Give feedback on the behavior, not the person. Describe the behavior and your perceptions of it. Relate the feedback specifically to the employee's action or behavior. This reinforces good performance or helps the employee change inappropriate behavior.
- While giving feedback, use "I" statements rather than "you" statements to indicate that these are your perceptions, thoughts, and feelings. For example, "I feel your behavior is not appropriate" instead of "you are not behaving appropriately."
- Ask the other person to clarify, explain, change, or correct inappropriate behavior.
- Give more positive feedback than negative feedback. Most people have difficulty hearing and accepting negative feedback. Start by complimenting employees on something done well, and then follow with constructive ideas on how to improve inadequate performance.

Interpersonal Skills and Their Relationship to Other Managerial Skills

All managerial skills are aided by good interpersonal skills. Interpersonal skills are especially important to leadership and oral communication, in which the manager is involved with others. Leadership demands that the manager be aware of the needs and feelings of others as well as motivate them and encourage input from them. These behaviors are interpersonal. Oral communication demands that the manager establish rapport and listen to others, both of which are interpersonal skills.

In the same way, interpersonal skills are aided by other managerial skills. For example, good perception and communication skills help the manager display sensitivity to the needs and feelings of others, develop rapport with others, and elicit their ideas, feelings, and perceptions. Good decision-making skills help the manager present feedback in a constructive manner, while flexibility skills help the manager deal with a wide variety of people.

The manager who is skilled in interpersonal behaviors usually develops a high level of self-awareness. It is important that as a manager you know your own personal needs and tolerance limits. To function effectively, you must find the managerial role a satisfying one. When your personal needs are in conflict with the needs of others, your ability to resolve conflict is critical. Such conflict resolution requires that you be aware of and understand yourself. In this context, "developing rapport" becomes self-acceptance; "listening to others" becomes self-awareness; "displaying sensitivity to others' needs and feelings" means being sensitive to your own needs and feelings; "eliciting ideas" means allowing yourself to think freely without censoring your feelings and perceptions; and "presenting feedback" means thinking through your thoughts, feelings, and perceptions so that you can use them constructively.

The process of solving problems in an organization is aided by managers' skills in interpersonal interactions. The manager with good interpersonal skills creates an atmosphere of trust. This makes others willing to share information and participate in the problem-solving process. Interpersonal skills help the manager separate personal from job-related problems and then deal with each appropriately.

In groups, interpersonal skills on the part of the manager will result in an open flow of suggestions for problem solving and a higher level of satisfaction with group participation and greater pride in group accomplishment. These are beneficial to both the company and the employees.

PRACTICING INTERPERSONAL SKILLS

Interpersonal skills require the ability to display sensitivity to the needs, feelings, and capabilities of others, develop and maintain relationships with others, and effectively interact with others regardless of differences in status, opinion, and temperament. Interpersonal skills consist of the following component behaviors:

- *Developing and maintaining rapport*—Managers develop and maintain rapport when they appear open to others and their ideas, demonstrate a friendly manner, show interest in others, and use humor in a way that diminishes tensions but does not belittle the concerns of others.
- *Listening to others*—Through active listening, managers encourage others to continue the interaction. Active listening behaviors include maintaining comfortable eye contact, rephrasing what has been said, listening for meaning underlying the overt meaning of the words that have been spoken, and observing the body language of the speaker.

- *Displaying sensitivity to others*—Managers show sensitivity when they are concerned about others and accept their individual differences and rights to privacy in personal matters.
- *Eliciting ideas, feelings, and perceptions from others*—This aspect of interpersonal skills means creating a safe environment where people can express their ideas, feelings, and perceptions.
- *Presenting feedback*—This is one of the most vital categories of interpersonal skills for the manager. It requires a fine balance of behaviors that permit the discussion of performance deficits while protecting the employee's self-esteem.

The next section of in-basket exercises focuses separately on each component of interpersonal skills we have been discussing. Each exercise is followed by questions that ask you to choose the best response(s) to the situation.

Before you begin the interpersonal skills exercises, take time to review your scores on the five parts of the ISI. Then, as you complete the exercises, keep in mind the behaviors noted in this questionnaire. The questions in the ISI deepen your understanding of basic interpersonal considerations.

Situation

You are Lee Maxwell, managing attorney in the firm of Caplan, Wentworth, Marbury, and Smith, P.A. Twenty junior attorneys are employed by the firm. As managing attorney, you are responsible for their general supervision and development.

The firm handles a broad span of legal matters, including labor relations cases, wills and probate, corporate and business matters, and negligence claims. Most junior attorneys are in a pool and are assigned to do research and information-gathering as needed. They also prepare routine briefs or assist the senior attorneys in their case preparation. Occasionally, one of the junior attorneys may be assigned as special assistant to a senior partner.

Today you are meeting with Jerry Blake, one of the young junior attorneys on your staff. Jerry joined your law firm immediately upon graduation from a prestigious school in the Northeast and has been employed by the firm for about a year. She was in the upper third of her class and very well recommended.

In the following in-basket exercises, you will deal with matters of concern both to yourself and Jerry. Some of the issues you discuss are personal. Others are job-related. All demand interpersonal skills if they are to be handled satisfactorily.

It is 10 A.M. on January 12, and Jerry is seated in your office. You must review the file of information (Exhibits 1 through 25) on your desk to prepare yourself for your discussion with her. Read the material and answer the questions in each in-basket exercise. As you answer the various questions, take into consideration all of the information from previous exercises and, if pertinent, use it in your answers.

IN-BASKET EXERCISE 1: DEVELOPING AND MAINTAINING RAPPORT

When you establish rapport, you achieve a comfortable relationship with another person. The ability to establish rapport is a major ingredient in effective interpersonal skills. Knowing some personal background about the person with whom you are meeting will show that you are interested in that person. It will also help make that person more receptive to what you have to say, and it will promote the open, honest atmosphere known as rapport. This section gives you some information about the purpose of your meeting and about Jerry Blake. Refer to Exhibits 1 through 3, and then answer the following questions to practice establishing and maintaining rapport with Jerry.

Your interpersonal skills focus:

- Demonstrate interest in the employee by taking time to learn something about her.
- Show that you are willing to address her concerns.
- Elicit her views during your discussion.
- Be supportive.

Questions for In-Basket Exercise 1:

1. Knowing some personal background about the person with whom you are meeting will show that you are interested in that person. It will also help make that person more receptive to what you have to say and will promote openness and honesty. This is rapport. Based on the memos you have examined, what do you know about Jerry that can help you establish rapport?

2. How would you use this information to establish rapport in your meeting with Jerry?

3. How could you begin to deal with some of the negative aspects of Jerry's performance that are noted in the memo from Gordon Keller and still maintain rapport?

4. In what way could you use the letter from James Holinshield of the Legal Assistance Group to maintain rapport with Jerry?

IN-BASKET EXERCISE 2: LISTENING TO OTHERS

A major component of interpersonal skills is listening to what others have to say. Listening carefully and letting the sender know that his or her message has been heard and understood conveys respect for that person.

Using the information in this section and the preceding section, you will practice behaviors needed for effective listening. After reviewing Exhibits 4 through 9, respond to the questions that follow.

Your interpersonal skills focus:

- Note the importance of observing body language.
- Attend to the implied as well as stated message.
- Emphasize the importance of hearing *all* of the message.
- Rephrase what you have heard or thought you heard.

Questions for In-Basket Exercise 2:

1. You (Lee Maxwell) are meeting with Jerry Blake. Jerry is explaining her encounter with Dana Wilson, the librarian. You want your body language to demonstrate that you are interested in what she is saying. Describe what you would do.

2. Jerry tells you that she is surprised that Dana Wilson has complained about her. Dana seemed so friendly that there appeared to be no harm in asking for a small favor. Using Jerry's November 16 reply to you, show Jerry that if she had really listened she would have recognized Dana's unwillingness to do what she had asked.

3. Restate Jerry's memo of November 18 in a way that demonstrates that you understand what she said. Do not express your own point of view.

4. Mrs. Sanderson wrote you a letter expressing concern that Jerry, who did some fact-gathering for the office, is incompetent. She stated that she understood that you were going to handle her case personally. Restate Mrs. Sanderson's message in a way that shows that you listened to what she said in her letter.

5. Jerry protested that she was unfairly passed over for a job as Steinberg's assistant. Steinberg let you know that he told Jerry why he did not select her for the position. Say something to Jerry to show that if she had really listened in her interview with Lou Steinberg she would not have written her memorandum of December 7.

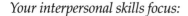

IN-BASKET EXERCISE 3: DISPLAYING SENSITIVITY TO OTHERS

Displaying sensitivity to the needs and feelings of others lies at the heart of interpersonal skills. You show sensitivity when you let others know that you are concerned about their well-being, that you understand their problems, and that you respect their rights to privacy. You also show sensitivity to others when you prevent their personal problems from becoming job problems.

The following section focuses on showing sensitivity. Use Exhibits 10 through 12, and any relevant information in the preceding exercises, to answer the questions.

Your interpersonal skills focus:

- Show that you are aware of others' problems.
- Try to help others resolve conflicts between personal demands and job demands.
- Satisfy the self-esteem and status requirements of others.
- Reassure others of your support for their job-related goals and objectives.

Questions for In-Basket Exercise 3:

1. Jerry explained that she has been tardy at Monday morning staff meetings due to conditions beyond her control. She appears to be genuinely upset that she has been unable to be prompt at the meetings. In this situation, Jerry's personal problems appear to conflict with office routine. What would be an appropriate way to show sensitivity to Jerry's personal concerns under these circumstances?

2. In a memo in the preceding in-basket exercise, Jerry objected to the office dress code. Now Jerry objects to being asked to empty her own ashtrays. In fact, both of Jerry's memos convey that she places much importance on being treated as a professional. Say something to Jerry that shows that you are sensitive to this need.

3. Jerry has tried to see you many times and you have indeed been difficult to reach. Prior to your current meeting, she wrote to you on three separate occasions to request a meeting with you. In all likelihood, Jerry feels that she is being ignored. Deal with this feeling, now that you are meeting with her.

4. Jerry indicated a strong desire to move ahead in her career. Because of her mother's accident, she has been unable to complete the judicial workshop, a workshop that would help her move forward. How could you show Jerry that you recognize both her disappointment in missing the workshop and her desire to advance in her career?

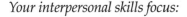

IN-BASKET EXERCISE 4: ELICITING IDEAS, FEELINGS, AND PERCEPTIONS FROM OTHERS

As a manager, you will actively seek others' ideas, feelings, and perceptions. You need to create an environment in which participants in a discussion feel free to express themselves honestly. Open-ended questions promote the exchange of information. So does assurance that people's ideas and feelings are of value and will be treated seriously.

In this section, you focus on eliciting Jerry's ideas, feelings, and perceptions as you continue your meeting together. Use the information in Exhibits 13 and 14, and in all of the preceding sections, to respond to the questions below.

Your interpersonal skills focus:

- Encourage individuals to examine rather than explain/defend their own behaviors.
- Ask open-ended questions.
- Demonstrate that you value others' opinions.
- Ask for information in a helping context.
- Share personal experiences.

Questions for In-Basket Exercise 4:

1. Stacy Locke has complained that Jerry Blake is uncooperative and antagonizes other attorneys. Jerry has another point of view. Make a statement that is open-ended and is likely to elicit Jerry's ideas, feelings, and perceptions. Explain how your statement will work in this situation.

2. From the deluge of complaints, it looks as though Jerry is not getting along too well with others. Say something that will elicit her feelings and perceptions regarding the situation. Explain how your statement will work to get Jerry to open up.

In-Basket Exercise 5: Presenting Feedback

Presenting feedback constructively is a major component of interpersonal skills in management. Constructive feedback means evaluating the performance of another person in a way that will encourage growth.

In this final practice section, you are given additional information relating to Jerry Blake. Using Exhibits 15 through 17, as well as any of the relevant data from the preceding sections, you are asked to present constructive feedback to Jerry.

Your interpersonal skills focus:

- Search out positive behaviors and reinforce them with positive remarks.
- Depersonalize negative behaviors and refer to them in terms of job requirements.
- Present your performance appraisal in a helping context.
- Encourage the employee to evaluate herself.
- Work with the employee to develop a plan for improvement or advancement.

Questions for In-Basket Exercise 5:

1. Using all of the information in this file (all exercises), review Jerry's performance with her in a way that will assist her professional development and advance her in your firm.

2. How and why would you involve Jerry in her own performance evaluation?

3. How will your feedback to Jerry improve her work performance and protect her self-esteem?

ASSESSING CHANGE

The purpose of this module has been to help you develop your interpersonal skills as a manager. You have worked through exercises requiring you to use each category of behaviors in interpersonal skills. A series of questions has been used to help you focus on these target skills. You have seen that interpersonal skills involve:

- *Developing and maintaining rapport*—As Lee Maxwell, managing attorney for Caplan, Wentworth, Marbury, and Smith, P.A., you were required to establish rapport with junior attorney Jerry Blake.
- *Listening to others*—As Lee Maxwell, you had to demonstrate active listening skills in your meeting with Jerry Blake.
- *Displaying sensitivity to the needs and feelings of others*—Continuing in your role as Lee Maxwell, you were called upon to display sensitivity to Jerry Blake's needs and feelings.
- *Eliciting ideas, feelings, and perceptions from others*—Your task as Lee Maxwell was to elicit ideas, feelings, and perceptions from Jerry Blake.
- *Presenting feedback*—Finally, as Lee Maxwell, you had to talk constructively with Jerry Blake about performance issues.

At the beginning of this module, you completed the ISI questionnaire to provide a baseline against which you could measure improvements in your interpersonal skills. Now it is time to assess some of these changes.

First, you will retake the ISI. A comparison of your before- and after-practice responses will demonstrate the extent to which you have increased the frequency and appropriateness of your interpersonal behaviors. When you have retaken this questionnaire, compare your answers with those you gave earlier to see how much you have strengthened your interpersonal skills.

The Interpersonal Skills Inventory (ISI)

Use the following scale to rate the frequency with which you perform the behaviors described in each question. Place the corresponding number (1–7) in the blank space preceding the statement.

Rarely	Irregularly	Occasionally	Usually	Frequently	Almost Always	Consistently
1	2	3	4	5	6	7

_____ **1.**　I am available when others want to speak to me.

_____ **2.**　I greet others in a friendly manner.

_____ **3.**　I use humor to lighten tense situations.

_____ **4.**　I indicate my concern for others while speaking with them.

_____ **5.**　I am open to the views and opinions of others, even when they challenge my own views and opinions.

_____ 6. I face the person I am interacting with and maintain comfortable eye contact.

_____ 7. I lean toward the person who is speaking to me.

_____ 8. I rephrase what is said to me to make certain that I have understood.

_____ 9. I listen for messages underlying what is actually being said.

_____ 10. I note the body language of those with whom I interact (facial expressions, stance, vocal inflections, etc.).

_____ 11. I am comfortable with individual differences.

_____ 12. I respect the right to privacy.

_____ 13. I show that I understand the problems of others, though I avoid becoming personally involved in these problems.

_____ 14. I try to prevent others' personal problems from becoming job problems.

_____ 15. I let others know that I am concerned about their well-being.

_____ 16. I encourage others to express their ideas, feelings, and perceptions.

_____ 17. I create a nonthreatening environment in which ideas, feelings, and perceptions may be safely expressed.

_____ 18. I ask questions that will help others think through the matters under discussion.

_____ 19. To promote a free flow of information, I ask open-ended questions rather than questions that require specific responses.

_____ 20. I communicate to others that their ideas, feelings, and perceptions are of value.

_____ 21. I identify the positive aspects of another person's performance and accomplishments and reinforce these with compliments and encouragement.

_____ 22. I discuss negative behavior objectively by reviewing guidelines and current standards.

_____ 23. I present feedback in a helpful manner and with a workable plan for improvement if required.

_____ 24. I ask others to evaluate themselves.

_____ 25. When presenting feedback to others, I protect their self-esteem.

ISI Scoring and Evaluation

Follow the scoring directions found on page 5 and in Figure 1. Complete the after-practice assessment column for the ISI and compare your before- and after-practice assessment totals. You will also need to plot your after-practice scores in Figure 2. In which categories did your scores improve? Think about what has made your progress possible. Perhaps you can apply your insights to categories where your performance has lagged.

The Interpersonal Choices Questionnaire (ICQ)

In the Interpersonal Choices Questionnaire (ICQ), you assume a variety of managerial positions and are placed in situations where you must exercise your interpersonal skills.

Described on the following pages are ten different situations. Following each paragraph is a list of five possible responses. Mark the response that, in your opinion, reflects the greatest degree of interpersonal skills. Please select only one response.

1. You are Jee Yeun Lee, sales manager for Table-Tops Unlimited, a small retail furniture shop. You are meeting with Tim Evans, sales representative, to discuss Tim's declining sales performance. Tim quickly becomes angry, defensive, and refuses to accept any blame. Tim states that sales are down all over, and it is not his fault. What should your next step be, interpersonally speaking?

_____ a) Present your supporting data factually and impersonally. Then, invite Tim to work with you on a plan for improving his performance.

_____ b) Reschedule the meeting for another time.

_____ c) Give Tim a list of ways in which his performance can be improved.

_____ d) Immediately place Tim on probation.

_____ e) Inform Tim that the purpose of the meeting is to help rather than to censure him.

2. Simply Elegant is a large chain of specialty clothing shops. Its stores are located throughout the southeastern United States, primarily in shopping malls. Tracy is a salesperson at the Downeast Mall store. Recently, the mall tenants all agreed to institute a uniform closing time. All mall stores will close at 9 P.M. The Simply Elegant store had been closing at 7 P.M. A coworker informs Tracy of the new closing hours. Tracy's personal work schedule has not been changed. Nevertheless, Tracy is upset. She feels that you, the store manager, should have informed her personally of the change. Tracy angrily confronts you regarding this matter. Which of the following responses would best demonstrate your interpersonal skills in this situation?

_____ a) Apologize for the oversight.

_____ b) Berate Tracy for her demanding attitude.

_____ c) Tell Tracy that the change does not affect her personal work schedule.

_____ d) Ask Tracy if she would like to work during the later hours.

_____ e) Inform Tracy that you appreciate her interest in store operations.

3. In a meeting of the sales staff of Imperial Office Supplies, Lesley Warren, senior sales representative, appears bored and distracted, unlike his usual self. He asks irrelevant questions, and much information must be repeated for his sake. You are the sales manager conducting the meeting. You confront Lesley immediately after the meeting. Select an opening statement that best demonstrates your interpersonal skills.

_____ a) "You seem to have something on your mind, Lesley. Would you like to talk about it?"

_____ b) "I don't understand what I did to turn you off, Lesley. You sure didn't seem interested in the meeting."

_____ c) "What's the matter, Lesley? Rough night?"

_____ d) "I'm afraid I'm going to have to make a note of your behavior in your personnel file."

_____ e) "Pretty boring meeting, wasn't it?"

4. You, Britt Wallace, are the manager of the United Savings Bank. You have called Chris Littlebird into your office for a conference. Until recently, Chris has been an exemplary employee. She has frequently been commended for her ability to get along well with both customers and coworkers. Only a few months ago, Chris was promoted to the position of head teller. Over the past few weeks, however, Chris' performance has declined. She is moody and openly rude to customers. When you ask Chris to explain her behavior, she states that the complaints are exaggerated. You know that Chris' mother is seriously ill. To best demonstrate your interpersonal skills, you would:

_____ a) Recommend that Chris seek professional help for her moodiness.

_____ b) Inform Chris that her personal problems do not excuse her rudeness to customers.

_____ c) Suggest that Chris take a leave of absence until her problems at home are settled.

_____ d) Ask Chris about her mother's illness, and encourage her to discuss her home problems.

_____ e) Transfer Chris to a job where she will have less customer contact.

5. Canyon Electronics is a growing company that produces small computers. You are the service manager. You have called Pat Morris, a member of your service team, into your office for a quarterly performance appraisal. Pat has always been a superior employee, but lately Pat's quality and quantity of work have diminished. She has not completed assigned tasks on time, and she has had several more absences than company standards allow. In discussing Pat's performance, you would best display interpersonal skills by saying:

_____ a) "You've been goofing off, Pat. We're not used to that from you."

_____ b) "Matched against the last three quarters, your absences have increased by 50 percent. Also, the customer complaints we have received about your work have tripled. Let's talk about that."

_____ c) "Your record for this quarter is really bad. If this keeps up, we'll have to assume that you are no longer interested in working here."

_____ d) "What's the matter with you? Can't you do the job anymore?"

_____ e) "Pat, you've always been one of our best employees. However, lately it looks as if you're having some problems. Your absences are up, and so are customer complaints about your work. Want to talk about it?"

6. In a recent conversation, two employees of the Tennyson Research Corporation were discussing various aspects of company operations. Their comments indicated that they felt they were being treated unfairly. You, their manager, inadvertently overheard their conversation. Under the circumstances, you could best demonstrate interpersonal skills by:

_____ a) Ignoring the matter completely.

_____ b) Informing the employees that their conversation was overheard and inviting them to discuss their feelings.

_____ c) Doing nothing immediately, but sometime later scheduling a meeting in which employees would be encouraged to air complaints.

_____ d) Transferring one of the employees to a different department.

_____ e) Reprimanding the employees for their negative attitudes.

7. Today, you, Lou Edwards, manager of Master Woodworking and Design, Inc., are meeting with your design staff. The purpose of the meeting is to brainstorm new design formats for commercial accounts. During the meeting, Lynann Lee, a staff artist, says, "Why do we waste time with these meetings? I don't need anyone's help. I have my own ideas." You would best demonstrate interpersonal skills by saying:

_____ a) "Ok, Lynann. It's good that you vented your feelings. Can anyone here answer Lynann's question?"

_____ b) "That's the wrong attitude. You should be willing to share your ideas."

_____ c) "These meetings are part of your job. You are expected to participate in them."

_____ d) "You do have good ideas, Lynann. And we'd like you to share them with us."

_____ e) "Your ideas are okay, Lynann, but if you listen, you may get better ones."

8. You are the vice president of the Conners Candy Company. At your monthly meeting with your managers, Terry White, manager of retail sales, wanted to talk about the decline in sales. You refused Terry's request, saying that sales were no problem and were at expected levels. After the meeting, Terry asked to discuss the sales situation with you privately. Which of the following responses to Terry's request would best demonstrate interpersonal skills?

_____ a) "Sorry, Terry, I don't have the time."

_____ b) "Why are you so persistent? I'm satisfied with things as they are."

_____ c) "I see that you are really concerned. Stop at my office and we'll talk about it."

_____ d) "There are some things that we cannot control. More talk would be futile."

_____ e) "You worry too much. Relax. You're doing a good job."

9. In an employee survey conducted by the Personnel Department of Emory Electronics Company, 78 percent of the employees stated that they would welcome an opportunity for participation in management decisions. You, Juan Ortiz, personnel manager, share these results with Jesse Wallace, operations manager. Wallace listens and then comments, "That's nonsense. What do you people at personnel know about management anyway?" You would demonstrate interpersonal skills best by saying:

_____ a) Nothing.

_____ b) "You're a fine manager, Jesse. But other firms have found that employee participation is good for everyone. Why not think about it?"

_____ c) "Perhaps you've misunderstood what we're trying to do. We're not criticizing you. We want to help."

_____ d) "Personnel knows a lot more than you think. After all, we're the department that deals with people."

_____ e) "Seems to me that you're angry because you think we're interfering with your department. Actually, all we want to do is give you the information."

FIGURE 3
Interpersonal Choices Questionnaire (ICQ) Scoring

Question	a	b	c	d	e	Response
1						
2						
3						
4						
5						
6						
7						
8						
9						
10						

10. You are the production manager of Solar Systems Manufacturing Company. You are meeting with Jan Weldon, first line supervisor. During the meeting, Jan states that several employees have complained that they are overworked. Jan goes on to say that there is some merit to the employees' complaints because overtime has been excessive during the past few months. Which of the following possible responses to Jan would demonstrate your interpersonal skills best?

_____ a) "Sorry, we really don't have time to talk about that right now."

_____ b) "They should be happy about the chance to make some extra money, what with prices the way they are."

_____ c) "Thanks for bringing this to my attention, Jan. We'll look into it."

_____ d) "I appreciate the fact that you are so sensitive to employee needs, but we are here to discuss other company concerns."

_____ e) "We can't do anything about that. The orders must get out on time."

ICQ Scoring and Evaluation

Complete the ICQ scoring form in Figure 3. Compare your responses with the feedback your instructor will provide about the most appropriate responses for the ten interpersonal situations.

SUMMARY

Since much of management involves working with and through others, good interpersonal skills are important for managers. The more you practice developing these skills, the more competence you gain as a manager. In this module you found that interpersonal skills are displayed in your interactions with others in five areas: (1) developing and maintaining rapport, (2) listening to others, (3) displaying sensitivity to others, (4) eliciting ideas, feelings, and perceptions from others, and (5) presenting feedback.

In working through this module, you have taken part in exercises that have tested your own interpersonal skills. You have had the opportunity to develop and maintain rapport, show appropriate listening behaviors, display sensitivity to others' feelings and concerns, and present feedback in a constructive way. You are now ready to apply the experience gained in this module to a work situation or a group project in a class or an organization in which you are a member. If so, you may well experience the pleasure of positive feedback from others. Feedback from persons with whom you work will help you gauge whether or not you are using your interpersonal skills in an appropriate manner. Remember that successful and competent managers continually work to improve their interpersonal skills.

To remember key steps in practicing effective interpersonal skills and to identify situations in which the skills are needed, use the action guide shown in Figure 4. Frequent review of the information will help you become a better manager.

FIGURE 4
Interpersonal Skills Action Guide

You Show Interpersonal Skills When You:
- Develop and maintain rapport
- Listen actively
- Display sensitivity to others
- Elicit ideas, feelings, and perceptions from others
- Present constructive feedback

You Should Show Interpersonal Skills When:
- Rapport must be established
- Listening to others express their ideas and feelings
- Others need to know you are sensitive to their ideas and reactions
- Trying to elicit ideas, feelings, and perceptions from others
- Constructive feedback would be useful

SKILL-BUILDING EXERCISES

EXERCISE 1 ■ LISTENING TO OTHERS: ONE-WAY VERSUS TWO-WAY COMMUNICATION

Choose a partner for the following exercise. One of you will act as the speaker, giving instructions verbally, and the other will be the listener, drawing the figure on paper according to the information the speaker provides. Your instructor will provide the figure. You will remain in these roles for both parts of the activity. Sit so that you cannot hear the interaction between other participants.

Activity 1: Have the listener draw the described figure. Time 5 minutes.

Speaker: Sit with your back to the listener and describe the figure given you by your instructor. You are to give drawing instructions without allowing the listener to see you or the figure. You may not answer any questions.

Listener: Sit with your back to the speaker and draw the figure as it is described to you. Correct your drawing as you think necessary. Do not look at the speaker. You may not ask any questions.

Activity 2: Have the listener draw the described figure. Time 5 minutes.

Speaker: Sit facing the listener and describe the second drawing. You are to give instructions while looking at the listener and at his or her drawing. Be careful not to show the drawing to the listener. You may answer questions from the listener.

Listener: Sit facing the speaker and draw the figure as directed. You may ask questions as needed.

1. What problems did you have with these activities?
2. How accurate were the drawings in Activity 1? Activity 2?
3. For the listener, how good were you at listening? For the speaker, how clear were your instructions?
4. Provide feedback to each other for suggestions about being more accurate in your role.

EXERCISE 2 ■ EXAMINING INDIVIDUAL DIFFERENCES

Form a group of 4 to 5 class members, preferably people you do not know. As a group, respond to the following questions. Be prepared to report your responses to the whole class or your instructor.

1. Consider the uniqueness of your group members. In what ways do members *differ* from one another? What do group members share in common with one another?
2. What *strengths* do members bring to the group? What weaknesses do members bring to the group?
3. Why is it important to be able to work with individuals different from yourself? How do the differences affect interpersonal skills?

■ Use Exhibits 1–3 with In-Basket Exercise 1,
  Exhibits 4–9 with In-Basket Exercise 2,
  Exhibits 10–12 with In-Basket Exercise 3,
  Exhibits 13–14 with In-Basket Exercise 4,
  Exhibits 15–17 with In-Basket Exercise 5.

EXHIBIT 1
Legal Assistance Group Letter

LEGAL ASSISTANCE GROUP
20 COURT ALLEY

January 10
Lee Maxwell, Esq.
Caplan, Wentworth, Marbury, and Smith, P.A.
92 Broadhurst Road

Dear Lee:

The decision of your firm to allow us to use some of your younger attorneys for our more challenging cases is greatly appreciated. This is worth much more to us than any direct financial contribution you could make because, as you know, we never collect sufficient financial contributions to pay for the legal time we need.

We know how carefully you select your junior staff and how bright and well-qualified all your younger attorneys are. I am certain they will do a good job for us. I think they will also benefit from devoting some time to our cases. Some of the matters with which we deal are very challenging and involve important points of law. Occasionally, we come up with precedent-setting cases.

Again, thank you for your contribution of time and expertise in the persons of your junior staff.

Best Regards,

James Holinshield, Associate

CAPLAN, WENTWORTH, MARBURY AND SMITH, P.A.

MEMORANDUM

TO: Lee Maxwell, Managing Attorney
FROM: Gordon Keller, Attorney
DATE: November 7
RE: Jerry Blake

Jerry has been sounding off to clients about the lack of opportunities afforded female attorneys. She is particularly miffed about the fact that most of our trial attorneys are male. This has not been a deliberate policy, I am sure.

Most of the women on our staff do not particularly like courtroom proceedings. Nevertheless, it could be an embarrassing issue, especially since we are representing Bentwell, Inc. in a sex discrimination matter.

Perhaps you can talk to Jerry and calm her down. She's very bright and sees possibilities and implications in cases that others often overlook.

We don't want to lose her, but we don't need trouble either.

EXHIBIT 2
Caplan Memorandum

EXHIBIT 3
Caplan Memorandum

CAPLAN, WENTWORTH, MARBURY, AND SMITH, P.A.

MEMORANDUM

TO: Lee Maxwell, Managing Attorney
FROM: Jerry Blake, Junior Attorney
DATE: October 1
RE: Duties and Responsibilities

I am writing you this note because I have not been able to make an appointment to see you in person. Your secretary, Susan Lester, tells me that you are too busy.

Anyway, I wanted to talk to you about my work assignments at this office. Most of the work I do is routine — background investigations, simple case law, and things like that. You know that I was in the top third of my class at my law school in Boston. I am not sure that you also know that I won the inter-school moot court competition in the Northeast. All of my professors told me that I have special talents as a trial attorney.

I would greatly appreciate a chance to become more actively involved in court proceedings. That is where I want to go with my career, and I need development. Is that at all possible?

Caplan, Wentworth, Marbury, and Smith, P.A.

MEMORANDUM

TO: Lee Maxwell, Managing Attorney
FROM: Jerry Blake, Junior Attorney
DATE: December 7
RE: Assignments

I believe that I am competent and can handle more responsibility than my present assignments require. Recently, Lou Steinberg selected Corey Childress as his assistant, although I have been here longer than Corey. I do not understand why I am not getting the same opportunities as my coworkers. I am certainly qualified to do the job that Corey was chosen to do. In fact, Lou Steinberg himself told me that I was competent and intelligent.

I am unaware of any problems with my work performance. Any errors I have made have been minor ones, and I have received a lot of compliments for the work I have done.

EXHIBIT 4
Caplan Memorandum

EXHIBIT 5
Caplan Memorandum

CAPLAN, WENTWORTH, AND MARBURY, AND SMITH, P.A.

MEMORANDUM

TO: Lee Maxwell, Managing Attorney
FROM: Lou Steinberg, Senior Attorney
DATE: December 9
RE: Jerry Blake, Junior Attorney

Regarding your inquiry about passing over Jerry Blake for the position of assistant to me:

As you know, I am in charge of our negligence division. Recently, I interviewed all junior attorneys. I was interested in selecting an assistant for myself, as my workload is escalating rapidly.

In my interview with Jerry Blake, I was impressed with her intelligence and knowledge. She is very competent and well trained, and I told her this. However, I also had to tell her that she is brusque, demanding, and seems to have a chip on her shoulder. I explained to Jerry that since my assistant is required to have a lot of client contact her abrupt manner would be detrimental in that job.

I believe that I made clear to Jerry why I felt that she was not suited for the position of assistant to me.

EXHIBIT 6
Sanderson Letter

November 20

Dear Mr. Maxwell:

As you know, your law firm is representing me in a negligence case against Movemore, Inc., the firm at which I am employed. Three days ago, one of your associates, Jerry Blake, came to my place of employment to examine the staircase on which I tripped and broke my leg. She also took some pictures.

While she was at my place of employment, she spoke to my boss, Collie Cone. Collie told me later that Jerry was a "flaky female," and he doesn't think that I have a chance of winning my case with "that kind of dame" on the team. It was my understanding that you were going to handle my case personally. I don't want a "flaky female" taking over.

Sincerely yours,

Mrs. James Sanderson

Mrs. James Sanderson

EXHIBIT 7
Caplan Memorandum

CAPLAN, WENTWORTH, MARBURY, AND SMITH, P.A.

MEMORANDUM

TO: Lee Maxwell, Managing Attorney
FROM: Jerry Blake, Junior Attorney
DATE: November 18
RE: Dress Code

The dress code of this office is antiquated, in my opinion. I think I do better with clients when I dress in a way that is appropriate for the climate and setting. For example, on really hot days, I don't see where stockings add anything to my job performance. And when I am doing research in the back, I work better in jeans than in a dress.

Perhaps we can have a staff meeting to vote on an appropriate dress code. Better still, I would appreciate an opportunity to speak with you in person.

EXHIBIT 8
Caplan Memorandum

CAPLAN, WENTWORTH, MARBURY, AND SMITH, P.A.

MEMORANDUM

TO: All Personnel
FROM: Lee Maxwell, Managing Attorney
DATE: November 15
RE: Professionalism

Let me again stress the importance of presenting a professional image. This means that attorneys and support staff must dress appropriately both at the office and when representing the firm anywhere.

A coat and tie for men and suitable business attire for women is required. All staff members must adhere to this policy.

Thank you for your cooperation.

CAPLAN, WENTWORTH, MARBURY, AND SMITH, P.A.

MEMORANDUM

TO: Lee Maxwell, Managing Attorney
FROM: Dana Wilson, Librarian
DATE: November 15

As librarian, you know that I always am happy to assist the staff in searching for information. However, I do not consider it part of my job to do their work. Jerry Blake, one of the Junior Attorneys, has been asking me to do her case searches. I am perfectly willing to show Jerry and anyone else where casebooks are, but I think that is where my responsibility ends. I do not feel that I am responsible for delivering books and files to her office, duplicating case abstracts on the copier, or researching material. I would appreciate it if someone would let Jerry know where my responsibilities end and hers begin.

FORWARD TO: Jerry Blake, Junior Attorney
FROM: Lee Maxwell, Managing Attorney
DATE: November 15

I'd like to know what's going on. Dana has been with us for four years, and she seldom complains about anyone. What happened?

REPLY TO : Lee Maxwell, Managing Attorney
FROM: Jerry Blake, Junior Attorney
DATE: November 16
RE: Dana Wilson

I really was rushed the other day, and I asked Dana if she would mind running off some copies of abstracts on the copier. I had these clearly marked. She has always seemed so friendly that I thought she would not mind doing me a favor. She was a little hesitant. I told her I really needed the material in a hurry. She did copy what I asked for and was a little huffy, but I thought that was because the copier was not working properly. I don't expect her to do these things for me ALL the time.

EXHIBIT 9
Caplan Memorandum

EXHIBIT 10
Caplan Memorandum

CAPLAN, WENTWORTH, MARBURY, AND SMITH, P.A.

MEMORANDUM

TO: Lee Maxwell, Managing Attorney
FROM: Jerry Blake, Junior Attorney
DATE: December 5
RE: Monday Morning Meetings

I have just received a memo from Corey James regarding promptness at Monday morning meetings. I have been late for several of these meetings and may have to be late again.

The morning traffic in my area is horrendous and backs up for miles. Frequently, there are snarls and accidents that cause delays. I want to obey the rules about promptness, but I honestly don't know what I can do about this, short of moving from my home area.

Is it possible to start these meetings a little later? It is difficult for me to leave any earlier than I leave now because I have to take care of my mother in the mornings. Several weeks ago, she fell and broke her leg. It's in a cast, and she needs a lot of assistance in getting up and dressed.

CAPLAN, WENTWORTH, MARBURY, AND SMITH, P.A.

MEMORANDUM

TO: Lee Maxwell, Managing Attorney
FROM: Jerry Blake, Junior Attorney
DATE: December 12
RE: Judicial Workshop

I just received the memo congratulating the attorneys who completed the judicial workshop. You probably noticed that my name was missing from the list.

I started the workshop but could not continue to attend because my mother fell and broke her leg. I had to take her to the doctor on Saturdays. That was the only time we could schedule appointments for the therapy she needed.

I'd appreciate a chance to take this workshop when it is offered again. I am aware of its importance in my own development as an attorney, and I am terribly disappointed that circumstances prevented me from completing the course.

EXHIBIT 11
Caplan Memorandum

EXHIBIT 12
Caplan Memorandum

CAPLAN, WENTWORTH, MARBURY, AND SMITH, P.A.

MEMORANDUM

TO: All Personnel
FROM: Lee Maxwell, Managing Attorney
DATE: November 25
RE: Break Areas

I've noticed dirty cups and cigarette butts in the break area. We can't expect the secretaries to pick up after us. They have other things to do! Please empty your own ashtrays and wash your own cups. Some of you ask clients to have coffee with you in the break area, and we don't want them to be greeted by a mess!

MEMORANDUM

TO: Lee Maxwell, Managing Attorney
FROM: Jerry Blake, Junior Attorney
DATE: November 25
RE: Your Memo on Break Areas (11/25)

As an attorney, I must tell you that I feel that your request is demeaning and certainly not an appropriate request to a professional. My job description does not include emptying ashtrays, that incidentally are filled by clients as well as staff. I suggest bigger ashtrays and/or a better cleaning service.

CAPLAN, WENTWORTH, MARBURY, AND SMITH, P.A.

MEMORANDUM

TO: Lee Maxwell, Managing Attorney
FROM: Stacy Locke, Senior Attorney
DATE: November 25
RE: Personnel Problem

I have noticed that Jerry Blake does not work well with the other attorneys on our staff. For example, on several occasions, I have requested that Jerry Blake do case law research for me in the law library, and Jerry has avoided doing any more than absolutely necessary. Moreover, Jerry antagonizes the other attorneys when they agree to help me out.

We all need to work together for the good of the firm. Please speak with Jerry and try to get this cleared up.

EXHIBIT 13
Caplan Memorandum

EXHIBIT 14
Moran Letter

Robert Moran
400 Highland Street
Center City, FL

December 12

Caplan, Wentworth, Marbury, and Smith, P.A.
92 Broadhurst Road
Attention: Lee Maxwell

Dear Lee:

I have had dealings with your firm on several occasions and have always been satisfied with the results. However, I am puzzled about the behavior of one of your staff — Jerry Blake. Blake showed up at my residence without an appointment last Wednesday and spoke with my wife while I was at work. According to my wife, Blake asked many personal questions.

My wife is quite upset and fears that she may have given Ms. Blake the wrong impression. She said that Ms. Blake insisted that she answer all her questions. I'd like some assurance that Jerry Blake has gotten the facts straight. And I must say that I think Blake used too much pressure on my wife.

Sincerely,

Robert Moran

Robert Moran

CAPLAN, WENTWORTH, MARBURY, AND SMITH, P.A.

MEMORANDUM

TO: Jerry Blake, Junior Attorney
FROM: Lee Maxwell, Managing Attorney
DATE: December 19
RE: Rizo Case

Congratulations for a job well done!

Jerry, I want to thank you for the help you gave me last week on the Rizo case. If it hadn't been for your turning up that old law that is still on the books, I never would have won that case.

It is initiative and persistence that makes a good attorney, and it looks like you have both.

Keep up the good work and thanks again.

cc: Personnel file

EXHIBIT 15
Caplan Memorandum

EXHIBIT 16
Caplan Memorandum

CAPLAN, WENTWORTH, MARBURY, AND SMITH, P.A.

MEMORANDUM

TO: Lee Maxwell, Managing Attorney
FROM: Corey James, Administrative Assistant
DATE: December 27
RE: Work Quantity Evaluation - Jerry Blake

Jerry works rapidly and well. She exceeds all other members of the junior staff in quantity of output.

The quality of her work, as you are aware, is excellent. She is thorough in her research and seldom misses a relevant case citation.

EXHIBIT 17
Blake Quarterly Performance Review

CAPLAN, WENTWORTH, MARBURY, AND SMITH, P.A.

QUARTERLY PERFORMANCE REVIEW
December 31

NAME: Jerry Blake

POSITION: Junior Attorney

COMMENT ON EACH AREA NOTED.   DOCUMENT YOUR COMMENTS.

ATTITUDE:
Jerry is ambitious (October 1 memo from Jerry), competent, and well trained (December 9 memo from Lou Steinberg, December 7 memo from Jerry Blake). She is eager to further her professional development and wants to forge ahead, especially as a trial attorney. Based on her performance in moot court competition, she appears talented in this area. However, she tends to be abrasive (December 9 memo from Lou Steinberg) and demanding (November 15 memo from Dana Wilson) with others on the staff. She is sometimes seen as unco-operative (November 25 memo from Stacy Locke). Occasionally, she is abrasive and indiscreet in her dealings with clients (December 12 letter from Robert Moran, November 7 memo from Gordon Keller).

ADHERENCE TO OFFICE RULES AND REGULATIONS:
Jerry is outspoken in her opposition to a formal dress code (November 18 memo from Jerry Blake) and to the imposition of duties she regards as unprofessional and outside of her realm of responsibility (November 25 memo from Jerry Blake). She has been late frequently for Monday morning junior staff meetings (December 5 memo from Jerry Blake) and has offered the excuse that she is delayed by having to care for her mother.

QUANTITY/QUALITY OF WORK:
Quantity and quality of work are excellent. Jerry is thorough, original and incisive in her thinking (memos of December 19 from Lee Maxwell, December 27 from Corey James).

PARTICIPATION IN CONTINUING EDUCATION:
Jerry failed to complete the Judicial Workshop offered to junior attorneys in order to familiarize them with the local courtroom procedures and personalities. We consider this essential for advanced trial work. Jerry explained that she was unable to complete this because of obligations to take her mother to therapy at the time the workshop was offered (memo of December 12 from Blake).

CLIENT RELATIONS:
Jerry is sometimes indiscreet and abrasive in her dealings with clients (November 7 memo from Gordon Keller, December 9 memo from Lou Steinberg, December 12 letter from Robert Moran).

RELATIONS WITH OTHER STAFF MEMBERS:
Jerry is seen as brusque, pushy, and demanding by other members of the staff (memo from Steinberg, December 9, memo from Wilson, November 15). She is also seen as uncooperative (memo from Locke, November 25).

GENERAL COMMENTS:
Jerry is bright, talented, well-trained and ambitious. She is outspoken and firm in her beliefs. She seems to know what she wants and is not afraid to pursue her goals. She is not easily intimidated.

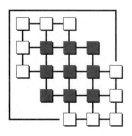

MODULE 2
LEADERSHIP SKILLS: PROVIDING DIRECTION

INTRODUCTION

Leadership means taking charge and guiding and controlling the activities of others. Managers use leadership skills to get others to accept direction and take initiative. They use leadership skills to convince employees to follow rules and procedures and also to accept changes in those rules and procedures. They also use leadership skills to motivate others to develop their own ideas as well as to support the leader's ideas. But how does leadership work? The concept of leadership is often seen as elusive and hard to define.

Leadership involves the appropriate exercise of authority and the ability to motivate, initiate, make assignments, and enforce accountability. These activities are basic to any managerial role. Managers are responsible for guiding and directing activities and employees within a unit, and they need leadership skills to carry out these responsibilities. Good leaders make other people work with and for them. Without leadership skills, managers may find that decisions and plans that depend on others are never completed or are only partially completed.

In managerial settings, leadership skills can be observed and measured. In this module, we are going to examine five categories of leadership skills: (1) initiating and maintaining action; (2) directing and coordinating; (3) motivating and stimulating others; (4) assigning and delegating tasks; and (5) holding others accountable.

The purpose of this module is to help you develop and strengthen your leadership skills. You will assume the role of manager in a variety of situations. In each situation, you will be provided with memos, charts, letters, graphs, and other pieces of information—samples of material that typically find their way to the manager's desk. As manager, you will practice using leadership skills to solve a potential problem. By actually participating in the situations, you will learn and practice leadership skills.

The module is organized so that you will develop a before-practice assessment of your leadership skills by completing the Leadership Behaviors Questionnaire (LBQ). This questionnaire is an assessment instrument that measures your

49

leadership skills at the present time. An overview of leadership and a brief discussion of leadership theories, styles, and influencing techniques follows. Next, through in-basket exercises, you will practice leadership behaviors. The exercises focus on one category of leadership behavior at a time. Feedback from your instructor will help you judge the quality of your responses and will provide guidance on improving specific behaviors.

After you have finished the exercises, you will retake the LBQ and compare your after-practice results with your earlier results. You will also complete the Leadership Experience Scale (LES). This assessment instrument examines how you actually behave in situations where leadership skills are needed. It will give you more insight into your behaviors in situations requiring leadership skills.

After completing this module, you may find that the exercises result in immediate improvement, or you may find that improvement is more noticeable after you have had opportunities to perform on the job, in a classroom, or in a group situation.

ASSESSING LEADERSHIP SKILLS

Complete the LBQ on the following pages before proceeding with the rest of the module. It is both a teaching tool and a means of evaluating your present leadership skills. Take time to complete the instrument carefully. You answers should reflect your behaviors as they are now, not as you would like them to be. Be honest. This questionnaire is designed to help you discover where you are now so you can work to improve your leadership skills.

The Leadership Behaviors Questionnaire (LBQ)

The Leadership Behaviors Questionnaire (LBQ) deals with categories of behavior that define leadership skills. If you do not have experience in a management position, consider a group you have worked with either in the classroom or in an organization such as a fraternity, sorority, club, church, or service group. You will find the questions applicable to your own experience even if you are not yet a manager.

Use the following scale to rate the frequency with which you perform the behaviors described in each question. Place the corresponding number (1–7) in the blank preceding the statement.

Rarely	Irregularly	Occasionally	Usually	Frequently	Almost Always	Consistently
1	2	3	4	5	6	7

_____ **1.** When starting a new task, I note its objective and inform others who might be involved.

_____ **2.** I let others know what is expected of them.

_____ **3.** I look for more efficient ways to accomplish a task.

_____ 4. I see what has to be done and make sure that it gets done without waiting for others to call my attention to it.

_____ 5. I give instructions to others in simple, clear language or rephrase instructions so that they are simple and clear.

_____ 6. I note whether situations require prescribed methods or new approaches.

_____ 7. I keep informed and inform others about due dates and deadlines.

_____ 8. I discourage questions and requests for information that interfere with getting the job done.

_____ 9. In my own work habits, I provide a good example for others to follow.

_____ 10. I encourage others to learn from their mistakes.

_____ 11. I set personal achievement goals and help others set goals.

_____ 12. I let others know when they have done a good job.

_____ 13. When assigning tasks to others, I inform them of the importance and urgency of the assignment.

_____ 14. When appropriate, I delegate tasks to others in accordance with their experience and capabilities.

_____ 15. When assigning tasks to others, I help them develop by giving them new responsibilities.

_____ 16. I assign tasks to others in a way that encourages them to use their initiative as much as possible.

_____ 17. When assigning work to others, I require them to accept responsibility for finishing the task.

_____ 18. I hold others, and myself, responsible for the quantity, quality, and timeliness of completed assignments.

_____ 19. I provide immediate feedback to others so that it is clearly associated with the task being evaluated.

_____ 20. When giving others feedback, I review their actual performance in terms of assignment and responsibility.

LBQ Scoring

The scoring sheet in Figure 1 summarizes your responses for the LBQ. It will help you identify your existing strengths and pinpoint areas that need improvement. Right now, fill in the before-practice assessment column for each skill area by adding your scores for each item. Add the five category scores to obtain a total score. Enter that total score in the space indicated. After completing the module, you will take the LBQ again and fill in the after-practice assessment column.

FIGURE 1
Leadership Behaviors Questionnaire
(LBQ) Scoring

Skill Area	Items	Assessment	
		Before Practice	After Practice
Initiating and maintaining action	1,2,3,4		
Directing and coordinating	5,6,7,8		
Motivating and stimulating others	9,10,11,12		
Assigning and delegating tasks	13,14,15,16		
Holding others accountable	17,18,19,20		
TOTAL SCORE			

LBQ Evaluation

Figure 2 shows score lines for your total score and for each individual category measured on the LBQ. Each line shows a continuum from the lowest possible score to the highest. Place the letter B (before-practice) where your personal score falls on each of these lines.

The score lines in Figure 2 show graphically where you stand with regard to five leadership behaviors. If you have been honest with yourself, you now have a better idea of your relative strengths and weaknesses in the categories of behavior that make up the skills of leadership.

Learning to Use the LBQ Skills

You have now completed the initial evaluation of your leadership skills. In the LBQ, you rated the frequency with which you demonstrate behaviors in the five categories of leadership. This questionnaire provides a baseline against which you will assess improvements that have taken place after you have completed this module.

Before moving on, think about what you have learned about yourself in this evaluation. In what area of leadership skills are you weak? These will require more of your attention during the remainder of the module. What areas are your strongest? Use this module to fine-tune these areas so you may take full advantage of them. For these stronger areas, learning only one or two new things may be all you need for significant improvement in your leadership skills.

The LBQ will help you identify leadership behaviors that are appropriate for the management situations described in this module. After you have completed the module and have put into practice what you have learned, retake the LBQ.

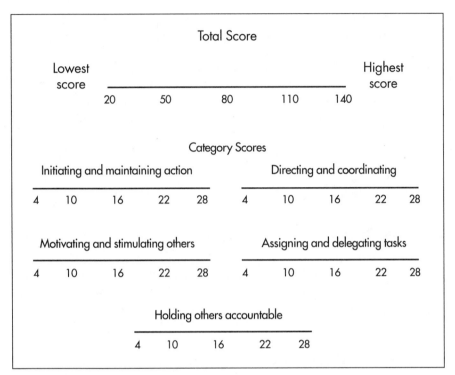

FIGURE 2
Leadership Behaviors Questionnaire
(LBQ) Evaluation

Then, compare your after-practice scores with your before-practice scores. This comparison will show you where you have progressed and where further work is needed.

UNDERSTANDING LEADERSHIP

In primitive social organizations, hierarchies of power and influence appeared and a dominant figure emerged. Personal characteristics such as forcefulness, attractiveness, and resourcefulness were associated with leadership, and it was believed that these qualities were inborn. A person who did not inherit these characteristics would have no way of achieving leadership skills. Thus the earliest leadership theorists searched for genetic traits that characterized a leader. Early anthropologists and historians, however, found it impossible to single out any personal traits that consistently predicted leadership or were consistently characteristic of leaders. For example, some leaders were forceful and were effective. Others were forceful and were ineffective. Frequently, in fact, leaders were just as different from each other as they were from the population at large.

These differences inspired a second approach to leadership theory. It was suggested that leaders differed from each other because they functioned in widely different situations. As situations differed, so did the persons who rose to leadership positions. This was not to say that the persons themselves changed to meet the situational needs but that persons of different genetic qualities were required in different situations. There was still no suggestion that a person could be taught how to act like a leader.

Neither of these theories could explain the fact that some persons clearly *learned* their leadership behaviors. Shy, quiet, and retiring persons could learn to demonstrate initiative, persuade and guide others, and act in a way that made others look to them to take charge. Thus another concept of leadership came into being. In this approach, leadership was seen as deriving from the performance of certain behaviors. Interest centered on identifying those behaviors. It was believed that systematic methods could be used to teach those identified behaviors, and that leadership skills could be learned and leaders developed. This approach is basic to the leadership practice in this module.

Influencing Others

Leaders influence others in order to move them toward specific actions and goals. As a manager, you may exert different kinds of influence. In this next section, we will briefly examine five types of influence. You may recall past situations in which one or more of these influences were used.

Legal Influence

Influencing others through one's official position or authority is referred to as legal, or legitimate, influence. Managers have the legal or contractual authority to lead others toward the goals of the organization. By virtue of their position, managers may command or demand that others comply with their directions and with established rules and policies.

Legal influence is based on perceptions about the obligations and responsibilities associated with particular positions in an organization or social system. It exists when people go along with the wishes of a person because they believe that person has the legitimate right to influence them and they have a duty to accept that influence. For example, presidents, supervisors, and professors have a certain degree of legitimate influence simply because of the position they hold. Other people accept this influence, as long as it is not abused, because they attribute legitimacy to the position and to the person who holds the position.

Expert Influence

A major source of influence in organizations comes from people who have expertise in solving problems and performing important tasks. Expert influence means using knowledge, ability, or information to lead others. Expertise rather than authority establishes leadership. Computer specialists often have substantial expert influence in organizations because they have technical knowledge that others need. The expertise of tax accountants and investment managers gives them substantial influence over the financial affairs of business firms. A secretary who knows how to run the office may have expert influence, although no legal influence.

Referent Influence

Referent influence operates when people want to follow a leader because of his or her personal characteristics. For example, the socially charismatic individual exercises referent influence. Charisma is not easily defined, but it exists when leaders use personal characteristics to move people in a particular direction. The charismatic leader may display an inordinate amount of energy, drive, or personal magnetism. People who demonstrate charisma are sure of themselves, and this sureness of purpose is displayed in their voice, their mannerisms, and their belief that others will *want* to follow their lead.

Reward Influence

Frequently, rewards or incentives influence the behaviors of others. Reward influence is derived from control over tangible benefits such as a promotion, a better job, a better work schedule, a larger operating budget, a larger expense account, or formal recognition of accomplishments. Reward influence is also derived from status symbols such as a larger office or a reserved parking space.

Punitive Influence

Punitive influence is derived from withholding rewards, withdrawing incentives, or administering some form of punishment. As a source of leadership control, punitive influence is important largely as a potential, rather than an actual, influence. For example, the threat of being disciplined for not arriving at work on time is effective in influencing the arrival time of most employees. The possibility that we might get a speeding ticket is enough to cause most of us to drive within the speed limit.

When you think about situations in which you were influenced toward a goal by another person, you probably can see that leaders usually exert more than one type of influence. For example, the person with a charismatic personality (referent influence) may also have knowledge you need or want (expert influence). The person who can influence you through incentives (reward influence) may also be able to withhold those rewards (punitive influence).

As a leader, you may use all five types of influence to motivate others. Each type can produce good effects under the right circumstance. However, not all types fit every situation, nor will all types be effective with every person. To use these types of influence effectively, you must first analyze the particular situation and consider the needs of the person involved. As a manager, you evaluate the types of influence available and then select the one to use based on two considerations: What are the chances that you will get the job done using this approach? What could be the consequence of your chosen approach?

Leadership Styles

Many different styles of leadership can be used to move others toward specific goals. Figure 3 depicts various leadership styles, from a highly centralized approach to one in which employees participate fully.

FIGURE 3
Leadership Styles: Degrees
of Authoritativeness

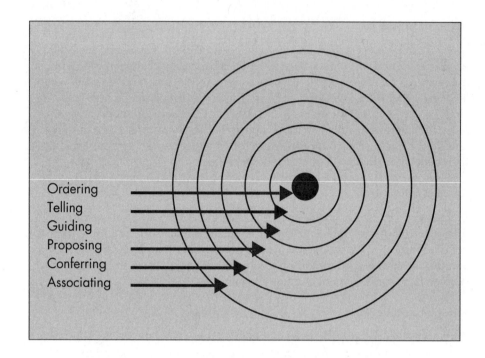

Each ring on this diagram indicates a different degree of authoritativeness and permits those being led different amounts of freedom. The further away a style is from the center of the circle, the more the leader shares authority with group members. No style is right or wrong; different situations require different styles or approaches to leadership. While one situation requires a leader to be direct and authoritarian, another situation may call for the leader to share authority with others. An effective leader selects the appropriate style for the particular situation.

The choice of leadership style also depends in part on the beliefs and attitudes of the manager. Some managers feel uncomfortable with highly authoritarian styles; they tend to ask employees to participate in leadership activities. Others feel that they are responsible for issuing orders to those they supervise. Managers who are confident in their leadership abilities will feel more confident conferring with employees.

The factors that influence the choice of leadership style include the manager's assessment of his or her own competencies, the needs and competencies of the employees, the nature of the situation, the amount of time available, and the organization.

If a manager believes that employees need to be told what to do in order to complete a task, that manager may use a highly authoritarian or leader-centered style. The more direction employees need, the more appropriate is a directive leadership style. Employees who can accept responsibility need less direction, so a less directive leadership style is appropriate.

Many times the situation itself determines which leadership style to use. In an emergency, such as a fire, it would be foolish for the leader to consult with employees on whether they should leave the building. Ordering is clearly the most appropriate leadership approach. In situations that are not emergencies, the leader should look carefully at the task at hand. Some tasks are better accomplished by conferring with employees; others require the use of a direct style.

Time also influences a manager's choice of leadership style. If immediate action is needed, the manager may choose a highly directive style; if there is time for long-range planning, a more participatory style may produce the best results.

The organization itself is another factor. Some organizations encourage employee participation. Others do not. Thus, the culture of the organization can influence the manager's selection of style.

Leadership Skills and Their Relationships to Other Managerial Skills

Leadership is closely intertwined with other managerial skills such as perception, flexibility, organizing and planning, decision making, decisiveness, communication, and interpersonal skills. For example, managers must perceive when to initiate action in a group. When motivating others to accomplish certain activities, they must show consideration for and sensitivity to others. When delegating tasks or providing instructions, they must carefully plan and organize what has to be done. To command the attention of others, a manager must communicate ideas convincingly. You can see that managers must develop all of their managerial skills to exercise leadership effectively.

Leadership Behaviors Required of Managers

Managers must demonstrate competency in five areas of leadership: (1) initiating and maintaining action; (2) directing and coordinating; (3) motivating and stimulating others; (4) assigning and delegating tasks; and (5) holding others accountable. Using these behaviors, managers perform two types of functions for the groups they supervise. The first type, task functions, is concerned with accomplishing work duties assigned to the group. The second type, building and maintenance functions, is concerned with developing and cementing group relationships, promoting feelings of group identity, and furthering employee growth and development. All five categories of leadership behavior are used for each type of function. In the next section, we will discuss the five categories of behavior that define the skills of leadership.

Initiating and Maintaining Action

Leaders initiate action so that followers can accomplish tasks. To initiate action, managers must explain objectives, define roles and tasks, generate rules and policies, and give instructions. Managers must first understand the tasks to be done before they can move others to complete those tasks.

When something interrupts or blocks the group's work, the manager must identify the information needed to remove the block and determine the best means of obtaining that information. To maintain action, the effective leader must also involve others, suggest new approaches, outline what is expected of others, and develop methods to facilitate job performance.

Directing and Coordinating

Leadership is often described as the process of getting the job done through and with the help of other people. In general, directing and coordinating means making sure that work flows smoothly and that activities are carried out with a minimum of conflict among individuals or groups.

Directing and coordinating employees involves clarifying job responsibilities by issuing clear directives as well as arranging and issuing assignments. Effective leaders demonstrate this skill by explicitly linking similar or related tasks, identifying task guidelines, and integrating instructions to the organization's or unit's goals. Directing and coordinating also involves being aware of deadlines, providing information needed to complete the task, establishing time frames, responding to questions about task assignments, and linking performance to rewards.

Motivating and Stimulating Others

Motivation means encouraging others to act in a particular way. Managers must motivate employees to behave in ways that further the goals of the organization. Keeping employees motivated over time is one of the universal tasks of leaders. One of the greatest sources of frustration for managers is the common misconception that people join organizations to pursue the organization's goals. In fact, most people join organizations to pursue their own goals. Therefore, it is important that managers motivate employees to work toward the goals of the organization by rewarding them for behaviors that help the organization.

Managers must recognize that individuals are spurred to action in different ways. They can use a variety of techniques to motivate employees, including reinforcing past successes and linking personal goals to organizational goals. Some people respond to positive attention and individual recognition; they can be motivated by praise and compliments. Other people need close monitoring from a strong manager. Whatever motivation technique is used, managers must take into account individual differences in employees. Not everyone is motivated in the same way or for the same reasons. The more managers are able to identify individual needs, the more successfully they will motivate and stimulate others.

Assigning and Delegating Tasks

The ability and willingness to delegate are essential to successful leadership. This aspect of leadership requires that the manager recognize employees' competencies and assign them tasks that will extend their competencies.

Delegation is typically defined as giving assignments to subordinates. It provides the manager with more time and allows him or her to focus attention on significant issues. While the manager's primary responsibility is to make certain that a job is accomplished, he or she is also responsible for providing opportunities that will expand employees' capabilities. As such, delegation may also be viewed as a key to the training and development of subordinates as well as the wise allocation of organizational resources.

By developing an effective work team, the manager can be assured that the task will be done adequately. If subordinates perform well, the manager will not have to fear the loss of power. Mutual confidence is an important foundation for effective delegation to take place. Assigning and delegating tasks accomplishes the following goals:

1. Establishes goals and clarifies objectives.
2. Defines responsibility and authority.
3 Establishes adequate controls.
4. Provides training.
5. Provides feedback, incentives, and rewards.

Holding Others Accountable

Accountability is the degree to which an individual is responsible or liable for the results of a decision or an assignment. Holding others accountable means that the manager must encourage subordinates to accept responsibility for their assignments and must offer clear and specific criteria for successful performance.

The techniques used in this aspect of leadership are monitoring and feedback. The manager makes certain that assignments are performed and that, in general, commitment and action are maintained. To enforce accountability, the manager must continually evaluate performance and offer feedback as progress is made.

PRACTICING LEADERSHIP SKILLS

Leadership skills cover a range of behaviors that relate to influencing, guiding, directing, and coordinating the activities of others. Leadership skills consist of the following component behaviors:

- *Initiating and maintaining action*—Informing others of your objectives and expectations, taking steps to avert possible problems, and taking needed action without waiting for others to direct you are some of the behaviors that are included under initiating and maintaining action.
- *Directing and coordinating*—Clear directions and simple instructions characterize this aspect of leadership skills.
- *Motivating and stimulating others*—Leadership is commonly associated with inspiring others. As a manager, you lead through encouraging, activating, and reinforcing employees in your unit.
- *Assigning and delegating tasks*—Leaders give assignments to others that not only use but build upon and enhance their competencies.
- *Holding others accountable*—Leadership skills are demonstrated by the manager who requires others to accept and live up to the responsibilities of their jobs.

The next section of in-basket exercises focuses separately on each component of leadership skills. Each exercise is followed by questions that ask you to choose the best response(s) to the situation.

Before you begin the leadership skills exercises, take time to review your scores on the five parts of the LBQ. Then, as you complete the exercises, keep in mind the behaviors noted in this questionnaire. The questions in the LBQ deepen your understanding of basic leadership considerations. Now practice the various components of leadership skills in the following in-basket exercises.

In-Basket Exercise 1: Initiating and Maintaining Action

Initiating and maintaining action is a critical leadership function. In the following situation, you assume the role of a manager who must demonstrate this aspect of leadership in dealing with a problem.

Situation:

You are Kerry Burns, the director of security for Canyon State University. The university is primarily a commuter campus. Only 5,000 of the 20,000 students live in college-owned facilities on campus: three high-rise dormitories that house 1,500 students each, a small community of 50 duplexes for married students, and two apartment complexes for married and unmarried students.

Recently, there has been a rash of break-ins at three of the facilities. These break-ins have occurred between the hours of 4 P.M. and 10 P.M. when most students are studying at the library or involved in extra-curricular activities.

You have to examine the current security system and find ways of providing more security to the students on campus. Because the budget has been frozen, you cannot get additional funding for security guards.

On your desk are the materials and memos shown in Exhibits 1 through 4 that relate to the security problem and provide information for you about the campus and crimestopper programs. Read these and then answer the questions that follow.

Your leadership skills focus:

- Know where the action is.
- Be aware of the objective of the action.
- Identify possible actions that will lead to the objective.
- Involve others.
- Clearly outline to others what is expected of them.
- Take steps to avert possible problems that can block action.

Questions for In-Basket Exercise 1:

1. As Kerry Burns, director of security at Canyon State University, you are responsible for dealing with the rising rate of non-violent crime on campus. Write a memo to your security staff that will initiate action on this matter.

2. Lt. Oshman of the city police department has sent you a memo (Exhibit 3) stating that at least 30 percent of the students on campus must be involved if the city police are to inaugurate a Crimestopper program. What will you do to initiate action to involve students in this program?

3. Pat Hower, resident director of apartment complex 1, has invited you to conduct a student meeting at the complex (Exhibit 4). You accept the invitation, and you are now at the meeting. What will you say that will begin a discussion with the students about their security concerns?

IN-BASKET EXERCISE 2: DIRECTING AND COORDINATING

The responsibilities of a manager include directing and coordinating the work of others. In the following in-basket exercise, you are a manager who directs and coordinates the sales division of a radio station.

Situation:

You are Asha Zaidi, sales manager of radio station WXXX, a 5,000 watt FM station with an MOR (middle of road) or easy-listening music format. Your primary advertisers cater to an affluent, mature, well-established population.

You have five sales representatives reporting directly to you. They are paid on a system of draw against commission. The weekly draw is $175 and the commission rate on their advertising sales is 20 percent of their weekly billing. In addition to selling commercial advertisements, sales reps write their own advertising copy and produce the commercials they sell.

You are responsible for directing and coordinating the efforts of all your reps so that each of them sells enough to earn the weekly draw or higher. You are responsible also for meeting overall sales objectives. Currently, the monthly billings are down. The station manager is concerned and has given you three weeks to reverse this downtrend in sales.

Today is July 2. You are meeting with your sales staff in order to direct their activities so that you can achieve this goal. On your desk are the materials from Exhibits 5 through 7 that pertain to the purpose of your meeting. Read these and then answer the questions that follow.

Your leadership skills focus:

- Clarify job responsibilities.
- Issue assignments and instructions.
- Coordinate activities.
- Link performance to rewards.

Questions for In-Basket Exercise 2:

1. The general manager of the station has given you three weeks to show progress in increasing monthly billing. Direct your staff to meet this deadline. Explain how you will demonstrate this leadership skill.

2. All sales reps are instructed to write and produce the commercials for their own accounts. Terry states that some of the sales reps do not do this. Direct your staff to carry out these instructions. Explain how you will demonstrate this leadership skill.

3. The six months' sales report (Exhibit 5) shows that Maria Perez and Hilbert Smith are the top producers in sales. However, they do not write and produce their own commercials. Explain how you will direct them to do this.

4. Last year, department stores and auto supply stores were the station's biggest customers. This year, sales to these businesses have declined sharply. Direct your staff to increase their sales efforts in these two areas. Be specific about the methods to use.

In-Basket Exercise 3: Motivating and Stimulating Others

For the manager, an important component of leadership skills is the ability to motivate and stimulate others to accomplish personal, departmental, and organizational goals. In the situation below, you are asked to motivate and stimulate others in the role of Kim Allen, sales manager for a health products manufacturer.

Situation:

As Kim Allen, sales manager of the eastern division of Naturin Health Products, Inc. (NHP), you are responsible for sales of NHP products in five eastern states. NHP manufactures and distributes a complete line of nutritional items, including natural foods and a line of natural vitamins. Buyers are large supermarket chains, retail drug and health food chains, and regional buyers. Sales growth in your division has been steady in all product lines except vitamin sales. Because overall sales are moving ahead and commission payments to the sales staff are increasing, you are pleased with general sales, but you want the vitamin line to move upward.

Today is September 1, and you are meeting with your sales staff. Your task is to motivate the sales staff to increase their sales of vitamin products during the coming quarter. On your desk are the materials from Exhibits 8 through 11 that relate to this problem. Read these and proceed to the questions that follow.

Your leadership skills focus:

■ Reinforce past accomplishments of the persons on your staff.
■ Identify and clarify individual goals.
■ Emphasize the need for action.
■ Link personal and company goals.
■ Arouse team spirit.
■ Promote competition.
■ Offer incentives.

Questions for In-Basket Exercise 3:

1. Although sales of other NHP products are increasing in the eastern division, sales of vitamins are down. The development and manufacture of vitamins represents a major investment for NHP. Therefore, you want the sales staff to increase their efforts to sell vitamins. How can you motivate the sales staff to do this?

2. The letter from Al Kirby (Exhibit 9) suggests that part of the reason for the decline in vitamin sales may be a case of mistaking NHP products for those of another manufacturer who has been cited for various violations. Al's way of dealing with this has been to back off until the problem solves itself. How can you motivate Al to take a more active role in overcoming the negative effects of mistaken product identity?

3. You (Kim Allen) have alerted your sales staff to the fact that the eastern division is behind other divisions in the sale of vitamins but ahead of others in all remaining NHP products. Say something to motivate your staff to accept a sales goal for the eastern division that will put them in first position for vitamins also. Explain how your statement motivates.

4. Frequently you want to motivate others to set personal goals for achievement that will further the management goal you want to achieve. How will you accomplish this for the members of your sales staff?

IN-BASKET EXERCISE 4: ASSIGNING AND DELEGATING TASKS

A manager demonstrates leadership skills by assigning and delegating tasks to others. In the following situation, you practice this aspect of the skill of leadership in the role of Carey Nelson, manager of products at Procall Corporation.

Situation:

You are Carey Nelson, manager of products at Procall Corporation. Procall manufactures beepers, pagers, and car telephone equipment. You coordinate product shipments to field representatives, so your office serves as a clearinghouse and control center. The field representatives place orders with you and you, in turn, coordinate the shipment schedules and delivery dates with the inventory department.

You have an assistant, Nada Everett, whose primary function is to develop cost projections and manage budgetary information based on reports filed by the field representatives. Nada has worked with you just over one year now and is a competent, efficient worker.

You also have one secretary, Lynn Scofield, who assists both you and Nada with general office work. Lynn has been with the company for fourteen years.

You are leaving on vacation for two weeks beginning Monday. It's now Friday afternoon, August 26, and you have to finish up before you leave the office. Some of your tasks will have to be delegated to others. A file on your desk contains memos (Exhibits 12 through 14) that outline these matters. As you answer the questions that follow, you will practice assigning and delegating tasks to others.

Your leadership skills focus:

- Encourage employees to use initiative.
- Enlarge employees' responsibilities.
- Note the importance of assignments.
- Consider experience and capabilities of the employees.
- Inform employees of the urgency of the assignments.

Questions for In-Basket Exercise 4:

1. Assign work to Nada Everett, your assistant manager. Explain how your assignments demonstrate the leadership skill of assigning and delegating tasks.

2. Delegate work to your secretary, Lynn Scofield.

3. What considerations have guided you in assigning tasks to Lynn? Explain how these are consistent with the leadership skills of delegation.

IN-BASKET EXERCISE 5: HOLDING OTHERS ACCOUNTABLE

Holding others accountable for the responsibilities assigned to them is a managerial function and an important component of leadership skills. Techniques used in this aspect of leadership are monitoring and feedback. The manager makes certain that assignments are performed and in general ensures that commitment and action are maintained. In the following situation, you will practice holding others accountable in the role of Pat White, quality assurance director of the Cresset Corporation.

Situation:

You are Pat White, quality assurance director of the Cresset Corporation. Cresset owns and operates residential health care facilities throughout the Southeastern states. The Quality Assurance Office oversees the operation of the individual homes in order to maintain high levels of service and quality and hold expenses at levels that ensure a reasonable return to investors.

Each of the homes is run by an administrator under the supervision of the quality assurance staff. The staff consists of you and six quality assurance specialists, who are assigned to a number of facilities. These specialists consult with the administrators of the residential facilities. They make certain that required standards of diet, sanitation, and nursing care are met. They also assess staffing needs and recommend budgets.

Today, May 30, you are meeting with Dave Turner, one of your quality assurance specialists, to discuss budgetary problems at three of the facilities assigned to him. To conduct this meeting properly you need to review the pertinent material from Exhibits 15 through 19. Then, respond to the questions that follow.

Your leadership skills focus:

- Require your specialists to accept responsibility for the assigned task despite changing circumstances.
- Provide for follow-up and feedback.
- Monitor performance.

Questions for In-Basket Exercise 5:

1. It is May 30. You (Pat White) are meeting with quality assurance specialist Dave Turner to discuss Dave's progress in reducing variances from budget at three residential home facilities. What steps would you take before this meeting to hold Dave accountable for keeping expenditures in line with budget?

2. Explain how feedback to Dave in the memo of May 21 informs Dave that the task of keeping spending in line with the budget still continues and that Dave is still accountable for results.

3. Dave informs you that part of the problem relates to a lack of storage space at the facilities. This makes it difficult to take advantage of price discounts on quantity purchases. Further, the storage space shortage was unforeseen at the time the budget was prepared. Under these circumstances, is it appropriate for you to hold Dave accountable for enforcing budgetary limits at the residential facilities in question? Explain.

4. What steps can you now take to ensure that Dave will continue on task until expenditures match budget at the residential facilities?

ASSESSING CHANGE

The purpose of this module has been to help you develop your leadership skills through in-basket exercises. Your attention has been focused on five components of leadership skills. You have seen that leadership skills involve:

- *Initiating and maintaining action*—As Kerry Burns, director of security at Canyon State University, you were required to get an action started and see that it progressed toward a goal.
- *Directing and coordinating*—In the role of Asha Zaidi, sales manager of radio station WXXX, you had to direct and coordinate the activities of the sales force.
- *Motivating and stimulating others*—Your task as Kim Allen, sales manager at NHP, was to motivate and stimulate your sales force to correct the down-trend in one item of NHP's otherwise successful product line.
- *Assigning and delegating tasks*—You assumed the role of Carey Nelson, manager of products at Procall Corporation. With your vacation about to begin, you found it necessary to delegate some of your duties to your staff.
- *Holding others accountable*—Finally, as Pat White, quality assurance director of the Cresset Corporation, you had to hold your staff members account-able for the results of their actions and recommendations.

At the beginning of this module, you completed the LBQ questionnaire to provide a baseline against which you could measure changes in your leadership behaviors. Now it is time to assess some of these changes.

First, retake the LBQ. A comparison of your before- and after-practice responses will demonstrate the extent to which you have improved your leadership behaviors. When you have retaken this questionnaire, compare your answers with those given earlier to see how much you have strengthened your leadership skills. Then take the Leadership Experience Scale (LES) that follows the LBQ.

The Leadership Behaviors Questionnaire (LBQ)

Use the following scale to rate the frequency with which you perform the behaviors described in each question. Place the corresponding number (1–7) in the blank preceding the statement.

Rarely	Irregularly	Occasionally	Usually	Frequently	Almost Always	Consistently
1	2	3	4	5	6	7

_____ **1.** When starting a new task, I note its objective and inform others who might be involved.

_____ **2.** I let others know what is expected of them.

_____ **3.** I look for more efficient ways to accomplish a task.

_____ **4.** I see what has to be done and make sure that it gets done without waiting for others to call my attention to it.

_____ **5.** I give instructions to others in simple, clear language or rephrase instructions so that they are simple and clear.

_____ **6.** I note whether situations require prescribed methods or new approaches.

_____ **7.** I keep informed and inform others about due dates and deadlines.

_____ **8.** I discourage questions and requests for information that interfere with getting the job done.

_____ **9.** In my own work habits, I provide a good example for others to follow.

_____ **10.** I encourage others to learn from their mistakes.

_____ **11.** I set personal achievement goals and help others set goals.

_____ **12.** I let others know when they have done a good job.

_____ **13.** When assigning tasks to others, I inform them of the importance and urgency of the assignment.

_____ **14.** When appropriate, I delegate tasks to others in accordance with their experience and capabilities.

_____ **15.** When assigning tasks to others, I help them develop by giving them new responsibilities.

_____ **16.** I assign tasks to others in a way that encourages them to use their initiative as much as possible.

_____ **17.** When assigning work to others, I require them to accept responsibility for finishing the task.

_____ **18.** I hold others, and myself, responsible for the quantity, quality, and timeliness of completed assignments.

_____ **19.** I provide immediate feedback to others so that it is clearly associated with the task being evaluated.

_____ **20.** When giving others feedback, I review their actual performance in terms of assignment and responsibility.

LBQ Scoring and Evaluation

Follow the scoring directions found on page 51 and in Figure 1. Complete the after-practice assessment column for the LBQ and compare your before- and after-practice assessment totals. You will also need to plot your after-practice scores in Figure 2. In which categories did your scores improve? Think about what has made your progress possible. Perhaps you can apply your insights to categories where your performance has lagged.

The Leadership Experience Scale (LES)

A second method to assess change in your leadership skills is the Leadership Experience Scale (LES). In the LES, you assume the role of a manager in several different situations. You are asked to choose the most appropriate leadership behavior from among several possible responses given the information available. This instrument helps you see how you actually behave in situations that require leadership skills.

The LES describes ten different situations. Select the response that demonstrates the most appropriate leadership behavior. Check the corresponding space at the left of the responses. Please choose only one response for each situation.

1. You are the plant manager of the Insbrun Company, a manufacturer of industrial brushes. You are in a conference with the personnel, production, warehouse, and shipping managers to discuss the high employee turnover. One out of three new employees is either fired or quits during the first three months of employment. At this meeting, you demonstrate leadership skills by:

_____ a) Initiating a discussion on how to deal with the turnover problem.

_____ b) Directing each division manager to develop an incentive program that will make remaining on the job more attractive.

_____ c) Announcing a new orientation program.

_____ d) Asking that all division managers give more personal attention to new employees.

_____ e) Directing the personnel department to screen all new employees more carefully.

2. You are the manager of the financial analysis department of Topsoil Incorporated. This landscape designing firm charges customers according to the amount of time needed for planting, as well as for landscape design and purchase of plants. In a meeting with the members of your department, you learn that the installation people have not been logging in their time and that the financial staff has estimated installation time on the basis of the number and cost of plants installed. You demonstrate leadership skills by:

_____ a) Complimenting the financial staff on their initiative in handling the problem.

_____ b) Admonishing the financial staff that they have acted in an unauthorized manner.

_____ c) Explaining that actual time must be used as the basis for billing and that reports from installers that do not show actual time spent on the job must be returned to them for completion.

_____ d) Arranging a meeting with the installation manager to discuss the matter.

_____ e) Reviewing the billings to see that they are reasonable.

3. At Marchon, Inc., a marketing firm that develops promotional materials for products of manufacturing firms, you are the manager of the creative materials department. You have called the department staff together to discuss a new contract with an office supply firm. The contract calls for the development of illustrated brochures that will describe the unique features of a new type of storage unit. You have decided to assign a team to handle the new contract. You demonstrate leadership skills by:

_____ a) Initiating a discussion on how to handle the contract and then choosing a team.

_____ b) Announcing the contract and assigning members to the team without further discussion.

_____ c) Assigning a staff member to lead the team and then asking the team leader to choose the team.

_____ d) Reviewing the previous experience of the staff at the meeting and deferring your selection to give yourself time to think about what you have learned.

_____ e) Announcing that you have decided to assign the contract to a team and asking for volunteers.

4. As the manager of the maintenance department of Shapro, Inc., you are chairing a meeting of the problem-solving team that you have been assigned. The team has been asked to develop a list of recommendations about plant safety. As the meeting begins, the vice president of operations walks in and asks if she can join the group. Of course, you agree. There is a sudden silence, and group members appear reluctant to continue the discussion. In this situation, you demonstrate leadership by:

_____ a) Remaining silent until someone speaks out.

_____ b) Stating a recommendation and asking for comments.

_____ c) Dividing the group into two subgroups, with directions to each subgroup to generate a recommendation that would then be shared with the general group.

_____ d) Inviting the vice president to state her ideas.

_____ e) Using a brainstorming technique in which each member in turn is asked to generate an idea very quickly and uncritically. Ideas will then be discussed more seriously.

5. This morning, the president of the Ellsworth Company resigned unexpectedly. As the accounting manager, you have scheduled a meeting for 10 A.M. to finalize budget recommendations for the fiscal quarter. You are meeting now, and staff members want to discuss the president's resignation. As manager you are responsible for turning in the recommendations by 4 P.M. today. You demonstrate leadership skills by:

_____ a) Canceling the meeting and preparing the recommendations yourself.

_____ b Rescheduling the meeting to noon to give the excitement a chance to die down.

_____ c) Informing the staff that the budget must be in that afternoon and directing them to attend to the task of the meeting.

_____ d) Suggesting to the staff that the news about the president can be discussed after the recommendations have been prepared.

_____ e) Making clear to the staff members that the president's resignation will not affect the recommendations they make but that a delay in the budget will affect their performance evaluations.

6. The Sushah Company has an honor system for its employees' work hours. Company policy has always been that people can be reasonably flexible with their time as long as all stations are covered and all work assignments are completed on time. Lately, some employees have been coming in late and leaving early; also, their work is not up to standard. As their manager, you must deal with the problem. To demonstrate leadership skills, you:

_____ a) Install a time clock in order to document all employees' time at work.

_____ b) Ask only the employees who are abusing the system to develop a workable solution.

_____ c) Bring the problem to the attention of all employees. Ask them to develop a solution to the problem.

_____ d) Establish a new policy in the department requiring employees who arrive late or leave early without completing their work to take a half day of vacation time.

_____ e) Inform the employees that they are responsible for monitoring the honor system if they wish it to continue. Suggest that they apply peer pressure to those who abuse the existing system.

7. Because an office employee of Hi-Di Rentals, Inc., completes her work efficiently and quickly, she is able to leave work 20 to 30 minutes early while other employees are still finishing their work. The situation is affecting the morale of the department; co-workers are complaining that it's not fair. As office manager, you are reluctant to "punish" the efficient employee. How can you demonstrate leadership skills in this situation?

_____ a) Tell the employee that although she completes her work and it is of excellent quality she nevertheless needs to stay until the end of the day.

_____ b) Ask the employee to assist others when she has finished her own work.

_____ c) Ask the employee to spend time writing some professional career goals that you might help her reach.

_____ d) Direct the employee to develop a project that she could work on in addition to her regular responsibilities.

_____ e) Broaden the current job responsibilities of the employee and increase her salary accordingly.

8. As manager of the public affairs department of the Toehod Bus Lines, you are frequently called upon to speak at meetings of social clubs and service

organizations. You have just checked your calendar and noticed that you are scheduled to address a meeting of the Landlocked Travel Club one week from today. This is a special meeting of the group, and it is important that the bus lines are represented. However, your vacation is scheduled to begin in three days, and you will be away for at least two weeks. Your office staff consists of one new departmental assistant who has recently received a master's degree in communication and one secretary who has been with the firm for five years. You have never heard your assistant speak publicly. Under the circumstances, you demonstrate leadership skills by:

_____ a) Directing your assistant to speak in your place.

_____ b) Directing your secretary to speak in your place.

_____ c) Postponing your vacation until after the meeting.

_____ d) Calling the travel club and canceling your talk.

_____ e) Asking the assistant to represent the firm at the meeting and to read your speech.

9. The Glynmore bank has purchased automatic teller machines that will be installed tomorrow. As planning manager, you have developed a safety procedure that requires three people to be in attendance whenever the money and the envelopes are emptied from the machine. While you are explaining the procedure to the employees of the bank, one of the employees declares that your procedure is a waste of time and personnel. She states that she has devised a safety system that would not require so many people to be in attendance each time. To demonstrate your leadership skills, you should:

_____ a) Encourage full discussion of possible alternatives to your plan.

_____ b) Direct that, at this point in time, it will have to be done as already arranged.

_____ c) Inform the employees that your procedure will be evaluated after it has been in operation for a designated period and that alternative procedures may be considered then.

_____ d) Ask the employee who spoke to outline the proposal fully during this meeting.

_____ e) Inform the employee that you have already considered possible alternatives and that your plan is the most feasible.

10. As the new manager of the shipping department of Stolon, Inc., you have received many complaints from field representatives that orders are not being shipped on time. Upon inquiry, you find that, indeed, there has been little coordination between order receipts and order shipments. You have called a meeting to discuss this matter with the members of the department. At the meeting you demonstrate leadership skills best if you:

_____ a) Instruct employees to ship the orders as they are received.

_____ b) Inform employees that they must meet a shipping quota.

_____ c) Direct each employee to comment on the complaints of the field reps.

_____ d) Compliment the employees on their efforts and state that the field representatives' complaints may be excuses for their own poor work.

_____ e) Require employee input on developing a plan to better coordinate the receipt and shipment of orders.

LES Scoring and Evaluation

Complete the LES scoring form in Figure 4. Compare your responses with the feedback that your instructor will provide about the most appropriate responses for the ten leadership situations.

SUMMARY

The more systematically you examine your leadership skills and the related styles and influencing techniques you use, the more effective you will become as a manager. In this module you found that leadership skills require a manager to demonstrate five categories of behavior: (1) initiating and maintaining action, (2) directing and coordinating, (3) motivating and stimulating others, (4) assigning and delegating tasks, and (5) holding others accountable.

Question	a	b	c	d	e	Response
1						
2						
3						
4						
5						
6						
7						
8						
9						
10						

FIGURE 4
Leadership Experience Scale (LES) Scoring

FIGURE 5
Leadership Skills Action Guide

You Show Leadership Skills When You:

- Initiate and maintain action
- Direct and coordinate
- Motivate and stimulate
- Assign and delegate
- Enforce accountability

You Should Show Leadership Skills When:

- Action must be initiated and continued
- Others must be directed and their activities coordinated
- Others must be motivated and stimulated to accomplish goals
- Tasks must be assigned and responsibilities delegated
- Others must be held accountable for results

To lead, you must move employees to accomplish goals. To do this, you can exert legal, expert, referent, reward, and punitive influence.

The style of leadership you use is also important in moving others toward a goal. This module examined six different styles of leadership: ordering, telling, guiding, proposing, conferring, and associating. Your choice of leadership style is influenced by the particular situation, your beliefs and attitudes as a manager, time factors, and the culture of your organization.

In working through this module, you have learned about the various components of leadership and you have practiced several aspects of leadership in a variety of exercises. If possible, you are applying the experience gained in this module to a work situation or a group project in a class or an organization in which you are a member. If so, you may well experience the pleasure of positive feedback from others. Feedback from persons with whom you work will help you gauge whether you are using your leadership skills in an appropriate manner. Remember that successful and competent managers continually work to improve their leadership skills.

To remember key steps in practicing leadership skills and to identify situations in which the skills are needed, use the action guide shown in Figure 5. Frequent review of the information will help you become a better manager.

SKILL-BUILDING EXERCISES

EXERCISE 1 ■ IDENTIFYING INFLUENCING TECHNIQUES

In each of the following situations, identify the influencing technique and provide a brief explanation.

Situation 1: You have a major contract that must be finished today. You have been told by your boss that you are to keep everyone at work until the task is finished. You meet with your employees and tell them, "I am responsible for seeing that this work is finished on time. No one will be allowed to leave until the work is finished."

Situation 2: You have one employee who has missed the last four deadlines. You have spoken with her after each one she missed, and she always agrees that she will meet the next one. You want her to change, so you tell her that the next time she is late, you will put her on probation.

Situation 3: You have an employee who is beginning to take classes at the local university in business administration. You have an undergraduate business degree as well as an MBA and you recommend a list of courses to your employee.

EXERCISE 2 ■ LEARNING MORE ABOUT DELEGATING TASKS

Conduct an interview with a manager and ask him or her to identify several tasks that he or she currently delegates to someone else. Each task should be defined in terms of the nature of the task, the type of individual who has assumed the responsibility, and the type of influence the manager used. Ask the manager if he or she encountered any difficulties in delegating. Be prepared to report your findings to a small group or to the class as directed by your instructor.

■ Use Exhibits 1–4 with In-Basket Exercise 1,
Exhibits 5–7 with In-Basket Exercise 2,
Exhibits 8–11 with In-Basket Exercise 3,
Exhibits 12–14 with In-Basket Exercise 4,
Exhibits 15–19 with In-Basket Exercise 5.

EXHIBIT 1
Map of Canyon State University

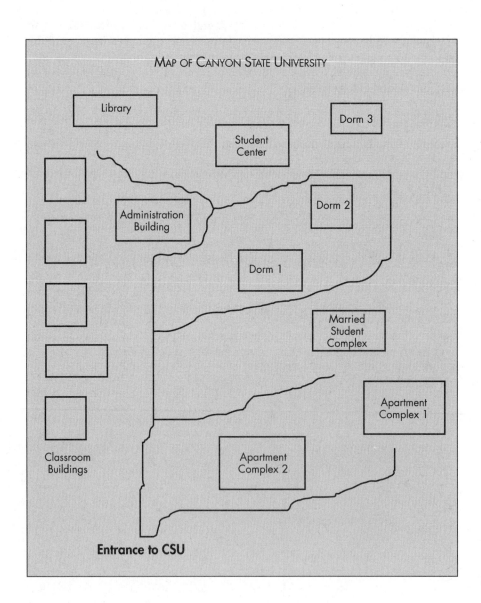

MAP OF CANYON STATE UNIVERSITY

Library

Dorm 3

Student Center

Dorm 2

Administration Building

Dorm 1

Married Student Complex

Apartment Complex 1

Classroom Buildings

Apartment Complex 2

Entrance to CSU

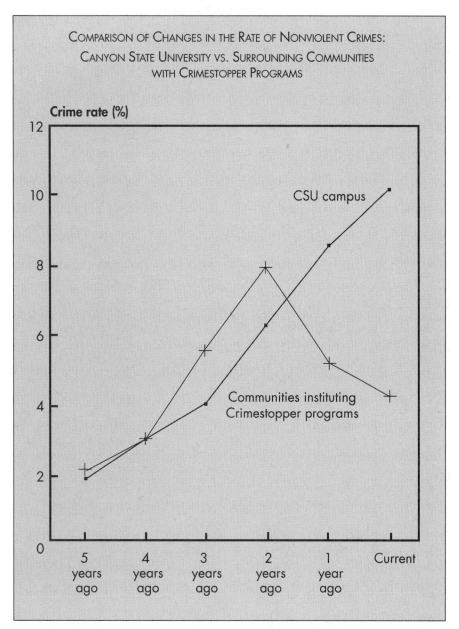

COMPARISON OF CHANGES IN THE RATE OF NONVIOLENT CRIMES:
CANYON STATE UNIVERSITY VS. SURROUNDING COMMUNITIES
WITH CRIMESTOPPER PROGRAMS

Crime rate (%)

CSU campus

Communities instituting
Crimestopper programs

EXHIBIT 2
Comparison of Changes in the Rate
of Nonviolent Crimes

EXHIBIT 3
City Police Memorandum

CITY POLICE DEPARTMENT

MEMORANDUM

TO: Kerry Burns, Director of Security
         Canyon State University
FROM: Lt. Randy Oshman
         Public Affairs Officer
         City Police Department
DATE: February 11

I appreciate your inquiry about Spring City's Crimestopper program. We have found the program to be of great help in our overall plan to reduce crime in the city.

For your information, I am enclosing a chart which shows the rate of nonviolent crime (NVCR) reported at Canyon State University over the past 6 years. The NVCR of surrounding communities that have instituted the Crimestopper program is also shown. You can see that in communities using the Crimestopper program, the NVCR has been lowered dramatically.

For any group wishing to begin this program, we first suggest that there be an overall commitment to becoming involved. When you can obtain at least 30% commitment to this program from the total number of residents in your facilities, then I would be glad to attend a University meeting and help you implement this program. We cannot commit the police department's involvement with less than 30% of your students taking an active role; the program would not work with less.

Because of funding limitations, the Police Department of Spring City is unable to provide as much direct contact with community members as we would like. Our officers are already stretched thin. The Crimestopper program is a valuable aid and frequently gives us the extra eyes and ears we need to hold crime in check.

CANYON STATE UNIVERSITY

MEMORANDUM

TO: Kerry Burns, Director of Security
         Canyon State University
FROM: Pat Hower, Resident Director, Apt. Complex 1
DATE: February 14

The students at my complex are very concerned about the number of break-ins since the beginning of the school year. Although all of the break-ins have occurred in their absence, the students are frightened about these incidents and are fearful for their safety.

At our last dorm meeting, there were lots of ideas tossed around about how we could step up security measures. The students really want to do something right away!

We are having another dorm meeting on Friday, February 19, at 4 P.M. Can you attend and conduct this meeting? Perhaps you can get us started on some preventive and protective measures.

EXHIBIT 4
Canyon State University
Memorandum

EXHIBIT 5
Six Month Billing Evaluation for Sales
Representatives

SIX MONTH BILLING EVALUATION FOR SALES REPRESENTATIVES						
RADIO STATION WXXX						
		H. Smith	M. Perez	T. Ames	D. Fitch	M. Allbrite
January	Billing	$8,000	$6,000	$2,500	$3,500	$4,000
	Commission	1,600	1,200	500	700	800
February	Billing	10,000	7,500	2,900	3,300	4,200
	Commission	2,00	1,500	580	1,160	840
March	Billing	11,500	13,500	3,000	3,300	8,000
	Commission	2,300	2,700	600	760	1,500
April	Billing	7,500	8,000	1,800	4,000	3,500
	Commission	1,500	1,600	360	800	700
May	Billing	9,000	10,000	2,200	3,800	3,200
	Commission	1,800	2,000	440	750	640
June	Billing	12,500	9,000	3,200	2,100	4,000
	Commission	2,500	1,300	640	420	800
Jan-June	Billing	53,000	54,000	15,500	25,000	25,900
TOTAL	Commission	11,700	10,800	3,120	5,200	5,380

Commission Rate = 20 Percent

WXXX
"EASY LISTENING"

MEMORANDUM

TO: Asha Zaidi, Sales Manager
FROM: Terry Ames, Sales Representative
DATE: June 26
RE: Commission

Look, I know I'm not meeting my draw of $175.00 per week against my commission. But I seem to be spending most of my time in the production room with Don editing the other reps' work. Maria and Hilbert have said they don't have the time to produce commercials because they are closing on sales. Don and I have to take care of their "extras."

I think being paid by commission is unfair when we are forced to spend many hours doing nonsales work, and work for other reps' clients at that. It wouldn't get done if Don and I didn't do it.

I think you should do something.

EXHIBIT 6
WXXX Memorandum

EXHIBIT 7
Radio Station WXXX – Time
Purchases

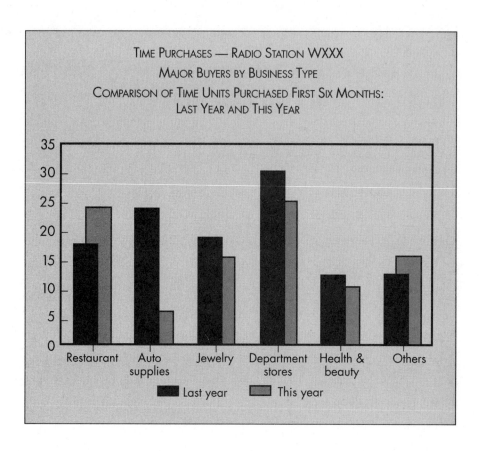

TIME PURCHASES — RADIO STATION WXXX

MAJOR BUYERS BY BUSINESS TYPE

COMPARISON OF TIME UNITS PURCHASED FIRST SIX MONTHS:
LAST YEAR AND THIS YEAR

■ Last year   ▢ This year

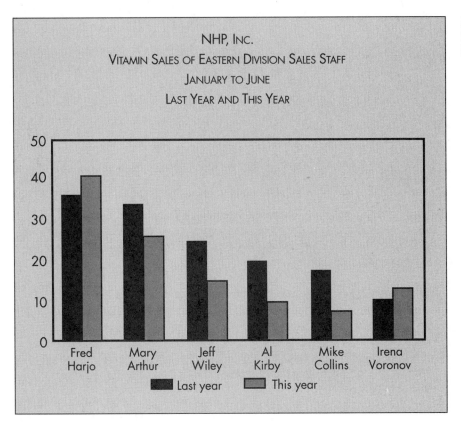

EXHIBIT 8
NHP, Inc. – Vitamin Sales of Eastern Division Sales Staff

EXHIBIT 9
NHP, Inc. Memorandum

NHP, INC.

MEMORANDUM

TO: Kim Allen, Sales Manager
FROM: Al Kirby, Sales
DATE: August 10
RE: Violation citation for Neutron-Holt, Inc.

You probably know that in January, Neutron-Holt, Inc., was cited for several violations by the government regulatory agencies. Their vitamins were found to be contaminated, their manufacturing processes unsafe, and their labels inaccurate.

For some strange reason, my accounts have been telling me that consumers are confusing our products with those of Neutron-Holt. I have told them to simply ignore the matter and it will solve itself when the Neutron-Holt business dies down.

In the meantime, I'm not pushing vitamins. There's no problem with the other products.

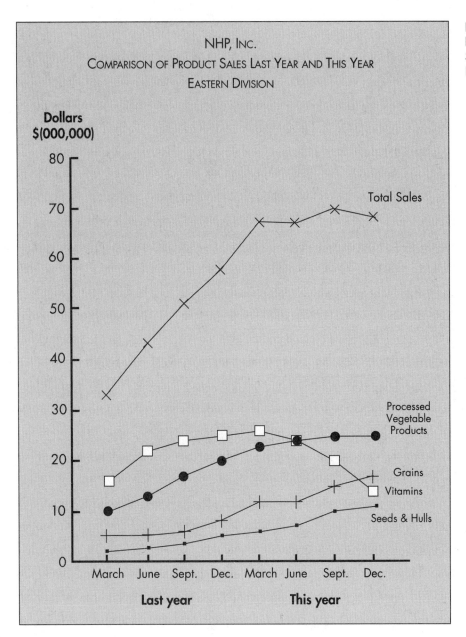

EXHIBIT 11
NHP, Inc. Memorandum

NHP, Inc.

MEMORANDUM

TO: Sales Staff
FROM: Kim Allen, Sales Manager, Eastern Division
DATE: August 30
RE: Decline in vitamin sales

Although our overall sales have moved up steadily, sales of vitamins are down in this division. Vitamins, an important part of the product line offered by NHP, represent a major investment of research and production dollars. Moreover, our vitamins are excellent and we take great pride in them. Other divisions are showing continued growth in vitamin sales. In fact, vitamins are the only product line where the eastern division is not tops in the country. We'll be talking about this at our meeting tomorrow. We need your ideas!

In the meantime, here is some natural food for thought. We have never been cited by the regulatory agencies for any type of violation. We belong to the Organic Manufacturers Association (OMA), a group that regulates processing methods in the organic products industry. Based on their inspections, we have been given the top rating (AAAA). OMA's standards are far more stringent than the government's. Your accounts need to know this. Although we stress these points in the trade magazines, you need to repeat them as well.

Finally, for the eastern division only, during the next three months, NHP is offering a 2 percent override above regular commission rates on vitamin sales which exceed your last year's December levels. That's a nice little stocking stuffer for the holidays!

PROCALL CORPORATION

I N T E R O F F I C E   M E M O R A N D U M

TO: Carey Nelson, Products
FROM: Rich Delta, Inventory Control
DATE: August 26
RE: Inventory check

There seems to be a discrepancy in the inventory figures you sent us. This discrepancy will cause problems in all the other departments unless it is resolved.

Please recheck your figures and send me a written reply. We need this as soon as possible.

Thanks.

EXHIBIT 12
Procall Corporation Memorandum

PROCALL CORPORATION

I N T E R O F F I C E   M E M O R A N D U M

TO: Carey Nelson, Products
FROM: Barb Esther, Comptroller's Office
DATE: August 25
RE: Briefing on new budget procedures

We are having a two-hour briefing session on the new budget procedures next Wednesday at 3:00 in the LRC.

I think your department will benefit greatly from the session. The new system may seem confusing at first, and this seminar should help make things clear.

EXHIBIT 13
Procall Corporation Memorandum

EXHIBIT 14
Procall Corporation Memorandum

PROCALL CORPORATION

INTEROFFICE MEMORANDUM

TO:　　Carey Nelson, Products
FROM:　Hu Yuyin, Audio Visual Department
DATE:　August 24
RE:　　Request for projector

I know you said you needed either a projector or an overhead for your presentation in April, but I forget which. I also need to know the dates you will use the equipment.

Please call me so that I can schedule you well in advance. The limited number of machines are in great demand.

Have a good vacation.

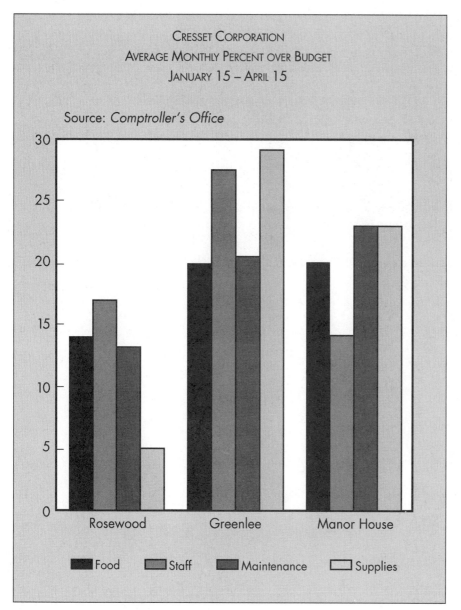

EXHIBIT 15
Cresset Corporation – Average
Monthly Percent Over Budget
January 15 – April 15

EXHIBIT 16
Cresset Corporation Memorandum

CRESSET CORPORATION

MEMORANDUM

TO: Pat White, Quality Assurance Director
FROM: Dave Turner, Quality Assurance Specialist
DATE: April 27
RE: Budget Variances

I am monitoring expenditures at Manor, Rosewood, and Greenlee. For the time being, all purchases, new hires, and overtime must be cleared with me.

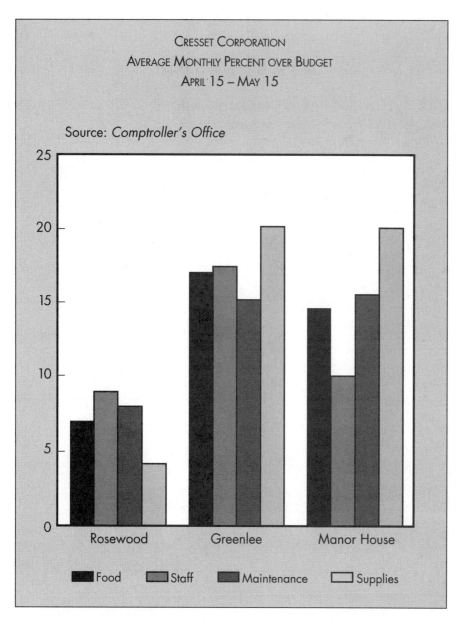

EXHIBIT 17
Cresset Corporation – Average
Monthly Percent Over Budget
April 15 – May 15

EXHIBIT 18
Cresset Corporation Memorandum

CRESSET CORPORATION

MEMORANDUM

TO: Dave Turner, Quality Assurance Specialist
FROM: Pat White, Quality Assurance Director
DATE: May 21
RE: Variances from Budget

Congratulations. The picture is improving at Manor House, Rosewood, and Greenlee. Monitoring expenditures was a good idea. However, all three facilities are still over budget. You need to take further measures to bring expenditures into line.

I've scheduled a meeting with you on May 30, at 10 A.M. At that time, I'd like a report on what additional steps you have taken to bring spending into line with budget.

EXHIBIT 19
Cresset Corporation Memorandum

CRESSET CORPORATION

MEMORANDUM

TO: Pat White, Quality Assurance Director
FROM: Dave Turner, Quality Assurance Specialist
DATE: May 23
RE: Vendors – Manor House, Rosewood, Greenlee

I have been reviewing the vendors used by the above three facilities. I find that the facilities frequently use local vendors whose prices are higher than those of larger firms. Also, they make many small last-minute purchases of food and cleaning supplies rather than making larger purchases on which they could get quantity discounts.

Administrators at all three homes complain of a shortage of storage space which has come about because some of the storage rooms have been converted to recreational spaces for residents in order to conform to revised state licensing requirements. This was not foreseen when the budget was prepared.

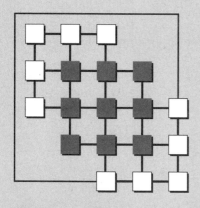

PART 2
COMMUNICATION SKILLS: COMMUNICATING EFFECTIVELY IN ORAL AND WRITTEN FORMATS

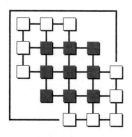

MODULE 3
WRITTEN COMMUNICATION SKILLS:
WRITING TO OTHERS

INTRODUCTION

Writing is communicating. The ability to communicate in writing—to accurately express ideas, feelings, and information—is demonstrated when others clearly perceive the intended message of the written communication. Everything you write is a chance to make a good impression! Clear writing is the sign of an effective manager. Those who capture their ideas on paper stand out as fluent, confident, and persuasive.

To demonstrate effective written communication, the manager uses the following building blocks: vocabulary, spelling, grammar, punctuation, sentence structure, transitions, and paragraphs. These are tools, and when used correctly, they help convey the written message to the reader.

Most management skills are demonstrated through communication with others. Much of this communication is in written form. If the written message is not clear and if it is not understood by the readers, these other management skills may be lost in the resulting confusion. In a managerial context, written communication skills can be divided into three behaviors: (1) pre-writing activities (determining objectives, organizing needed material, and considering the reader), (2) writing activities (choosing words, selecting word forms, and constructing the written communication), and (3) post-writing activities (reviewing and editing).

This module focuses on the skills needed to write effectively and efficiently. The exercises in the module will help you develop and strengthen these skills. You will assume the role of manager in a variety of situations. In each situation, you will be provided with pieces of information—materials that typically find their way to the manager's desk. As manager, you must use your writing skills to solve potential problems. By actually participating in these situations, you can learn and practice written communication skills.

The module is organized so that you will develop a before-practice assessment of your writing skills by completing the Written Communication Process Questionnaire (WCPQ). This questionnaire is an assessment instrument that measures your writing skills at the present time. We then examine the basic communication model along with some of the barriers to effective communication. Next, we present a brief discussion of the components of written communication. To better understand the skills associated with written communication, you will practice these skills through in-basket exercises. The exercises focus on one category of written communication at a time. Feedback from your instructor will help you judge the quality of your responses and will provide guidance on improving specific behaviors.

After a review and summary, you will have an opportunity to retake the WCPQ and compare your after-practice assessment results with your earlier results. You will also complete the Written Communication Technical Skills Questionnaire (WCTS). This assessment instrument measures your skills regarding rules of writing, including your use of grammar.

Once you have completed this module, you may find that the exercises result in immediate improvement, or you may find that improvement is more noticeable after you have had opportunities to perform on the job or in a non-work-related situation.

Assessing Written Communication Skills

Before proceeding with the rest of this module, complete the questionnaire on the following pages. It is both a teaching tool and a means of measuring your present level of written communication skills. Take time to complete the questionnaire carefully. Your answers should reflect your behaviors as they are now, not as you would like them to be. Be honest. This instrument is designed to help you discover where you are now so you can work to improve your writing skills.

The Written Communication Process Questionnaire (WCPQ)

The Written Communication Process Questionnaire (WCPQ) examines your current written communication skills in six areas. These skills are essential to managerial effectiveness. When responding to the questions, consider your work experience or relate the questions to your experience in classroom, fraternity, sorority, club, church, or service organization. You will find that the questions apply to your own experience even if you are not yet a manager.

After you have completed this module and have had an opportunity to put into practice the writing skills you have learned, you will retake the questionnaire. Comparing your before- and after-practice results will help you evaluate the effectiveness of your learning in this module.

Use the following scale to rate the frequency with which you perform the behaviors described in each question. Place the corresponding number (1–7) in the blank preceding the statement.

Rarely	Irregularly	Occasionally	Usually	Frequently	Almost Always	Consistently
1	2	3	4	5	6	7

_____ **1.** I clearly establish the general purpose of each of my written communications.

_____ **2.** I clearly establish the specific objective(s) of each of my written communications.

_____ **3.** I systematically obtain the necessary and relevant information to include in my written communications.

_____ **4.** I sort through and organize information to be included in my written communications (e.g., organize by topic, source, problem, or time frame).

_____ **5.** I outline (in writing) the sequence or structure of my written communications.

_____ **6.** I familiarize myself with the background, expectations, and experiences of my reader(s).

_____ **7.** I take note of my reader's probable point of view.

_____ **8.** I consider the level of knowledge that the reader possesses.

_____ **9.** I recognize the needs of the reader and their effect on the reception of my written communications.

_____ **10.** I determine ways to adapt my written communications to meet the needs of or gain acceptance from the reader.

_____ **11.** I quickly and correctly choose words that clearly express my intended meanings.

_____ **12.** I review various connotations of words I use.

_____ **13.** I consider the fact that words often contain hidden messages and make sure that these messages convey my intended meaning.

_____ **14.** I seek feedback from readers to make certain that my words are understood.

_____ **15.** I avoid using words that might not be part of the reader's vocabulary.

_____ **16.** I use concrete nouns as opposed to abstract nouns in my written communications.

_____ **17.** The pronouns I use accurately reflect the gender and number of the persons to whom I refer.

_____ **18.** I am careful to avoid the use of extreme adjectives or other "loaded language" when my objectivity as the writer is important.

_____ **19.** I do not repeat myself needlessly in my writing.

_____ **20.** I avoid the use of technical jargon.

_____ **21.** My sentences express one main idea.

_____ **22.** I compose paragraphs so that ideas and information concern one main theme that is expressed in the topic sentence.

_____ **23.** I use transition ideas and sentences to lead from one paragraph to another.

_____ **24.** I use an outline form or subheadings to structure my written communications.

_____ **25.** I stick to the point of my communication.

_____ **26.** After completing a written communication, I carefully read it to make sure the style and tone of the message are what I want.

_____ **27.** When editing, I reduce the number of words in my written communication.

_____ **28.** When editing, I substitute shorter words for longer ones if they have the same meaning.

_____ **29.** I check for spelling errors and use a dictionary when in doubt.

_____ **30.** I review my original purpose and objectives to determine whether the final written product accomplishes them.

WCPQ Scoring

The scoring sheet in Figure 1 summarizes your responses for the WCPQ. It will help you identify your existing strengths and pinpoint areas that need improvement. Right now, fill in the before-practice assessment column and add the six category scores to obtain a total score. Enter that total score in the space indicated. After completing the module, you will take the WCPQ again and fill in the after-practice assessment column.

FIGURE 1
The Written Communication Process Questionnaire (WCPQ) Scoring

Skill Area	Items	Assessment Before Practice	After Practice
Determining objectives and organizing needed material	1,2,3,4,5		
Considering the reader	6,7,8,9,10		
Choosing words	11,12,13,14,15		
Selecting word forms	16,17,18,19,20		
Constructing the written communication	21,22,23,24,25		
Reviewing and editing	26,27,28,29,30		
TOTAL SCORE			

	Total Score	
Lowest score		Highest score
	30 66 102 138 174 210	

Category Scores

Determining objectives and organizing needed materials	Considering the reader
5 12.5 20 27.5 35	5 12.5 20 27.5 35

Choosing words	Selecting word forms
5 12.5 20 27.5 35	5 12.5 20 27.5 35

Constructing the written communication	Reviewing and editing
5 12.5 20 27.5 35	5 12.5 20 27.5 35

FIGURE 2

The Written Communication Process Questionnaire (WCPQ) Evaluation

WCPQ Evaluation

Figure 2 shows score lines for your total score and for each category measured on the WCPQ. Each line shows a continuum from the lowest score to the highest. Place the letter B (before-practice) where your personal score falls on each of these lines.

The score lines in Figure 2 show graphically where you stand with regard to six written communication behaviors. If you have been honest with yourself, you now have a better idea of your relative strengths and weaknesses in the categories that make up the skills of written communication.

Learning to Use the WCPQ Skills

You have completed the initial evaluation of your written communication skills. In the WCPQ, you rated the frequency with which you demonstrate behaviors in the six categories of written communication. This questionnaire provides a baseline against which you will assess improvements that have taken place after you have completed this module.

Before moving on, think about what you have learned about yourself in this evaluation. In what areas of written communication skills are you weak? These will require the most attention during the remainder of the module. What areas are your strongest? Use this module to fine-tune these areas so you may take full advantage of them. For these stronger areas, learning only one or two new things may be all you need for significant improvement in your written communication skills.

The WCPQ will help you identify written communication behaviors that are appropriate for the management situations described in this module. After you have completed the module and have had an opportunity to put into practice what you have learned, retake the WCPQ. Then, compare your after-practice scores with your before-practice scores. This comparison will show you where you have progressed and where you need further work.

UNDERSTANDING COMMUNICATION

Human beings are distinguished from other animals not so much by our ability to communicate as by our ability to develop *systems* of communication. To understand the communication process, you need to recognize two things. First, communication is the *exchange* of information and the *transmission* of meaning. Second, the purpose of communication is to bring about change or influence action.

People communicate through language. The language they use reflects their personality, culture, and environment. You are likely to respond to other people's written communications according to the situation you are in and your own predispositions, and your communications are likely to be determined by your environment and culture. In the next section, we will look at a model of the communication process.

The Communication Model

A model of the communication process is shown in Figure 3. You can see that first an idea must be encoded, or put into language, by the sender. Next, the sender relays the message through a variety of channels to a receiver. The receiver must then decode the message and arrive at the idea being sent. The channel serves as a filter and either aids or hinders the two-way communication process via feedback. Although this model seems straightforward, it can break down for many reasons, leading to situations where the idea the receiver receives is not much like the idea the sender intended to send.

Our main focus in this module is on the written communication channel. As a manager, the memos, letters, and reports you write will occur in an organizational culture. This culture has rules (implicit and explicit) for written communication that must be followed. For example, when you submit a written report to a manager two levels up in the organization, you may use a different format or style than you would use for a note or memo to someone in the organization who reports to you.

Effective writing skills are the tools or techniques for increasing the probability that the sender's intended message will be accurately received by the receiver. However, as previously noted, many things can interfere with this process and

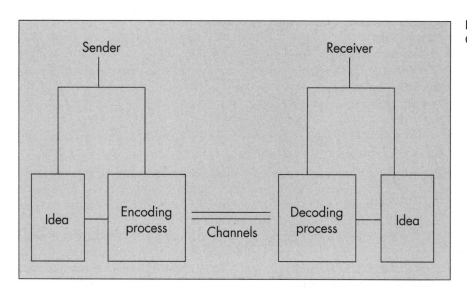

FIGURE 3
Communication Model

decrease the likelihood that the reader accurately decodes the message. Let's look at some of these barriers to effective written communication.

Barriers to Effective Written Communication

When we talk about the effectiveness of communication, we should be able to document this effectiveness. It doesn't matter how much you write or how many people read your memos, letters, or reports. What matters is the extent to which the intended reader accurately receives and understands your message. But how do you know if someone "receives and understands" your letter? You know by that person's behavior. In other words, you become aware of the reader's responses to your communications. If these responses indicate that you have not been understood, what could have gone wrong? The following explains some of the barriers or roadblocks in written communication, including sender, channel, and receiver problems.

Sender Problems

First, the sender must have a purpose or reason for communicating. If you as sender do not state this purpose, the reader must guess it. The reader may guess incorrectly, and this could certainly influence the manner in which the communication is interpreted.

Second, the sender must have an idea. You get ideas from thinking, reading, listening, and seeing, among other things. If your idea is incomplete, vague, or too abstract, you may have difficulties stating the idea to others in writing.

Third, the sender must encode ideas into language. This is why vocabulary is so important. If your vocabulary is inadequate, you will have trouble putting your ideas into words. Also, you must choose words from the reader's vocabulary to express your ideas. If you choose words that are not part of the reader's vocabulary, the communication process can break down. You may make an incorrect assumption about the reader's familiarity with a concept or technique.

The sender composes the written communication using words, sentences, and paragraphs. All languages have rules governing the use of these elements. When you violate these rules, you risk a breakdown in the message you are sending.

Channel Problems

One of the most severe channel problems results from too much information, or what we call information overload. Overload occurs when people receive a great amount of written communications. Often when you write to someone you are competing with other messages for attention. In the business environment, you need to stick to the point and write briefly when possible.

When people receive written material, they may put it down or throw it away if it does not grab their attention. Unlike face-to-face communication, no one is standing in front of the receiver demanding that they listen. Writing must earn and maintain the reader's attention.

Written words carry connotations, shades of meaning, or implications. People "read between the lines." Since written communications are not accompanied by tone of voice, facial expressions, or gestures, these shades of meaning are very important. In the written communication channel you must choose your words carefully. For example, suppose you start a letter to a client by saying, "Thank you for your unusually prompt reply to my recent letter." You may have meant this as a compliment, but the client might think you are implying that he or she usually does not respond promptly. There may be a better way to say what you mean.

Written feedback from the reader to the sender takes time and effort. Therefore, don't rely on feedback, because many readers simply won't respond.

Receiver Problems

The receiver is an active participant in the communication process. He or she has needs, experiences, moods, and pet peeves. You cannot know how all of these factors will influence the interpretation of your written communication, but certainly you should consider as many of these factors as possible. Failure to consider the reader can result in a total breakdown of the communication process.

Solutions and Guidelines

Now that we have reviewed some barriers to effectively communicating in writing, let's look at solutions to these problems.

- Always state clearly the purpose of your communication. For example, statements like "I am writing to inform you" or "I am writing to express my concern over your decision to change the allocation of funds" clearly express the purpose of your communication.
- Make sure your ideas are clearly thought out and complete. Review the data on which your ideas are based.

- Develop your vocabulary so you can write smoothly and quickly. Keep a current dictionary and thesaurus at your desk at all times. Always look up a word if in doubt about its meaning.
- Remain sensitive to the reader's vocabulary and his or her needs as a receiver.
- If in doubt about the reader's level of knowledge or familiarity with a concept, don't assume that your reader knows what you know.
- Improve your knowledge of spelling, punctuation, grammar, and sentence and paragraph construction. These are important tools for effective writing. Refer to your dictionary, thesaurus, and grammar books if in doubt about your spelling, punctuation, or grammar.
- Recognize that communicating in writing is different from oral communication. Write directly and concisely, and be sure to stick to the point.
- Remember that you are competing for the reader's attention. Make the reader's task easier by clearly organizing your memos, letters, and reports.
- Be sensitive to possible attempts to "read between the lines." When revising or editing your work, ask yourself, "How could this phrase or sentence be misinterpreted?" Then reword it to avoid problems.
- Encourage your readers to provide feedback in the form of comments or questions. This can be done in writing when appropriate or in less formal ways. The important thing is that you provide opportunities for others to communicate their understanding of your intended messages. In this way, you can clarify any miscommunication.
- Remember to consider the reader. Analyze his or her needs and viewpoints. Shape your communications to meet both your needs and those of the reader.

Although the communication model shown in Figure 3 seems straightforward, it is apparent now that the process of communication can be very difficult. There are many potential ways for the process to break down. If you know what these barriers are and how to avoid them, you will be a more effective writer.

Written Communication Skills Required of Managers

We have reviewed some important concepts in effective written communication. In the following section, we are going to examine the specific written communication skills needed by managers.

Written communication skills are the ability to communicate in writing—to accurately express ideas, feelings, and information. When others clearly perceive the intended message of the written communication, it has been successful.

Managers use the following building blocks of written communication: vocabulary, spelling, grammar, punctuation, sentence structure, transitions, and paragraphs. These are tools, and when used correctly, they help get the written message to the reader.

Written communication skills may be divided into three components: (1) prewriting activities (determining objectives, organizing needed material, and considering the reader), (2) writing activities (choosing words, selecting word forms, and constructing the written communication), and (3) post-writing activities (reviewing and editing). In the next section, we will examine these three components.

Pre-writing Activities

The major reasons managers avoid writing or feel anxious about writing are not knowing how to begin, struggling to find the right words, and worrying about organizing the message. Managers can avoid these obstacles by developing effective pre-writing skills. First, it is important to determine your objective for the written message and then organize the needed materials. In this step you clearly establish both the general purpose and the specific objectives of your written communications. Obtaining and organizing relevant information and outlining your ideas are also important steps in written communication.

The next pre-writing activity is to consider the reader. Since effective written communication cannot occur without a reader, it is very important to remember your audience. Consider the reader's background, expectations, experiences, viewpoint, level of knowledge, and needs. Reader characteristics influence your (1) choice of words, (2) length of sentences, (3) degree of repetition, (4) organization of material, (5) complexity of information, and (6) style.

Writing Activities

There are basically three writing activities. First, it is important to choose the right words to convey a clear, concise, and logical meaning. Choosing words that clearly express your meaning and that seek feedback from readers demonstrates effective written communication.

The next step is selecting the correct word forms. Choose nouns over adjectives. Nouns are the names of people, places, and things our readers want to know about. Select verbs (action words) rather than adverbs. For example, consider the difference between "Geri went quickly to class" and "Geri rushed to class." Choose specific words over general words. The more specific you are, the sharper the picture you create in your readers' minds. Instead of telling your readers "The organization had a lot of problems," consider "The organization suffered from financial and human resource allocation problems."

Select the correct gender of pronouns and use nonsexist language. Words that favor one gender over the other have no place in business or any other kind of writing. Sexist language includes using the generic third-person masculine pronouns (he, him, himself, his) and job titles that have a built-in gender preference (foreman, chairman, stewardess). Avoid using generic male pronouns when you are referring to individuals or job titles. For example, do not assume a manager is a he. Avoid terms such as chairman or policeman. Always use neutral nouns such as those given in the following examples:

Incorrect	Correct
fellow worker	peer
mankind	people
manned	staffed
all men	all individuals
mailman	letter carrier
salesman	sales representative
fireman	firefighter
chairman	chairperson

The major criticism of bureaucratic writing is that it is wordy and indirect. One cause of wordiness is the passive voice. The passive voice is a construction that makes the subject of a sentence the receiver of the action rather than the doer of the action. When we write "A decision was reached by the committee," the subject is "decision" and the subject is being acted upon. This is a passive voice construction. To make it active you make the subject the doer of the action: "The committee reached a decision." The second sentence is much clearer. Another way to avoid wordiness is to be specific and use concrete terms instead of generalizations or vague phrases.

The third writing activity that leads to effective written communication is the basic skill of sentence construction. Your sentences should be easy to understand, organized, and logically presented. The opening sentence should focus the reader's attention on your main topic. The rest of the sentences in the paragraph should follow logically. Be consistent and avoid shifting from one person to another, from one tense to another, or from singular to plural without good reason. Use transition words or phrases to help the reader go from one idea to the next.

Post-Writing Activities

After completing a written communication, you must read it carefully to look for mistakes and to tighten the language. Always proofread the final copy of your written work. Effective writers usually proofread their communications in two ways. First, they proofread the rough draft and final copy for the content of the message, making sure that the memo, letter, or report is logical, thorough, and concise. Next, they proofread for spelling or typographical errors. Reading from right to left helps focus your attention on one word at a time. Many writers find this a helpful way to locate spelling errors or mistakes in typing. When reviewing and editing your message, make sure your written communication is free of errors and that it conveys its intended purpose.

Practicing Effective Written Communication

Most management skills are demonstrated through communications with others, much of which is in written form. Many times the actual expression of your perceptions, decisions, plans, leadership, and flexibility occurs through writing to others. If the written message is not clear and not understood by your readers, these other management skills may be drowned in the resulting confusion. Thus writing skills are very important. Written communication skills consist of the following six behaviors, divided into three components:

Pre-writing Activities

- *Determining objectives and organizing needed material*—In this step you clearly establish both the general purpose and the specific objectives of your written communications, and you obtain and organize relevant information and outline the sequence of your ideas.
- *Considering the reader*—You review the background, expectations, and experiences of your reader, as well as the reader's viewpoint, knowledge level, and needs.

Writing Activities

- *Choosing words*—You choose words that clearly express your meaning and seek feedback from readers to make sure your meaning is understood.
- *Selecting word forms*—You use concrete nouns, select the correct gender of pronouns, and avoid extreme adjectives, repetitiveness, and jargon.
- *Constructing the written communication*—Basic skill in sentence construction is important. Place main ideas in sentences and paragraphs, use transitions, and outline your writing.

Post-writing Activities

- *Reviewing and editing*—After completing a written communication, read it carefully to look for mistakes and tighten the language. Make sure your written communication conveys its intended purpose.

This next section of in-basket exercises focuses separately on each component of written communication. In the first two exercises, you will focus on the pre-writing process. You will be asked to determine the objective of the written communication, organize the needed materials, and complete a reader analysis. The third exercise concentrates on frequently misused words. Next, you will practice the writing process and be asked to compose a written communication applying the principles of sentence and paragraph construction. The last exercise focuses on post-writing activities. In that exercise you will analyze what you have written, look for errors, and seek better ways to say what you mean. Each exercise is followed by questions that direct your attention to these components of written communication.

Before you begin the in-basket exercises, review your scores on the six parts of the WCPQ that you completed earlier. As you work to complete the exercises, keep in mind the behaviors noted in this measure of written communication. The questions in the WCPQ deepen your understanding of basic written communication skills.

IN-BASKET EXERCISE 1: DETERMINING OBJECTIVES AND ORGANIZING NEEDED MATERIAL

Clearly thinking through the general purpose and specific objectives of your written communication is an important first step. And organizing the information you need to present is an essential structuring activity. This exercise requires you to use these behaviors.

Situation:

In this situation you are Chris Allen, director of employee relations for the Midwestern Railway. Midwestern is a relatively small railroad that has operated in two states for the past forty years. The railroad receives approximately 80 percent of its revenues from freight-carrying services and only 20 percent from passenger service.

In recent years, your Employee Relations Office has assumed more and more responsibility for recruiting, selecting, and training employees. In addition, you handle all interactions with the union and its representatives.

In the past two years, there have been several challenges regarding the employment of women and minority group members by Midwestern. On your desk are some memos and letters, shown in Exhibits 1 through 4, that relate to this situation. Please read them and respond to the questions that follow.

Your written communication skills focus:

- Determine your general purpose.
- Determine your specific objectives.
- List the necessary information to include in the written communication.
- Outline the structure and sequence of your ideas in the written communication.

Questions for In-Basket Exercise 1:

1. You are going to write a letter to John Warset, head of the Employment Alliance Committee. What is the general purpose of your letter to Warset?

2. What specific objectives do you want to accomplish by means of the letter? List the necessary information to include in your letter.

3. Outline the structure of the letter by topic, source, or time frame.

4. Explain why it is helpful to outline your purpose(s), objective(s), and information before composing your written communication.

5. Now that you have been introduced to the situation at Midwestern Railway and have prepared the necessary information, compose the letter to John Warset, head of the Employment Alliance Committee.

IN-BASKET EXERCISE 2: CONSIDERING THE READER

Effective writing involves the reader's accurate reception of your ideas and information. You must consider the reader by constantly being aware of his or her characteristics. Although it isn't always necessary to complete a reader analysis every time you compose a memo or letter, reader analyses are an important tool of effective writing.

Situation:

Assume that you are a writer for a politician who is running for mayor of a medium-sized city in Ohio. The candidate has been asked to respond in writing regarding his views and positions on two topics of concern in the upcoming election—equal employment opportunity for minority groups and urban renewal. You are now planning how you will compose this letter. The letter is being sent to the Midtown Tenants Association (M.T.A.). A description of the M.T.A. is shown in Exhibit 5. Use this information to complete the Reader Analysis Questionnaire that follows.

Your written communication skills focus:

- Appraise reader characteristics.
- Ask, "Who is going to read this?"
- Examine choice of words, length of sentences, degree of repetition, and complexity of information.
- Organize material.
- Consider the style of the written communication.

Questions for In-Basket Exercise 2:

Defining the readership:

1. What is (a) the age range represented, (b) their economic status, (c) their background (urban or rural), (d) their level of education (educated or uneducated), (e) the ratio of sexes represented, and (f) the businesses, trades, and professions represented?

2. What special interests are represented?

3. Describe the allegiances or biases of the readers in the following areas: (a) economic, (b) political, (c) racial, (d) religious, (e) geographical, and (f) domestic.

4. Describe the attributes of your readers with regard to (a) special desires, (b) special needs, (c) sensitivities and preoccupations, (d) prejudices, and (e) preferences.

Applying the information:

5. Because of your analysis, what points would you avoid in writing for these readers? Why?

6. Explain how you might adapt the subject to your readers.

7. What general points would you consider most appropriate to address concerning the assigned topic?

IN-BASKET EXERCISE 3: CHOOSING WORDS

The English language is famous for its many irregular words. Because of this, many English words are frequently misused.

Situation:

Refer to the rules and examples of frequently misused words shown in Exhibit 6. As you complete the next exercise, follow the rules and avoid these errors.

Your written communication skills focus:

- Choose the proper word(s) to convey a clear, concise, and logical meaning.

Questions for In-Basket Exercise 3:

1. Circle the correct meaning to the right of each word in the following list:

Word	Meaning or usage	
1. below	a. underneath	b. following
2. affect	a. result	b. influence
3. alright	a. correct	b. (not appropriate)
4. between	a. two things	b. three or more things
5. number	a. can be counted	b. cannot be counted
6. as to	a. (not appropriate)	b. about
7. besides	a. next to	b. in addition to
8. may	a. permission	b. is able to
9. complement	a. praise	b. set
10. consensus of opinion	a. agreement	b. (not appropriate)
11. correspond with	a. write to	b. match
12. council	a. advice	b. group of people
13. creditable	a. believable	b. worthy of praise
14. criteria	a. a standard	b. measures
15. data	a. facts	b. fact
16. differ with	a. to disagree	b. to be unlike
17. eminent	a. impending	b. famous
18. accept	a. receive	b. exclude
19. further	a. degree	b. space
20. irregardless	a. (not appropriate)	b. not regarding
21. lay	a. put	b. recline
22. loose	a. part with	b. not confined

23. principle	a. main	b. rule
24. quiet	a. calm	b. fully
25. reason is because	a. because	b. because why
26. distribute the same	a. (not appropriate)	b. adjective
27. sometime	a. units of time	b. point in time
28. stationery	a. fixed	b. paper
29. more unique	a. (not appropriate)	b. really unique
30. were	a. plural	b. singular or plural

Check your answers with a dictionary or with your instructor. Review any discrepancies in your answers before proceeding to the next in-basket exercise.

IN-BASKET EXERCISE 4: CONSTRUCTING THE WRITTEN COMMUNICATION

In this in-basket exercise, you will practice two components of the writing process—selecting word forms and constructing the written communication. When composing a written communication, you should be aware of the principles of constructing sentences and paragraphs. Note that use of technical jargon, repetitive phrases, or extreme adjectives (such as *fantastic* or *unbelievable*) may detract from the effectiveness of your writing.

Situation:

For the purpose of this exercise, you are Kim Hamilton, marketing director for the Blackstone Luggage Company, headquartered in Boston, Massachusetts. It is your responsibility to increase sales.

During the past three years, sales figures at Blackstone have declined because of increased competition from other firms. The main problem has been Blackstone's failure to keep pace with advances in materials and the new technology of fabrication (e.g., fiberglass materials being molded into perfectly sized pieces for various types of luggage). The cost of the new technology is high at first, and Blackstone has been very conservative in spending. Also, there have been numerous complaints about service and pricing. Several accounts have been lost to competitors.

The president of Blackstone has finally realized that survival and prosperity depend on implementing new production techniques. Toward this end, he has purchased new equipment, implemented new fabrication procedures, and promised competitive pricing strategies. A totally new line of lighter weight but sturdier luggage will be ready for delivery in ninety days.

You are in the midst of a new "crash" marketing campaign development. You need to contact all past and present accounts to inform them of the new merchandise. In particular, the owner of Jackson Luggage Shop has written to Blackstone and needs a written reply.

Please read the materials shown in Exhibits 7 through 9 and respond to the questions that follow.

Your written communication skills focus:

■ Use concrete nouns to make your communication less formal and easier to understand.
■ Avoid the use of abstract nouns that may confuse your reader.
■ Avoid the use of extreme adjectives because you lose credibility when you use them frequently.
■ Use repetition for emphasis only.
■ Construct sentences that contain one main idea. However, combining your main idea with subordinate ideas will make your writing less choppy.
■ Link words, ideas, and paragraphs with transitional expressions.
■ Construct paragraphs to express a group of related ideas.

Questions for In-Basket Exercise 4:

1. Now that you know something about the Blackstone Luggage Company and H. B. Jackson's situation, compose your letter to Mr. Jackson.

2. In the letter you just wrote, how many concrete nouns did you use? Remember, a concrete noun is a name of a person, place, or thing that can be touched. (For example, *luggage* is a concrete noun.) Review your letter and count the number of concrete nouns.

3. How may abstract nouns did you use? An abstract noun is a word for a concept, process, or idea, something that cannot be touched (*satisfaction, competition,* or *promise* are examples of abstract nouns).

4. Did you use any extreme adjectives in your description of the new luggage? If you described or mentioned the improved new luggage, what words did you use to describe it?

5. Did you avoid using words repetitively? What important words did you use more than once?

6. Review your sentences to see if each one expressed one main idea. If you find problem sentences, rework them here.

7. How many paragraphs did your letter contain? Did each paragraph express a group of clearly related ideas? If you find a problem paragraph, rewrite it here.

8. Were there smooth transitions from one main idea (sentence or paragraph) to the next? In the following space, give examples of the transitions you used or could have used.

9. Did you stick to the point, or were some sentences slightly "off topic"? Write any "off topic" sentences here.

IN-BASKET EXERCISE 5: REVIEWING AND EDITING

After you have written a draft of a memo, letter, or report, the next step is reviewing and editing. In this step you analyze what you have written, look for errors, and seek better ways to say what you mean. Finding mistakes requires that you know the rules of spelling, grammar, and composition.

Situation:

For the purposes of this exercise you will again be Kim Hamilton, marketing director for the Blackstone Luggage Company. In the preceding exercise, you composed a letter to Mr. Jackson. Assume that the rough draft of your letter is shown in Exhibit 10. Refer to this draft as you respond to the questions that follow.

Your written communication skills focus:

- Correct spelling errors.
- Look for punctuation problems.
- Shorten phrases.
- Make sure the letter accomplishes its purpose.
- Evaluate the tone of the letter.

Questions for In-Basket Exercise 5:

1. Carefully review the draft of the letter in Exhibit 10. Look for spelling errors, punctuation problems, and phrases that are too long. In general, does the letter accomplish its purpose? Also, pay attention to the "tone" of the letter. Tone is typically defined as the reader's impression of the writer's attitude toward the subject. Put yourself in Mr. Jackson's position and read the letter from his viewpoint. Does this letter's "tone" reassure him about the quality of your products and service?

2. Rewrite sections of the letter to Mr. Jackson that are not clear, concise, and correct.

ASSESSING CHANGE

The purpose of this module has been to help you develop your written communication skills through several in-basket exercises. You have focused on the behaviors that make up written communication skills. You have seen that written communication skills involve:

- *Determining objectives and organizing needed material*—As Chris Allen, director of employee relations for the Midwestern Railway, your task was to write a letter about a touchy discrimination allegation. You had to organize your needed material and evaluate the objectives of your letter.
- *Considering the reader*—As a writer for a politician running for mayor of a medium-sized city in Ohio, your task was to put in writing his views and positions on two topics of concern in the upcoming election. You completed a Reader Analysis Questionnaire in order to evaluate the members of the Midtown Tenants Association, to whom you were going to write a letter. By reviewing their background, expectations, experiences, viewpoint, knowledge level, and needs, you had a better sense of how to develop the message and address your readers.
- *Selecting the words*—Your task in the third in-basket exercise was to review the rules for frequently misused words and then test yourself on their correct meanings or usages.
- *Constructing the written communication*—Your task as Kim Hamilton, marketing director for the Blackstone Luggage Company, was to compose a letter in response to the owner of the Jackson Luggage Shop regarding concerns about your products and service. You had to be aware of the principles of constructing sentences and paragraphs and limit your use of technical jargon, repetitive phrases, and extreme adjectives, all of which could detract from the effectiveness of your writing.
- *Reviewing and editing*—In your role as Kim Hamilton, marketing director for the Blackstone Luggage Company, you were asked to review and edit the rough draft of a letter to Mr. Jackson. You had to analyze what you had written, look for errors, and seek better ways to say what you meant. To complete this exercise, you had to know the correct rules of spelling, grammar, and composition to make sure your written communication conveyed its intended purpose.

At the beginning of this module, you completed the WCPQ to provide a baseline against which you could measure improvements in your written communication skills. Now it is time to assess some of these improvements.

First, retake the WCPQ. A comparison of your before- and after-practice scores will show how much you have increased your skills. When you have retaken this questionnaire, compare your answers with those you gave earlier to see how much you have strengthened your written communication skills.

The Written Communication Process Questionnaire (WCPQ)

Use the following scale to rate the frequency with which you perform the behaviors described in each question. Place the corresponding number (1–7) in the blank preceding the statement.

Rarely	Irregularly	Occasionally	Usually	Frequently	Almost Always	Consistently
1	2	3	4	5	6	7

_____ 1. I clearly establish the general purpose of each of my written communications.

_____ 2. I clearly establish the specific objective(s) of each of my written communications.

_____ 3. I systematically obtain the necessary and relevant information to include in my written communications.

_____ 4. I sort through and organize information to be included in my written communications (e.g., organize by topic, source, problem, or time frame).

_____ 5. I outline (in writing) the sequence or structure of my written communications.

_____ 6. I familiarize myself with the background, expectations, and experiences of my reader(s).

_____ 7. I take note of my reader's probable point of view.

_____ 8. I consider the level of knowledge that the reader possesses.

_____ 9. I recognize the needs of the reader and their effect on the reception of my written communications.

_____ 10. I determine ways to adapt my written communications to meet the needs of or gain acceptance from the reader.

_____ 11. I quickly and correctly choose words that clearly express my intended meanings.

_____ 12. I review various connotations of words I use.

_____ 13. I consider the fact that words often contain hidden messages and make sure that these messages convey my intended meaning.

_____ 14. I seek feedback from readers to make certain that my words are understood.

_____ 15. I avoid using words that might not be part of the reader's vocabulary.

_____ 16. I use concrete nouns as opposed to abstract nouns in my written communications.

_____ 17. The pronouns I use accurately reflect the gender and number of the persons to whom I refer.

_____ 18. I am careful to avoid the use of extreme adjectives or other "loaded language" when my objectivity as the writer is important.

_____ **19.** I do not repeat myself needlessly in my writing.

_____ **20.** I avoid the use of technical jargon.

_____ **21.** My sentences express one main idea.

_____ **22.** I compose paragraphs so that ideas and information concern one main theme that is expressed in the topic sentence.

_____ **23.** I use transition ideas and sentences to lead from one paragraph to another.

_____ **24.** I use an outline form or subheadings to structure my written communications.

_____ **25.** I stick to the point of my communication.

_____ **26.** After completing a written communication, I carefully read it to make sure the style and tone of the message are what I want.

_____ **27.** When editing, I reduce the number of words in my written communication.

_____ **28.** When editing, I substitute shorter words for longer ones if they have the same meaning.

_____ **29.** I check for spelling errors and use a dictionary when in doubt.

_____ **30.** I review my original purpose and objectives to determine whether the final written product accomplishes them.

WCPQ Scoring and Evaluation

Follow the scoring directions found on page 104 and in Figure 1. Complete the after-practice assessment column for the WCPQ and compare your before- and after-practice scores. Plot your after-practice scores in Figure 2. In which categories did your scores improve? Think about what has made your progress possible. Perhaps you can apply your insights to categories where your performance has lagged.

The Written Communication Technical Skills Questionnaire (WCTS)

The Written Communication Technical Skills Questionnaire (WCTS) is a second method to assess your skills. In the WCTS, you are asked to respond to questions regarding technical written communication rules. This questionnaire assesses your knowledge of grammar.

Please answer questions 1 through 10 by placing a T for true or an F for false in the space next to each statement.

_____ **1.** A gerund is a verb form ending in "ing" that is used as a noun.

_____ **2.** Pronouns must agree in number with the person(s) to whom they refer.

_____ **3.** The subject of a sentence does not always agree in number with the verb used.

_____ **4.** An example of a split infinitive is "to see correctly."

FIGURE 4
Written Communication Technical
Skills Questionnaire (WCTS) Scoring

Written Communication Technical Skills Questionnaire (WCTS) Scoring

ITEM	YOUR ANSWER	CORRECT ANSWER
1		
2		
3		
4		
5		
6		
7		
8		
9		
10		
11		
12		
13		
14		
15		
16		
17		
18		

Give yourself 1 point for each correct answer. Scores range from 0 to 18.
Score _____

_____ **5.** When the subject of a sentence is the "doer" of action, the verb is active.

_____ **6.** Adverbs are used to describe only adjectives and other adverbs.

_____ **7.** Adjectives describe pronouns or nouns.

_____ **8.** The word "by" is a preposition.

_____ **9.** Hyphens are used to combine two words into a one-word modifier.

_____ **10.** Sentences should not end with prepositions.

For questions 11 through 15, circle the appropriate word inside the parentheses.

11. I saw (him, his) answering of the question as antagonistic behavior.

12. After the proposals were thoroughly discussed, the committee rejected (it, them).

13. She did (good, well)!

14. The union has bargained (real, really) effectively.

15. He demanded (up-to-the-minute, up to the minute) reports.

For questions 16 through 18, circle the *incorrect* word or words.

16. In terms of the training program, I am not very sure where he is at.

17. The data is clearly supportive of any attempt to quickly negotiate a settlement.

18. I really appreciated you returning the printout quickly.

WCTS Scoring and Evaluation

Complete the WCTS scoring form in Figure 4. Compare your responses with the feedback your instructor provides about the correct responses for the eighteen questions.

Summary

In this module, you have practiced the skills of effective written communication. These skills are not tied to specific places or events. Once learned, they apply whenever and wherever you need to communicate in writing. You will use them in all types of situations, managerial and otherwise. You will certainly be able to apply what you have learned here to your own workplace or classroom situation.

The purpose of this module has been to give you practice using the six skills of effective written communication. You have assumed many managerial roles, and you have been placed in situations that required you to develop better written communication skills. The six skills were grouped into three areas: pre-writing activities (determining objectives, organizing needed material, and considering the reader); writing activities (choosing words, selecting word forms, and constructing the written communication); and post-writing activities (reviewing and editing).

Working through this module, you have taken part in situations that have required you to write. You have examined memos, letters, and reports in order to evaluate how more effective written communication skills might have improved outcomes. The skill-building exercises at the end of this module will give you further practice with various components of written communication such as spelling, vocabulary, editing, and sentence construction.

Perhaps you are now applying the experience gained in this module to your work situation. If so, you already may have had the pleasure of receiving positive feedback from others. Feedback from your instructor or persons with whom you work will help you gauge whether you are using written communication skills well.

FIGURE 5
Written Communication Skills Action
Guide

You Show Written Communication Skills When You:

■ Determine objectives and organize needed material
■ Consider the reader
■ Choose appropriate words
■ Select proper word forms
■ Construct the written communication
■ Review and edit

You Should Show Written Communication Skills When:

■ The purpose and objectives of your message must be clear
■ The background and needs of the readers must be analyzed
■ Words must reflect intended meanings and the readers' knowledge level
■ Word forms must be concrete, nonrepetitive, and free from jargon
■ The construction of your message must be solid and to the point
■ The message must be reviewed and edited to ensure effectiveness

To remember key steps in practicing effective written communication skills and to identify situations in which the skills are needed, use the action guide shown in Figure 5. Frequent review of this information will help you become a more effective writer.

SKILL-BUILDING EXERCISES

EXERCISE 1 ■ USING FEEDBACK TO IMPROVE YOUR WRITING SKILLS

Bring two samples of your own writing to class. These can be samples from course work or from writing tasks you have completed on your job or in various organizations. Exchange samples with a classmate. Informally assess the strong points as well as areas that need improvement in each other's writing samples. Keep in mind that as editors or evaluators you are just operating as readers reacting to one another's writing. Provide feedback to your classmate. Suggest improvements in his or her writing sample. After each of you has provided feedback, make any changes in your own writing sample that you think are appropriate.

EXERCISE 2 ■ IMPROVING SPELLING

Which of the following words are spelled correctly? Place a **C** for correct or an **I** for incorrect next to each word. Refer to a dictionary, or your instructor will provide the correct answers.

_____ 1.	absense		_____ 21.	harrass
_____ 2.	acceptible		_____ 22.	hurriedly
_____ 3.	adolesent		_____ 23.	illogical
_____ 4.	accommodate		_____ 24.	incidently
_____ 5.	attendence		_____ 25.	inevitably
_____ 6.	beneficial		_____ 26.	inocuous
_____ 7.	changeable		_____ 27.	irrelevant
_____ 8.	conceit		_____ 28.	judgement
_____ 9.	dependant		_____ 29.	license
_____ 10.	desireable		_____ 30.	maintenance
_____ 11.	develope		_____ 31.	maneuver
_____ 12.	disappoint		_____ 32.	misspelled
_____ 13.	disatisfied		_____ 33.	neccessary
_____ 14.	elgible		_____ 34.	nuisance
_____ 15.	embarrass		_____ 35.	occassion
_____ 16.	exaggerate		_____ 36.	personel
_____ 17.	expense		_____ 37.	procede
_____ 18.	fasinate		_____ 38.	recommend
_____ 19.	forcibly		_____ 39.	scarcity
_____ 20.	guarantee		_____ 40.	unanimous

Follow up:

If you missed more than three of these words, you should do two things. First, use a dictionary when you are in doubt about the spelling or use of a word. Second, practice your spelling and consult references provided by your instructor.

EXERCISE 3 ■ IMPROVING VOCABULARY

Instructions: For the twenty words listed below, circle the letter that most closely defines the word.

1. manifest
   a) earmark   b) covered   c) reveal   d) insinuate

2. demagogue:
   a) gambler   b) tightwad   c) liar   d) rabble-rouser

3. supersede:
   a) enforce   b) necessitate   c) continue   d) replace

4. condone:
   a) counsel   b) trust   c) overlook   d) take exception

5. profligate:
   a) expansive   b) wasteful   c) abundant   d) lacking

6. gregarious:
   a) sociable   b) vicious   c) strong   d) calm

7. inveterate:
   a) clever   b) shameless   c) slapdash   d) habitual

8. anomalous:
   a) uncommon   b) sad   c) interesting   d) scornful

9. homogenize:
   a) change   b) blend   c) take apart   d) disintegrate

10. unequivocal:
    a) esoteric   b) confusing   c) clear   d) concise

11. debase:
    a) to break down   b) cheapen   c) assuage   d) assault

12. assent:
    a) concur   b) argue   c) disagree   d) to rise

13. perspicacity:
    a) faithfulness   b) trust   c) keenness   d) viciousness

14. retroactive:
    a) past matters   b) summarizing   c) suspected   d) fitting

15. juxtapose:
    a) put close together   b) separate   c) combine   d) disclose

16. glib:
    a) smooth   b) upsetting   c) quiet   d) secretive

17. placate:
a) help   b) appease   c) encourage   d) dissuade

18. evanescent:
a) fleeting   b) sparkling   c) colorful   d) demanding

19. indolent:
a) strong   b) idle   c) withdrawn   d) accusing

20. vicarious:
a) outgoing   b) feeling through   c) not self-   d) enjoyable
                   another   supporting

Check with your instructor to score your responses. If you missed more than three of these words, you may want to pursue vocabulary-building activities. Many popular books can help you do this, or your instructor can supply references.

EXERCISE 4 ■ SUBJECT–VERB AGREEMENT

Instructions: Read the following sentences and determine whether they are correct (C) or incorrect (I) in subject–verb agreement. Subjects and verbs must agree in terms of number (singular or plural) and person (first, second, or third).

Example: John always finishes reports on time.

____C____   *John* is the subject (third person), and the verb *finishes* is the third-person singular form of the verb *to finish*. Therefore, this sentence demonstrates subject–verb agreement.

_____ **1.**   The man, while occupied by other tasks, still give adequate support.

_____ **2.**   A brochure of training courses often attract trainees.

_____ **3.**   Both the union and management support the policy.

_____ **4.**   Everybody is going to the reception.

_____ **5.**   Either the president or the vice president are the chief negotiator.

_____ **6.**   Either the employees or their representative are going to present the report.

_____ **7.**   The new group have excellent performers in it.

_____ **8.**   There is too many problems in that unit.

_____ **9.**   John's only support is his insurance and social security.

_____ **10.**   The number of revisions is high.

Check with your instructor to score your responses.

EXERCISE 5 ■ PRONOUNS AND ANTECEDENTS

Instructions: Read the following sentences and decide whether they are correct (C) or incorrect (I) regarding agreement between the pronoun and its antecedent. The antecedent of a pronoun is the noun or pronoun to which it refers. The antecedent usually comes before the pronoun, but occasionally it may follow the pronoun. Pronouns and antecedents agree in person and number.

Example: Everyone brought their reports.

___I___   Generally, indefinite pronouns such as *everyone* take singular pronouns. Thus *their* in the above sentence should be *his or her*.

_____ **1.** An employee's attitude toward their work is important.

_____ **2.** The union symbolically left its work stations.

_____ **3.** The stockholders worried about their holdings.

_____ **4.** Each manager arrived at his or her office.

_____ **5.** Nancy or Jane should have voiced her opinion.

_____ **6.** The membership voted to include itself in the larger organization.

_____ **7.** Every person took their seats.

_____ **8.** No new supervisor feels comfortable in his or her position.

_____ **9.** After the holidays, the family went its separate ways.

_____ **10.** Neither the consultant nor the president will preside at his meeting.

Check with your instructor to score your responses.

■ Use Exhibits 1–4 with In-Basket Exercise 1,
   Exhibit 5 with In-Basket Exercise 2,
   Exhibit 6 with In-Basket Exercise 3,
   Exhibits 7–9 with In-Basket Exercise 4,
   Exhibit 10 with In-Basket Exercise 5.

MIDWESTERN RAILWAY

M E M O R A N D U M

TO: Chris Allen, Employee Relations Director
FROM: Wait Thomas, Vice President, Public Relations
DATE: October 15
RE: Letter from John Warset

Attached is a copy of a letter our office recently received from Mr. John Warset, head of the Employment Alliance Committee. The letter is quite disturbing, and I feel that we need to respond immediately in order to avoid further problems.

Would you please write Mr. Warset and let him know that Midwestern certainly does not condone or promote any discrimination on the basis of race or sex. In fact, our new budget specifically increases funding for fair employment activities by 15%.

Thanks.

EXHIBIT 1
Midwestern Railway Memorandum

EXHIBIT 2
Employment Alliance Committee Letter

EMPLOYMENT ALLIANCE COMMITTEE
140 7TH AVENUE

Mr. Wait Thomas
Vice President, Public Relations
Midwestern Railway

Dear Mr. Thomas:

For the last three months, the Employment Alliance Committee has been observing and documenting your recruitment and hiring practices. We are appalled by what we have seen. The percentage of blacks and women in lower-level jobs is extremely high, and pay seems to be inequitably distributed.

We have spoken to several of your employees and managers, and we have gotten no cooperation whatsoever. They tell us that your office is responsible for this situation.

Unless we hear from you within ten days, we plan to demonstrate in front of your local office. Also, we are considering a boycott against your passenger service and against products carried on your trains.

We feel we have clearly identified discriminatory actions on your part, and unless these situations are corrected quickly, we will take action against you as we see fit.

Sincerely,

John Warset

John Warset
President, Employment Alliance Committee

MIDWESTERN RAILWAY

MEMORANDUM

TO: Chris Allen, Employee Relations Director
FROM: Paul Rutkowski, Personnel Technician
DATE: October 1
RE: Employment Practice Questions

A Mr. John Warset of the Employment Alliance Committee has been calling us regularly to question our employment practices. We have told him that our female and minority employee statistics are improving, but he isn't satisfied.

As you know, our minority hiring has been a problem before.

I thought I'd let you know about this guy in case he calls you.

EXHIBIT 3
Midwestern Railway Memorandum

MIDWESTERN RAILWAY

FEMALE AND MINORITY GROUP STATISTICS

Female	Midwestern %		Industry %	
	Last Year	This Year	Last Year	This Year
Laborers	1.0%	1.0%	1.7%	1.2%
Semi-skilled	2.5%	3.0%	2.0%	2.0%
Managers	3.0%	3.0%	2.5%	2.5%
Professionals	6.8%	9.0%	9.0%	8.0%

Minority	Midwestern %		Industry %	
	Last Year	This Year	Last Year	This Year
Laborers	22.0%	25.0%	17.0%	17.6%
Semi-skilled	6.0%	7.0%	6.0%	4.0%
Managers	3.5%	3.5%	5.0%	6.0%
Professionals	1.0%	3.7%	6.0%	5.8%

EXHIBIT 4
Midwestern Railway Female and Minority Group Statistics

EXHIBIT 5
Midtown Tenants Asociation (M.T.A.)

MIDTOWN TENANTS ASSOCIATION (M.T.A.)

The M.T.A. is an organization of workers in the inner-city area. It was established in order to work for better living conditions for tenants in the inner city. Its scope has been expanded to include finding jobs for members of minority groups and seeking better working and living conditions in the inner city.

Members of the M.T.A. are primarily minority group members. They have relatively low incomes and few possessions. Many members are on welfare, and all are inner-city tenants. They are interested in social problems, including continually rising rents and food costs. They are all interested in ways to provide better education for their children and more job opportunities for the adults. The membership is 45 percent male and 55 percent female, and ages range from 19 to 80 years. The group members are not concerned with problems that are not specifically related to their area.

EXHIBIT 6
Rules and Examples of Frequently
Misused Words

RULES AND EXAMPLES OF FREQUENTLY MISUSED WORDS

1. **Above and below:** These words refer to positions in space. They should not be used to refer to information that comes before or after a statement.
    Incorrect: The chart below...
    Correct: The following chart...

2. **Affect** versus **effect:** *Affect* is a verb meaning to influence while *effect* is a noun meaning result.
    Incorrect: The new contract does not effect her working hours.
    Correct: The effects of the election will be felt for years to come.

3. **All right** versus **alright:** *Alright* is not considered acceptable and therefore should be eliminated from all written communication. You would never write *alwrong,* would you?

4. **Among** versus **between:** *Between* should be used in reference to two people or things. *Among* is used in reference to three or more people or things.
    Correct: Proceeds of the will were divided among the eight heirs.

5. **Amount** versus **number:** *Amount* refers to mass nouns (annual amount of rainfall; amount of money). *Number* refers to count nouns.
    Incorrect: The amount of voters was great.
    Correct: The number of people who were late was very high.

6. **As to** versus **about** or **on:** The use of *as to* should be avoided. Instead, use a one-word preposition such as *about* or *on.*
    Incorrect: What is your view as to the importance of this matter?
    Correct: May we have your reviewer comments on the relevant cases?

7. **Besides** versus **beside:** *Besides* means in addition to, while *beside* refers to the position next to.
    Incorrect: Beside these two negative points there were no others.
    Correct: Beside the chart was the color transparency (meaning the two objects were next to each other).

8. **Can** versus **may:** *Can* means is able to, while *may* indicates permission.
    Incorrect: You can go on now.
    Correct: Can you give me the final report by Friday?

9. **Complement** versus **compliment:** *Complement* refers to an amount necessary to complete a set. *Compliment* refers to an expression of praise.
    Incorrect: A full compliment of workers was present.
    Correct: He complimented her appearance.

10. **Consensus of opinion** versus **consensus:** *Consensus of opinion* is a redundant phrase and should be avoided. It means the same thing as *consensus.*

11. **Correspond to** versus **correspond with:** *Correspond to* means to match something or be similar to something, while *correspond with* means to exchange letters or memos.
    Incorrect: His figures correspond with mine.
    Correct: I have corresponded with him on two occasions.

12. **Council** versus **counsel:** *Council* is a decision-making group of people, while *counsel* means advice or to advise.
    Incorrect: The legal council was expensive.
    Correct: He often counseled his friends.

EXHIBIT 6 (CONTINUED)
Rules and Examples of Frequently
Misused Words

13. **Credible** versus **creditable:** *Credible* means believable while *creditable* means praise-worthy or worthy of commercial credit.
    Incorrect: His sources of information were creditable.
    Correct: Our team leader did a creditable job in that emergency situation.
14. **Criterion** versus **criteria:** A *criterion* is a measure or standard. The plural of criterion is *criteria.*
    Incorrect: We need to develop a selection criteria.
    Correct: The proposals were evaluated on the basis of four criteria.
15. **Datum** versus **data:** A *datum* is a fact or quality. Its plural is *data.*
    Incorrect: The data is here.
    Correct: The data indicate a financial recovery.
16. **Differ from** versus **differ with:** To *differ from* means to be unlike. To *differ with* means to disagree.
    Incorrect: I beg to differ from you.
    Correct: I may differ with your political views, but I'll listen to what you have to say anyway.
17. **Eminent** versus **imminent:** *Eminent* means distinguished, famous. *Imminent* means about to happen or impending.
    Incorrect: A downturn in the stock market is eminent.
    Correct: The eminent Nobel Prize winner has agreed to address the group.
18. **Except** versus **accept:** *Except* means to exclude. *Accept* means to take what is offered or agree to.
    Incorrect: They excepted the proposal with no changes.
    Correct: Everyone was there except the publisher.
19. **Farther** versus **further:** *Farther* means more distant in space. *Further* means more distant or advanced in time or degree.
    Incorrect: Each year he travels further than before.
    Correct: Let's pursue those arguments further.
20. **Irregardless** versus **regardless:** *Irregardless* is a redundant and nonstandard word. It is not acceptable. People mean regardless when they say or write irregardless.
21. **Lie** versus **lay:** *Lie* means to recline or rest. *Lay* means to place or put.
    Incorrect: I need to lay down and rest.
    Correct: I need to lie down and rest.
22. **Lose** versus **loose:** *Lose* means to part with unintentionally or to be defeated. *Loose* means not fastened or confined.
    Incorrect: It appears he may loose the appeal.
    Correct: Several loose connections caused the problem.
23. **Principal** versus **principle:** *Principal* means first in rank or importance. *Principle* refers to general truths, laws, or rules.
    Incorrect: The principle reason was the party stance.
    Correct: Various ethical principles were questioned.
24. **Quiet** versus **quite:** *Quiet* means calm or silent. *Quite* means fully or totally.
    Incorrect: The library was a very quite place to work.
    Correct: His summary of the proposal was quite thorough.

EXHIBIT 6 (CONTINUED)
Rules and Examples of Frequently
Misused Words

25. **Reason, because:** *Because* means "for the reason that." Therefore, it is redundant to say *The reason for his behavior was because he was angry.* Instead you might say *The reason for his behavior was his anger.*

26. **Same:** *Same* means identical. It should not be used as a pronoun to refer to a previously mentioned noun.
    Incorrect: I gave her the report and she typed same.
    Correct: I gave her the report and she typed it.

27. **Sometime** versus **some time:** *Sometime* refers to a point in time. *Some time* should be used to refer to units of time.
    Incorrect: I am asking you to present your ideas some time today.
    Correct: I have known the man for some time.

28. **Stationary** versus **stationery:** *Stationary* refers to remaining in one place or fixed. *Stationery* refers to writing material.
    Incorrect: He was so scared he remained stationery.
    Correct: The cold front became stationary during the day.

29. **Unique, complete, perfect:** The words are adjectives that do not have comparative or superlative forms. That is, if something is unique, complete, or perfect, it cannot be more unique or most perfect. There are no degrees of uniqueness, completeness, or perfection.
    Incorrect: His report was the most perfect one.
    Correct: Her campaign was unique. Her test score was perfect.

30. **Was** versus **were:** Use *was* with singular forms and *were* with plural forms.
    Incorrect: She mailed me the reports that was typed.
    Correct: The reports were upsetting in their content.
    However, it is also necessary to use *were* with the singular in the subjunctive mood. The subjunctive mood is used to express a wish or desire. It is introduced by conjunctions of condition, doubt, contingency, concession, or possibility. Examples include: *as if, though, lest, unless, till, and whether.*
    Correct: If he were to harm you...
    Correct: I wish the entire fiasco were not so well remembered.

31. **A lot** versus **alot:** Remember to use a lot as two words.

32. **Compare to** versus **compare with:** To *compare to* is to point out the similarities in different things. To *compare with* is to point out the differences between similar things. Life can be compared to a rat race; rat races can be compared with rush-hour traffic.

33. **Its** versus **it's:** *Its* is the possessive form of *it*. It means something belongs to whatever place or thing *it* stands for. *It's* is the contraction for *it is.*
    Correct: This computer is more expensive than most because its screen is so large and clear.
    Correct: It's a large and clear screen.

34. **Like** versus **as:** Except as a term of affection, *like* has to do with comparison. *As* can also be used in comparisons.
    Correct: That was not like him.
    Correct: He was as efficient as she.

EXHIBIT 7
Jackson Luggage Shop Letter

JACKSON LUGGAGE SHOP
3300 WILLS STREET

November 10

Kim Hamilton
Marketing Director
Blackstone Luggage Company

Dear Kim:

I have not written to you often in the past, but I'm afraid I can't let the current situation persist any longer. Frankly, I'm tired of waiting for your promised lines of more durable luggage sets.

Over a year ago, I received a letter from your sales supervisor, Mr. Arnold, in which he assured me that I would receive samples by last October and stock in time for the Christmas rush. Neither promise was carried out. Since then I have directly questioned him on the matter, and all I get is an incredible combination of evasive answers.

That is not the only problem. One of my best customers here in Toronto sent me the attached letter. As you will see, he is extremely upset about the quality and promptness of your repair of some of his luggage. The luggage was only three months old and obviously still under warranty.

I haven't complained about your products, and I have always been understanding of your situation. However, we need better service and better quality merchandise. I certainly don't mean to threaten you, but several of your competitors seem to be offering high quality merchandise and good service. We have a couple of Canadian firms that are rapidly improving. If we can't do something to change the situation, I will have to cancel my present orders for this year.

Sincerely,

H. B. Jackson

H. B. Jackson

EXHIBIT 8
Applegate Letter

October 27

Mr. H. B. Jackson
Jackson Luggage Shop
5500 Wills Street

Dear Mr. Jackson:

About four months ago, I purchased a matched set of luggage from your store in Toronto. On my first trip, the catch on the large bag broke, and a hinge pin fell out of my wife's smaller bag.

When I returned home, I immediately brought both bags to your shop. Your clerk, Eileen Pauliss, agreed they were to be repaired under warranty. She said the repairs would take no more than four weeks. I thought four weeks was a bit long, but I accepted it. I wish I had asked for a refund now.

It has now been over ten weeks and still no luggage. I realize this may be the fault of the manufacturer, but I still need my luggage. I'd like the repaired luggage within ten days or a full refund.

Yours truly,

Charles Applegate

EXHIBIT 9
Blackstone Luggage Company
Memorandum

BLACKSTONE LUGGAGE COMPANY

MEMORANDUM

TO: Kim Hamilton, Director of Marketing
FROM: Thomas Blackstone, President
DATE: November 15
RE: Jackson Luggage Shop

I understand that one of our clients, Jackson Luggage Shop in Toronto, is having some problems with our products.

Please see if you can satisfy Mr. Jackson. He represents one of our more stable and sizeable accounts.

Mr. H. B. Jackson
Jackson Luggage Shop
5500 Wills Street

Dear Mr. Jackson:

It was of some concern that I saw your recent letter complaining of the service rendered to one of your customers regarding damage to his luggage. An apology seems in order and we apologize.

My purpose in writing is to tell you how much we value your continued satisfaction with our products. I think we have some good news for you regarding new product lines. They are finished. New products will be available to you within ninety days. This new luggage will be lighter in weight and amazingly sturdy.

I am sorry for the promises made for your in the past and this time, promises will be kept. The salesman you mentioned had devastating affects on customers we dismissed him.

Regarding Mr. Applegate's complaint. I have personally seen that his luggage will be fixed in a manner such that he will be happy. We are now in the process of getting together new prices and structures that is going into effect soon.

Please except my apologies and trust that our products and service is returning quickly to it's original lofty posture.

Cordially,

Kim Hamilton

EXHIBIT 10
Rough draft of your letter to
Mr. Jackson

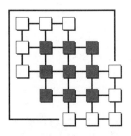

MODULE 4
ORAL COMMUNICATION SKILLS: TALKING AND LISTENING TO OTHERS

INTRODUCTION

Almost daily, candidates for management positions are observed and evaluated regarding their ability to handle people and situations. These evaluations are greatly influenced by the candidate's ability to communicate orally. In fact, skills in oral communication are frequently a prerequisite for assignment to a managerial position.

Oral communication skills enable the manager to make verbal messages clear to others. Anytime a manager interacts with other people (which is a good portion of the manager's time), he or she uses oral communication. The situations can be as diverse as one-on-one discussions, staff meetings, group discussions, or formal briefings and speeches. Sometimes the situation may be social. Many business communications take place in social situations, usually with the goal of simplifying a management task through better rapport. In all these situations, the manager relies on oral communication to achieve his or her purpose.

Oral communication skills are needed to *get* the job because they are needed to *do* the job. Imagine a television station with producers, actors, studios, and equipment creating programs and commercials twenty-four hours a day. Without transmitting equipment to send the signal into viewers' homes, all of the activity would be futile. For a message to have impact and influence, it has to be received by the persons to whom it is addressed. A manager who lacks effective oral communication skills may have serious problems carrying out his or her duties and responsibilities because important messages are not transmitted to, or understood by, others.

Oral communication means articulating a message and conveying ideas through language. But the speaker must make the message clear. Oral communication skills are used in both formal and informal situations to ensure

151

that what is said is received and understood by others. The skills of oral communication include (1) using the voice effectively, (2) employing nonverbal accompaniments, (3) structuring the message, (4) eliminating random noise, and (5) developing audience rapport.

The prospect of giving an oral presentation makes many business people apprehensive. Because of the emphasis on quantitative methods in business courses, many students have had little practice speaking formally. As a result, they feel more at ease working with numbers than with words. Yet the ability to communicate effectively is important in getting to the top in business.

The purpose of this module is to help you develop your oral communication skills or to strengthen skills you already have. You will assume the role of manager in a variety of situations. In each situation, you will be provided with information—samples of material that typically find their way to the manager's desk. As manager, you must use your oral communication skills to solve potential problems. By actually participating in these situations, you will learn and practice oral communication skills.

The module is organized so that you will develop a before-practice assessment of your oral communication skills by completing the Oral Communication Behaviors Questionnaire (OCBQ). This assessment instrument measures your oral communication skills at the present time. We then present a brief discussion of effective oral communication planning and the skills needed by managers. Next, you will work through a series of in-basket exercises in which you will assume the role of manager and practice different skills of oral communication. Feedback from your instructor and your peers will help you judge the quality of your responses and will provide guidance on improving specific behaviors. After a review and summary, you will have an opportunity to retake the OCBQ and compare your after-practice assessment results with your earlier results. You will also complete the Oral Communication Awareness Scale (OCAS). This assessment instrument examines how you actually behave in situations where oral communication skills are needed. It will give you more insight into your behaviors in situations requiring effective oral communication.

After completing this module, you will find that the exercises result in immediate improvement in your oral communication skills. Also, your skills will continually improve as you have additional opportunities to perform on the job or in a classroom situation.

ASSESSING ORAL COMMUNICATION SKILLS

Complete the OCBQ on the following pages before proceeding with the rest of the module. It is both a teaching tool and a means of evaluating your present oral communication skills level. Take time to complete the instrument carefully. Your answers should reflect your behaviors as they are now, not as you would like them to be. Be honest. This instrument is designed to help you discover where you are now so you can work to improve your oral communication skills.

The Oral Communication Behaviors Questionnaire (OCBQ)

The Oral Communication Behaviors Questionnaire (OCBQ) identifies behaviors that demonstrate the skills of oral communication and asks you to note the frequency with which you display these behaviors. Some of the behaviors in this instrument concern your voice and mannerisms. You will find it helpful to listen to how you sound by using either a videotape or an audiotape of a presentation you have made. In addition, you will need to become conscious of the body language you display when you are talking with others.

In order for this questionnaire to be useful to you, you must answer it truthfully. After you have completed the module, you will retake the questionnaire. Comparing your before-practice and after-practice scores will help you evaluate your improvement.

Use the scale shown below to rate the frequency with which you perform the behaviors noted. Place the corresponding number (1–7) in the blank preceding the statement.

Rarely	Irregularly	Occasionally	Usually	Frequently	Almost Always	Consistently
1	2	3	4	5	6	7

_____ 1. I speak loudly enough to be heard, yet not so loudly as to distract from what I am saying.

_____ 2. I vary the pitch and tone of my voice.

_____ 3. I match the pace and rhythm of my speech to my message.

_____ 4. My voice is pleasant and full.

_____ 5. I pronounce my words clearly.

_____ 6. I use gestures to enhance my message.

_____ 7. I establish eye contact with or frequently look at others.

_____ 8. My apparel is right for the message I wish to convey.

_____ 9. My posture is in tune with my message (for example, relaxed for casual communication, erect for formal communication).

_____ 10. My facial expressions (for example, frowns, smiles) reinforce my message.

_____ 11. I state the purpose of my communication.

_____ 12. I use vocabulary appropriate to my audience.

_____ 13. I match the detail and depth of what I say to the interest and understanding of my listeners.

_____ 14. My communication has a logical, easy-to-follow structure.

_____ 15. I use visual aids to strengthen my oral message.

_____ 16. My speech is free of extraneous sounds and words such as "you know" or "uh."

_____ 17. I stay on my topic and do not digress.

_____ **18.** I continue my train of thought despite interruptions.

_____ **19.** I avoid distracting mannerisms (for example, fidgeting, finger tapping, leg movements, hair pulling).

_____ **20.** The tone and inflection of my voice are in harmony with my message.

_____ **21.** I involve my audience in direct participation (for example, asking or answering questions).

_____ **22.** I vary my style of speech according to the situation (for example, conversational in one-on-one communication, formal in presentations before an audience).

_____ **23.** I use humor appropriately in my messages or presentations.

_____ **24.** I address my listeners' interests and concerns.

_____ **25.** My communications have a friendly tone.

OCBQ Scoring

The scoring sheet shown in Figure 1 summarizes your ratings for the OCBQ. It will help you identify your existing strengths and pinpoint areas that need improvement. Right now, fill in the before-practice score column for each skill area by adding your scores for each item. Add the five category scores to obtain a total score. Enter that total score in the space indicated. After completing the module, you will take the OCBQ again and fill in the after-practice score column.

FIGURE 1

The Oral Communication Behaviors Questionnaire (OCBQ) Scoring

Skill Area	Items	Assessment	
		Before Practice	After Practice
Using the voice effectively	1,2,3,4,5		
Employing nonverbal accompaniments	6,7,8,9,10		
Structuring the message	11,12,13,14,15		
Eliminating random noise	16,17,18,19,20		
Developing audience rapport	21,22,23,24,25		
TOTAL SCORE			

OCBQ Evaluation

Figure 2 shows score lines for your total score and for each category measured on the OCBQ. Each line shows a continuum from the lowest possible score to the highest. Place a B (before-practice) where your score falls on each of these lines.

The score lines in Figure 2 show graphically where you stand with regard to five oral communication skills. If you have been honest with yourself, you now have a better idea of your relative strengths and weaknesses in these skills.

Learning to Use the OCBQ Skills

You have just rated yourself according to the frequency with which you demonstrate good oral communication behaviors. This questionnaire provides a baseline against which you will assess improvements that have taken place after you have completed this module.

Before moving on, think about what you have discovered in this evaluation. What areas of your oral communication skills are least developed? In which categories would you like to improve? These will require the most attention during the remainder of the module. Which are your strongest skills? Use this module to fine-tune these areas so that you may take full advantage of them. In areas where you already perform well, learning some new things can lead to even greater accomplishments.

Keep your own special needs in mind as you proceed. Review the OCBQ frequently. Use it to guide you as you work through the material presented in this module.

LEARNING EFFECTIVE ORAL COMMUNICATION

Although in our daily work we speak more often than we write, many of us have not overcome the fear of having to speak to a group. If this applies to you, you are not alone! Numerous surveys point to public speaking as the number one fear of business people. Yet an oral presentation, whether it is a speech, a proposal to some outside business organization, or an outline of plans to an internal group of colleagues, is an important part of business communications.

The advantage of speaking rather than writing is that it permits immediate feedback. The speaker can respond to the audience's nonverbal reactions and clarify any confusing points. The listeners often can comment or ask questions. The disadvantage is that the audience cannot go back over material. Oral communication therefore is not a good channel for conveying a lot of detailed information. The message in an oral presentation has to be relatively simple if it is to have an impact on the audience. Simple does not mean simple-minded, however. Planning for an oral presentation is just as important as planning for a written one.

Effective Oral Communication Techniques

If you are going to improve your oral communication skills, it is important that you begin with a plan for using oral communication techniques. This plan can be developed by following the five-step process shown in Figure 3. Each of these steps builds on the previous step. Let's examine them more closely.

Establishing Goals

In this critical first step, it is important that you have a clear image of your goals or purpose. Ask yourself, what do I hope to achieve with this communication? What exactly do I want listeners to do, think, or feel? If you don't know what your goals are, you will find it easy to ramble, say the wrong things, or even communicate the right message in the wrong environment. Having clear goals in mind will also help you respond appropriately to anything unexpected that may occur during your delivery.

Consider whether your goal is to inform or persuade. If it is to inform, you should emphasize facts. If your goal is to persuade, you may consider an appeal to emotion as well as to reason.

In most communications, several goals will stem from your overall purpose. Write them down, so you can plan. These goals or desired outcomes are usually a combination of personal goals (career considerations), company goals (objectives or purpose of your job duties), and department goals (often involving interdepartmental relationships).

Analyzing the Audience

What kind of audience will you have? Knowing your audience will help you select appropriate content, attention getters, vocabulary, and visual aids, among other things. For most internal business presentations, it is fairly easy to assess

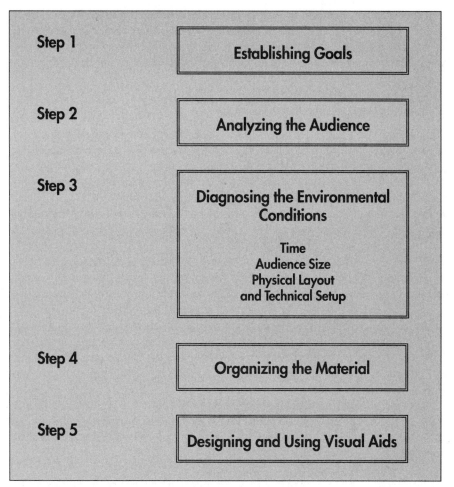

the audience. Most of them will be aware of your experience and why you are talking to them, so you won't have to establish credibility. They will be interested in your subject, since it will presumably have a bearing on the business as a whole. As business associates, they may be fairly homogeneous in their backgrounds or experience. Recognize, however, that differences among business associates exist and that each person has particular interests he or she is looking out for. Therefore, it is worthwhile to consider answers to the following questions:

- Who are the key decision makers or opinion makers, and what are their needs and concerns?
- What will the audience already know and what should I explain?
- Where might resistance to my ideas come from and how can I counter it?

When your audience is from diverse backgrounds or occupations, it is important to determine a common bond. Pinpoint some shared concerns members of the audience may have, whether they are economic, political, or cultural.

Whether your goal is to inform or persuade, a detailed audience profile that covers style preferences, attitudes, needs, knowledge level, and other factors will be helpful. Plan ahead. Make sure that your style and approach are consistent with your role and degree of credibility. Consider the possible responses from the audience when they listen to your message.

Diagnosing the Environmental Conditions

To be effective in a variety of communication environments (for example, in one-on-one discussions, meetings, leaderless group discussions, or formal speeches), you must diagnose the environmental conditions in which the communication will take place. Conditions such as time, audience size, physical layout, and technical setup can place different demands on the communicator. You will need to be flexible and adjust what you say and how you say it to the environmental conditions. Let's look at how a few of these conditions can affect your message.

Time   Whatever the length of time allocated, stick to it. If an audience expects a half-hour talk and you speak for only fifteen minutes, they may feel cheated, especially if they have given up valuable time—or paid money—to attend. Far worse than being too brief, however, is being long-winded. Even ten minutes beyond the expected length can seem like an eternity to an audience. Psychologists have suggested that most people's attention span is not longer than twenty minutes, and many people's thoughts begin to wander long before that. If your presentation is scheduled right before a meal, the audience may be even more restless.

Timing yourself in rehearsal will tell you how long your presentation is. If it looks as if you are going to be behind on your time, summarize the remaining material and end on time rather than push on relentlessly through the full speech.

Audience Size   Tailor your message and delivery to the size of the audience. To speak in a small group discussion as if you were addressing a large audience would be inappropriate, and probably counterproductive. To speak in one-on-one situations as if you were in a group would be similarly inappropriate. In general, the smaller the group, the less formality is needed. For example, a casual pitch and rate to your voice can be effective in a small group whereas the same voice may be out of place in a formal briefing. In one-on-one discussions, interaction with the audience is appropriate, and you must leave room for feedback in the form of questions and comments and pace your speech accordingly.

Physical Layout and Technical Setup   There are several considerations with respect to physical layout and technical setup. Find out in advance how large the room is and whether you will have (or need) a microphone. Are the doors placed so that anyone coming in late will distract the audience? What type of audiovisual aids will you need, and are they in good working order?

Will you be speaking in front of a lectern or a table? Using a lectern can be both an advantage and a disadvantage. It allows you to look at notes unobtrusively, and can hide nervous hands. On the other hand, a lectern presents a physical barrier between you and the audience, increasing the sense of formality and distance. If you are giving a short, informal talk or presentation, you are probably better without a lectern. If you choose to use one, recognize that you can move away from it to approach the audience periodically, creating visual relief while bridging the spatial gap between you and the audience.

Organizing the Material

It is important to organize your material so that your message can be followed easily. Whether exchanging ideas across a table with one person or presenting a formal briefing to a group, you need a logical flow of thought to help your listeners follow the message.

Organize your material with an introduction that previews, a body that develops, and a conclusion that reviews. When you organize the body of your presentation, start by sorting out the theme. The theme is a planning device that holds together the various ideas you want to discuss. If the theme of your presentation is informative, then the body should provide facts. If the theme is persuasive, the body should develop persuasive arguments.

Next, choose the basic method of organization. Ways to organize your message include order of importance, chronological order, known to unknown, simple to complex, problem to solution, or comparison. Even if you use the right vocabulary and match the listeners' level of interest, if you do not present your facts or story in a logical manner, your message may not get across. Think of your message's organizational structure as a map to help your listeners find their way to your ideas, concepts, thoughts. Rambling off course can take the audience down many blind alleys and, possibly, lose them entirely. On the other hand, if you organize your thoughts logically, your listeners will have no trouble following you.

How direct or indirect you should be in your organization depends on your analysis of the audience and your goals. In most cases, the direct approach works best. It is especially useful for a business presentation when you and the audience are in general agreement about objectives and goals. If the audience is likely to be opposed to your ideas, you may want to be indirect. You may choose to build gradually to your solution, keeping the most effective argument to the last. Another option for organizing the material is to direct the audience by pointing out in the introduction that you will be proposing a solution, but keep from disclosing the exact nature of the solution until you have laid the groundwork.

Designing and Using Visual Aids

Visual aids not only help to clarify material and give impact but also keep an audience alert. However, visuals can be overused. If you are a dynamic speaker, visual aids may lessen your momentum by shifting the focus away from what you are saying.

When designing visual aids, use the following guidelines:

- Keep the message or diagram simple and uncluttered. The audience should be able to understand it quickly.
- Break complex points into simple ones. Use overlays to show any complex relationships.

- Use a type size large enough to be seen from the back of the room. Although your choice of print size varies with the size of the room and with the font you choose, usually you should use at least 18-point type, and in some cases 24- or 36-point type on overhead slides.
- Avoid showing a long list of key points. Instead, break a list of items into subsections so that no major heading has more than three or four items.
- Use standard capitalization. Except for very short lines, capitalize only the first letter of a sentence or phrase.
- Use color sparingly. Use no more than three colors in a single illustration. Avoid a combination of green and red, since many color-blind people can't distinguish the difference.

All your work in designing visual aids will be wasted unless you use them effectively during your presentation. First of all, become familiar with the equipment. Practice with any piece of equipment you are going to use long enough so that you can use it easily.

Make sure that you show only the visual you are discussing. When you are no longer discussing a visual, get it out of sight. Turn off the projector when you are finished referring to the transparency, erase the board, or turn flip charts to blank sheets in between charts.

As you introduce each visual, remember that this is the first time the audience has seen it. Give them a chance to become acquainted with the visual before you start to talk about it.

When using visuals, look at your audience. You are there to interact with them, not with your visuals. Speakers tend to become so engrossed with their machinery or charts that they forget to look at their audience. Face your audience, not the screen or the projector. If possible, stand next to the screen.

Point to show the exact place where you want your audience to look instead of gesturing vaguely in the direction of your visuals. Be sure to face your audience as you point and point on the screen itself, not on the projector.

Learn to use handouts effectively. Be particularly cautious with handouts because people will always read ahead. Withhold handouts on detailed, complex information until the specific point in your presentation when you are discussing it; then give the audience some time to read what they have just been handed. Save detailed summary handouts until the end of the presentation.

A good rule of thumb for using visuals effectively is: Never use visual aids if they simply repeat the obvious. Use them to emphasize, clarify, or pull together important information.

Oral Communication Skills Needed by Managers

Up to this point we have been discussing how to plan the content of your oral communication message. Now we are going to examine some oral communication presentation skills. In the next section, we will examine (1) using the voice effectively, (2) employing nonverbal accompaniments, (3) structuring the message, (4) eliminating random noise, and (5) developing audience rapport.

Using the Voice Effectively

Many people underestimate the importance of the voice in determining credibility. Your voice can help or hinder your communication. If it is too loud or too soft, if your speech is too rapid or too slow, if your words are over-articulated or slurred, you are using your voice in a way that distracts your listeners. Also, if you speak in a monotone, you may bore your listeners unbearably, no matter what the content of your talk.

On the other hand, your voice, properly used, can enhance your communication immeasurably. Speak with expressiveness and enthusiasm, in a warm, pleasant tone, and with volume appropriate for the size of the room. Inflection refers to variations in your volume and pitch that make you sound expressive. When you use inflection effectively, your voice reflects your enthusiasm and interest. Inflect your voice down, never up. You shouldn't sound as if you are asking a question or seeking approval but rather are stating your objective.

Rate is the speed at which you speak. It's natural when you are nervous to speed up your talking. Unless you are normally a slow speaker, take the opposite approach. Before you start to speak, pause for a moment to get your bearing and look over the audience. Take a few deep breaths to relax. Then, when you begin speaking, vary your rate to avoid droning. Generally, keep it slow enough to be understood but fast enough to maintain energy. Use pauses before or after key terms, to separate items in a series, to indicate a major break in thought, and when you are changing your emphasis.

Fillers are verbal pauses such as *uh, um,* and *ya know.* Pause during your presentation to collect your thoughts. Don't fill the pauses with fillers.

Enunciation is the clarity of your pronunciation. Your listeners can understand you better when you pronounce your words clearly, without mumbling, running words together, leaving out syllables, or dropping final consonants.

Employing Nonverbal Accompaniments

Nonverbal accompaniments include use of time, space, aroma, physical environment and physical characteristics. All of these communicate messages. Body language, the type of nonverbal accompaniment that we are going to examine, includes gestures, posture, facial expressions, eye contact, and body movements. What messages are you sending nonverbally? Are these consistent with your goals?

Your body language starts "speaking" immediately, and first impressions are crucial. When you are addressing a group, think of yourself as onstage from the moment you enter the room until the moment you leave—even if you are waiting to start or listening to others.

Managers are often unaware of the nonverbal signals they are sending. The wrong signals may result in an ineffective presentation or a low evaluation. For example, slouching may communicate defeat or lack of power and may diminish the authority with which a message is communicated. An erect posture will convey power and self-confidence and increase the impact of the spoken word. By rehearsing your presentations in front of a mirror or watching a videotape of yourself, you will gain a clearer idea of how you are communicating nonverbally.

The most effective communicators use hand gestures, facial expressions, posture, and body motion to emphasize the meaning and spirit of what they're saying. Less effective communicators are often not aware how slouching, nail biting, or arm waving distracts from, instead of enhances, their key points. The following are some important nonverbal accompaniments that can influence your oral communication effectiveness:

- *Smiling.* People who smile a lot are happier than those who do not smile. When a smile comes naturally, great. Otherwise, think of something pleasant that will get you smiling.
- *Good posture.* A speaker who walks purposefully and stands erect conveys a sense of command and appears poised. Stand in a relaxed, professional manner. Align your feet under your shoulders. Do not slouch or drape yourself over a lectern. Be careful not to rock or sway from side to side or back and forth.
- *Appropriate and comfortable dress.* There is no point in distracting an audience from what you are saying by what you are wearing. Unless special clothing is a deliberate part of the drama you are creating—a kind of costume—it's better to be on the conservative side.
- *Eye contact.* Make eye contact; don't be afraid to look directly at the person you are speaking to. When you speak to a group, think of the audience as a number of individuals. Look for someone who is especially attentive and establish eye contact with that person. Try to hold your eye contact for a few seconds with one person before moving to another. This technique will help you feel comfortable with the audience and adapt to audience responses when necessary.
- *Natural gestures.* Gestures should be relaxed and complement your message. Natural gestures can be an effective way to reinforce points or express a mood. Artificial gestures and repetitive or fidgety movements can distract from your presentation. Use hand movements when they are natural. Avoid putting your hands in any one position—such as the "figleaf" (hand clasped in front), the "parade rest" (hands clasped in back), the "gunshot wound" (hand clutching opposite arm), and the "lectern clutch"—and leaving them there without change.
- *Natural body movements.* It is helpful to move around while talking. Although constant walking can be distracting, taking a few steps here and there, if you feel natural doing so, can be effective.

Figure 4 lists several commonly seen forms of body language and their interpretations. Remember, body language is a two-edged sword. Used competently, it can greatly enhance a speaker's effectiveness; used incompetently, it can hamper communication. Become aware of how these factors can work for you rather than against you.

Structuring the Message

Presenting information orally differs from presenting it in writing. A common prescription for speakers is: Tell them what you are going to say, say it, and then tell them what you have said. An effective oral presentation includes an opening, a preview of the main points, clearly demarcated main points, and a closing.

BODY LANGUAGE	COMMON INTERPRETATION
Facial Expressions	
Frown	Displeasure, unhappiness
Smile	Friendliness, happiness
Raised eyebrows	Disbelief, amazement
Narrow eyes, pursed lips	Anger
Biting lip	Nervousness
Gestures	
Pointing finger	Authority, displeasure, lecturing
Folded arms	Not open to change or communication
Arms at side	Open to suggestions, relaxed
Hands on hips	Anger, defensiveness
Hands uplifted outward	Disbelief, uncertainty
Jiggling coins in pocket	Nervousness
Voice	
Shaky	Nervous
Broken speech	Unprepared
Strong and clear	Confident
Body Postures	
Fidgeting, doodling	Boredom, nervousness
Shrugging shoulders	Indifference
Sitting on edge of chair	Listening, great interest
Slouching	Boredom, lack of interest
Shifting	Nervousness
Eye Contact	
Sideways glance	Suspicion
Steady	Active listening, interest
No eye contact	Disinterest

FIGURE 4
Interpreting Body Language

With an effective opening, you will get the audience to listen to you right from the start. From the audience's perspective, your opening should arouse their interest, show how the topic relates to them, establish your competence and credibility, and establish rapport.

Next, give your audience a preview. Think of a preview as a table of contents, an agenda, or an outline of what you will be covering in your presentation. One of the most common problems in business presentations is the lack of a preview. Your listeners have no idea what you will be covering unless you tell them. Always give an explicit preview before you begin discussing your main points.

After your opening and preview, launch into your main points. Be sure to limit the number of main points you make in a presentation, since listeners cannot process as much information as readers can. Most people cannot easily comprehend more than three to five main points in a speech. This doesn't mean that you say three things and sit down. It means that you should group your complex ideas into three to five major areas and select supporting visuals that will reinforce your main points. Use internal summaries to conclude each major section or subsection. Listeners may not remember information they hear only once.

Since your audience is likely to remember your last words, use an effective closing. Don't waste your closing by saying something like "Well, that's all I have to say" or "I guess that's about it." An effective closing uses strong, obvious transitional phrases such as *to summarize* or *in conclusion* to introduce concluding remarks. One effective closing is to summarize your main points. You may feel as though you're being repetitive, but this kind of reinforcement is extremely effective when you are explaining or instructing. Another effective closing is to refer to the rhetorical question, promise, image, or story you used in your opening.

Eliminating Random Noise

Random noise is any type of distraction that could interfere with your message. It is the "static" of oral communication. Random noise includes needless digressions, distracting mannerisms and extraneous sounds, as well as voice tone and inflections that distract the audience or contradict what you are saying. Random noise can occur anytime in the communication process, and the effective oral communicator must be prepared to free his or her communications from these distractions.

Unnecessary sounds, words, and mannerisms are random noises that detract from your message and may even communicate something other than what you intend. Digressions and contradictions between voice inflection and words also are random noises that may drown out your meaning. Through practice, you can learn to eliminate these noises from your speech.

Developing Audience Rapport

As a manager, you instruct, direct, persuade, and transmit information through oral communication. If you are going to be an effective manager, you must develop rapport with those to whom you communicate, or your messages may never be received. Remember that rapport improves all types of oral communication, whether group discussions, formal presentations, or one-on-one conversations.

Rapport with your audience serves two purposes—it gets them to listen and it persuades them to accept what you're saying. Without rapport, your audience may not even pay attention to what you are saying, or they may become antagonistic. Either of these reactions will hamper your ability as a manager to influence others or to make things happen.

Building rapport begins when you first meet your audience, not just when you begin your formal oral communication. Establishing rapport is easier to do if you plan ahead. This means learning about both your audience and the situation in which you meet with your audience. To build rapport you will want to note common goals, acknowledge their possible concerns, and demonstrate your willingness to relieve these concerns.

Rapport develops more quickly when you involve your audience in the communication. By asking audience members to participate, you keep them involved instead of losing their interest. This can be done simply by asking a question that requires raising a hand in response.

Although we discussed the use of eye contact as an important nonverbal accompaniment, we mention it again here because it is crucial for establishing rapport with your audience. Eye contact allows you to read visual clues about your audience's comprehension and opinion and allows your audience to feel a greater connection with you.

Oral Communication Skills and Their Relationships to Other Managerial Skills

Oral communication cannot be effective without the use of many other managerial skills. Competence in oral communication demands the ability to express ideas clearly and concisely, to be well organized, and to attract and maintain the interest of listeners. For this you need strong interpersonal and perception skills that will help you know your audience members, establish rapport with them, and anticipate their concerns. Organization and planning skills are also important. For example, you must plan what you wish to say and organize your ideas in a logical manner. To respond to feedback from listeners during your delivery requires you to adapt your strategies and communication. This is where flexibility skills come in.

Oral communication skills are frequently the vehicle through which other management skills, such as decision making and leadership, are expressed. Perhaps, this is one reason that managers who are perceived to be skillful oral communicators often move ahead quickly in their organizations.

PRACTICING EFFECTIVE ORAL COMMUNICATION

Oral communication skills cover a range of activities. They consist of the following behaviors:

- *Using the voice effectively*—Varying the pitch and tone of your voice and making sure that your voice is pleasant and full are ways to use your voice effectively. Also, it is important to speak loudly enough to be heard but not annoyingly loud, and to pronounce your words clearly and correctly. Your speech should be varied in rhythm and neither too fast nor too slow.
- *Employing nonverbal accompaniments*—Your dress, posture, facial expressions, and body movements should not detract from your message. Appropriate gestures and eye contact will add to what you are saying.
- *Structuring the message*—You will be more effective if you state the purpose of your communication clearly in an opening, provide a preview, demarcate the main points, and end with a strong closing. You also should

structure your message logically and use vocabulary appropriate for your audience.

■ *Eliminating random noise*—Extraneous sounds, needless digressions, distracting mannerisms, and voice tone and inflection that contradict what you are saying may all interfere with your message. Rid yourself of these distractions.

■ *Developing audience rapport*—Rapport will get your audience to listen and accept what you are saying. Involving your listeners in your communication through activity, humor (when appropriate), and friendliness will make them more receptive and enhance your oral communication.

The next section of in-basket exercises focuses separately on each component of effective oral communication. Before you begin these exercises, review your scores on the five parts of the OCBQ that you completed earlier. As you work through the exercises, think about the behaviors noted in the questionnaire. The questions in the OCBQ will deepen your understanding of basic oral communication considerations.

Each in-basket exercise is followed by questions that direct your attention to important aspects of oral communication skills. Work in groups of two or more to answer these questions so that you may have classmates watch your presentations.

All five in-basket exercises are set in interfacing divisions of Natori Sound Systems, Inc. The Product Development division is responsible for developing new products for the company; the Manufacturing division is responsible for producing products for mass marketing.

Natori Sound Systems, Inc., is a relatively new company in the field of stereo sound systems for professional and home use. It was formed just ten years ago but already has a line of three popular products in the marketplace with four more presently in development.

One of the projects in development is now ready to be moved into production. The product, called NAVOLESE, is a new concept in compact disc, cassette, and record players that allows the home user to file a CD, record, and tape library into a computer-controlled selection system. Once the filing is completed, the user merely enters the name of the selection, the composer, the performer, or even the type of music desired and the system automatically selects and plays it.

Although production is to start in January of the upcoming year, Product Development is continuing to work on additional features for future models. These include (1) a module that would permit the user to merely speak into the system to obtain the desired selection, (2) a tapehead and needle cleaner that automatically cleans the tapehead and needle to minimize wear and damage, and (3) an alert light to warn when the needle needs changing or the tapeheads need servicing.

As the product moves into production, close cooperation is necessary between Product Development and Manufacturing. The critical working relationship will continue in the future as the two departments work closely together to integrate advanced features and modifications into the manufacturing process.

IN-BASKET EXERCISE 1: USING THE VOICE EFFECTIVELY

As a manager, you must use oral communication skills to achieve a wide variety of management objectives. The manner in which you use your voice can either increase or reduce your effectiveness.

Situation:

You are Sandy Tuthill, manager of the Design department in the Product Development division of Natori Sound Systems, Inc. It is your responsibility to work with the Model Shop and Engineering departments to create the concept models of new products. As part of this job, you are often called on to explain the models and design concepts in formal briefings to top-level management. Your job also calls for informal communications in one-on-one and group discussions.

You have been asked by your director to give a briefing. Your job in this in-basket exercise is to read through the materials in your files (shown in Exhibits 1 and 2), prepare and conduct the briefing, and respond to the questions that follow. Use a tape recorder or, if possible, videotape your presentation. Use the speech prepared by Pat Cosgrove in the memo of December 21 (Exhibit 2). Respond to the questions that follow.

Your oral communication skills focus:

- Adapt the speed at which you present your message to lend emphasis to what you are saying.
- Adjust the volume of your voice to get the attention of your audience.
- Enhance your message by varying the rate of your speech.
- Speak distinctly and vary the rhythm of your speech.
- Alter your patterns of speech to the type of oral communication you are engaged in (formal presentation, group discussion, one-on-one exchange).

Questions for In-Basket Exercise 1:

1. As Sandy Tuthill, you have been asked to give a talk on the NAVOLESE system to a group of ten purchasing agents. Prepare and give your speech now to a group of at least ten peers. Review the tape (audio or video) of your speech and use the following criteria to critique your presentation:
   a. How clear and distinct was your voice in the talk you just gave? Note words you slurred and the effect they had on your talk.

   b. Did you speak loudly enough to be understood but not so loudly as to be distracting?

   c. Ask for feedback about the use of your voice from the group to whom you presented the talk.

2. Present the same speech again but this time in a one-on-one informal discussion with someone role-playing the manager of purchasing. Review the tape (audio or video) of your speech and use the following criteria to critique your presentation:

   a. How did your pitch, volume, and rate of delivery differ in this situation, compared to the formal briefing in question 1? Explain the difference.

   b. Ask for feedback about the use of your voice from the individual to whom you presented your talk.

3. Imagine that you are sitting in a meeting participating in a group discussion. You feel that this group should know some details about the NAVOLESE system. There is no formal agenda, and there is no designated discussion leader. Present the same information (from questions 1 and 2) to this group. Review the tape (audio or video) of your group meeting and use the following criteria to critique your discussion:

   a. How did your pitch, volume, and rate of delivery differ in this situation, compared to the formal briefing in question 1 or the one-on-one informal discussion in question 2? Explain the difference.

b. Ask for feedback about your presentation from the group to whom you presented it.

4. Explain why it is important to speak clearly and distinctly so that your words are not slurred.

5. How can you use your voice to gain the attention of a group so that they will listen to what you have to say?

6. Describe how you can use vocal pitch, volume, and rate of delivery for emphasis.

IN-BASKET EXERCISE 2: EMPLOYING NONVERBAL ACCOMPANIMENTS

When communicating orally, whether in formal briefings, informal one-on-one conversations, or group situations, your use of gestures and other nonverbal forms of communication can either enhance or detract from your message. Becoming aware of the impact of nonverbal accompaniments will help you strengthen your communication effectiveness.

Situation:

You are Bobbie Sterling, director of marketing for Natori Sound Systems, Inc. You have a staff of seven marketing managers, one for each of the Natori products. Each manager is responsible for all customer contacts regarding that product and for creating marketing plans and strategies. Each manager uses oral communication skills extensively, both inside the company and with customers.

You have received a memo from the vice president and general manager that is critical of your staff members, based largely on the image created by their nonverbal behavior. He has told you to do something about it. You have observed the behavior of your staff and decided that the criticism is valid.

This afternoon is your regular staff meeting. All your managers will be present. You have decided to use this meeting to begin improving the nonverbal skills of your staff by demonstrating your own proper behavior during this meeting. At the meeting, you want to bring up the monthly call report and brief your managers on a competitor's product. Videotape your presentation if possible. Members of the class can role-play the seven marketing managers. Respond to the questions that follow.

Your oral communication skills focus:

- Use erect body posture to communicate seriousness, solemnity, formality, and authority.
- Employ a relaxed body posture to communicate informality.
- Avoid slouching since it indicates a lack of seriousness and power.
- Use facial expressions to reinforce your spoken words and to convey approval or disapproval.
- Establish eye contact to interest your listeners.

Questions for In-Basket Exercise 2:

1. As Bobbie Sterling, prepare and conduct your staff meeting, paying special attention to how you can effectively use nonverbal accompaniments to express the seriousness of this matter. Review the videotape and use the following criteria to critique your use of body language:

    a. How effective was your use of posture to convey the seriousness of this matter?

    b. How did you use body language to convey your feelings?

    c. How effective was your use of facial expressions?

d. What other use of body language did you build into your discussion with your staff? Were these uses effective or ineffective?

e. Ask for feedback about your use of body language from the group to whom you presented.

IN-BASKET EXERCISE 3: STRUCTURING THE MESSAGE

You will find that in order to effectively communicate with others, you must structure your message so that it is clear. The key points you make, the details you present, and the vocabulary you use all must be chosen with the audience you are addressing and the context of your communication in mind. Structuring an effective oral presentation includes providing your audience with an opening, a preview of the main points, clearly demarcated main points, and a closing.

Situation:

You are Terry Johnson, manager of purchasing for the NAVOLESE system in the Manufacturing division of Natori Sound Systems, Inc. You report on a direct line to Robin Franks, manager of the NAVOLESE product for Manufacturing and on a functional line to Bob Sanchez, manager of purchasing in the Manufacturing division. You are responsible for all purchasing for the planned NAVOLESE production, a new product that is now in transition from Product Development to Manufacturing. Robin Franks has asked you to prepare and present a briefing on the status of purchasing for the NAVOLESE system.

The information on purchasing requirements is shown in Exhibits 3 through 7. Your job in this in-basket exercise is to read through those materials and prepare and conduct the briefing. Use a tape recorder or, if possible, videotape your presentation. Respond to the questions that follow.

Your oral communication skills focus:

- Identify your key points.
- Support these points with appropriate details.
- Express your message concisely.
- Tailor your message to the audience.

Questions for In-Basket Exercise 3:

1. Playing the role of Terry Johnson, present your briefing to a partner playing the role of Robin Franks. What are the key points you will communicate to Robin? What details will you give to Robin?

2. Demonstrate your ability to express content concisely by explaining to Robin, in one brief sentence, the essence of the memo you received from your buyer, Marilyn Boley. With a partner playing the role of Robin Franks, communicate this statement.

3. Instead of briefing Robin, imagine that you were asked to brief top-level management. Would you communicate key points to this audience differently than to Robin? Explain.

4. With a small group playing the role of top management, communicate this message. Ask for feedback from the group about the effectiveness of your message.

In-Basket Exercise 4: Eliminating Random Noise

Random noise is the static of oral communication. It diverts the attention of the audience and dilutes the clarity of what you are saying. Unnecessary sounds, words, and mannerisms detract from your message and may even communicate something other than what you intend. Digressions and contradictions between voice inflection and words also are random noise that may drown out your meaning. The effective oral communicator will consciously attempt to free his or her communications from these distractions.

Situation:

You are Robin Franks, manager of the NAVOLESE product in the Manufacturing division of Natori Sound Systems, Inc. Today is Thursday, November 18. You will be making a ten-minute formal presentation to the general manager and to staff members on the NAVOLESE sound system. You will talk specifically about the status of production plans for this product.

NAVOLESE is in the process of changing from Product Development to Manufacturing. Your position has been newly established to take care of this changeover and to manage the manufacturing process.

Shown in Exhibits 8 through 11 are materials you have requested from your staff. Included is information on the people you will address and notes you have made in preparation for your meeting with the general manager and staff. Read through this material and then prepare a ten minute presentation on the NAVOLESE system. Review your notes and determine what you are going to say. Give your briefing in front of a small group. If possible, videotape your presentation so that you can critique your presentation.

Your oral communication skills focus:

- Avoid sounds, words, and mannerisms that communicate something other than what you intend.
- Eliminate unnecessary distractions.
- Avoid digressions and contradictions between voice inflection and words.

Questions for In-Basket Exercise 4:

1. As Robin Franks, you have been asked to give a ten-minute formal presentation to the general manager and to staff members on the NAVOLESE sound system. Prepare and give your speech now to a group of peers. Review the tape (audio or video) of your presentation and use the following criteria to critique your presentation:

   a. What was the main topic? Did you stick to it, or did you digress? How did this affect your communication? What key points did you make?

   b. What did you do to ensure that your briefing would be clear and concise?

   c. Estimate the number of times you used words like "you know," made sounds like "uh," cleared your throat, or repeated yourself.

d. Were there any contradictions between your voice inflection and words?

2. Ask for feedback from the group to whom you presented. Ask them to use the following questions:
   a. What was the main topic? Did the presenter stick to the topic or did he or she digress? How did this affect the communication from the speaker to you?

   b. What key points did the speaker make?

c. Estimate the number of times the speaker used words like "you know," made sounds like "uh," cleared his or her throat, or repeated statements.

d. Were there any contradictions between the speaker's voice inflection and his or her words?

IN-BASKET EXERCISE 5: DEVELOPING AUDIENCE RAPPORT

As a manager, you instruct, direct, persuade, and transmit information through oral communication. If you do not establish rapport with the person(s) with whom you communicate, your messages may never be received. Without rapport, your audience may not pay attention to what you're saying.

Situation:

You are Pat Cosgrove, manager of the NAVOLESE project in the Product Development division of Natori Sound Systems, Inc. This product has been under your guidance for two years and is now being placed into production under the control of the Manufacturing division. You will be discussing this with other key managers involved in the transition. This discussion will take place in a meeting that has been scheduled for tomorrow morning, November 19.

The other people present at the meeting will include Robin Franks, manager for NAVOLESE, and members of Robin's team (Terry Johnson, manager of purchasing; Jill Ranks, manager of quality; and Judy Tarshall, manager of production control). The group also includes members of your own staff: Trish Potter, engineering manager, and Fred Summers, manager of design. You have never met Robin before and only slightly know Terry, Jill, and Judy. Cooperation between your group and Robin's group is essential in accomplishing the transition of the project into full production in manufacturing. A profile of these team participants is shown in Exhibit 12.

You are asked in this in-basket exercise to participate as Pat Cosgrove in a team-meeting discussion on the Navolese project with six other people role-playing the team members named in Exhibit 12. Before you begin the discussion, respond to the questions that follow.

Your oral communication skills focus:

- Establish rapport with others early in your meeting.
- Show a personal interest.
- Take personality differences into account.
- Be friendly; let your communications have a friendly tone.
- Do your homework so you can address the specific concerns of others.
- Get your audience to participate.

Questions for In-Basket Exercise 5:

1. What are your overall goals in this meeting?

2. What initial gestures of goodwill would be in order before the meeting starts?

3. What goal(s) do you share with Robin and others at the meeting?

4. What will probably be the main points of discussion at the meeting?

5. What messages will you need to give or explain at the meeting to build rapport?

6. Suppose that when you arrive at the meeting everyone is already assembled. Terry and Jill appear to be complaining to Robin about something. Trish and Fred are looking puzzled. Robin begins the meeting by stating that Manufacturing has heard that there are some design problems that have not been solved and that putting NAVOLESE into production is premature. You are asked to talk about this. As far as you are concerned, there are no design problems, yet you cannot guarantee that there will be no problems when the system is put into production. You have been put on the defensive. At least part of your audience appears to be hostile. What do you do to establish rapport under these circumstances?

ASSESSING CHANGE

The purpose of this module has been to help you develop your oral communication skills through practice. Your attention has been focused on the different components of behaviors that make up oral communication skills. You have seen that oral communication skills involve:

- *Using the voice effectively*—As Sandy Tuthill, manager of design at Natori Sound Systems, Inc., your task was to talk about a product in both formal and informal situations and to use your voice to add meaning to your message.
- *Employing nonverbal accompaniments*—As Bobbie Sterling, director of marketing for Natori Sound Systems, Inc., you were called upon to use nonverbal accompaniments effectively to demonstrate to your staff the impact of body language on the oral message.
- *Structuring the message*—You assumed the role of Terry Johnson, manager of purchasing in the Manufacturing division of Natori, and practiced behaviors you must use to present your message logically and clearly.
- *Eliminating random noise*—In the role of Robin Franks, manager of the NAVOLESE project in the Manufacturing division of Natori Sound Systems, you had to practice eliminating distracting sounds and mannerisms from your oral presentations.
- *Developing audience rapport*—As Pat Cosgrove, manager of the NAVOLESE project in the Product Development division of Natori, your job was to relate to your audience and gain their attention and interest.

At the beginning of this chapter, you completed the OCBQ questionnaire to provide a baseline against which you could measure improvements in your oral communication skills. Now it is time to assess some of these improvements.

First, retake the OCBQ. When you have finished, compare your scores with your before-practice scores to see how much you have strengthened your oral communication skills.

The Oral Communication Behaviors Questionnaire (OCBQ)

Use the scale shown below to rate the frequency with which you perform the behaviors noted. Place the corresponding number (1–7) in the blank preceding the statement.

Rarely	Irregularly	Occasionally	Usually	Frequently	Almost Always	Consistently
1	2	3	4	5	6	7

_____ **1.** I speak loudly enough to be heard, yet not so loudly as to distract from what I am saying.

_____ **2.** I vary the pitch and tone of my voice.

_____ **3.** I match the pace and rhythm of my speech to my message.

_____ 4. My voice is pleasant and full.

_____ 5. I pronounce my words clearly.

_____ 6. I use gestures to enhance my message.

_____ 7. I establish eye contact with or frequently look at others.

_____ 8. My apparel is right for the message I wish to convey.

_____ 9. My posture is in tune with my message (for example, relaxed for casual communication, erect for formal communication).

_____ 10. My facial expressions (for example, frowns, smiles) reinforce my message.

_____ 11. I state the purpose of my communication.

_____ 12. I use vocabulary appropriate to my audience.

_____ 13. I match the detail and depth of what I say to the interest and understanding of my listeners.

_____ 14. My communication has a logical, easy-to-follow structure.

_____ 15. I use visual aids to strengthen my oral message.

_____ 16. My speech is free of extraneous sounds and words such as "you know" or "uh."

_____ 17. I stay on my topic and do not digress.

_____ 18. I continue my train of thought despite interruptions.

_____ 19. I avoid distracting mannerisms (for example, fidgeting, finger tapping, leg movements, hair pulling).

_____ 20. The tone and inflection of my voice are in harmony with my message.

_____ 21. I involve my audience in direct participation (for example, asking or answering questions).

_____ 22. I vary my style of speech according to the situation (for example, conversational in one-on-one communication, formal in presentations before an audience).

_____ 23. I use humor appropriately in my messages or presentations.

_____ 24. I address my listeners' interests and concerns.

_____ 25. My communications have a friendly tone.

OCBQ Scoring and Evaluation

Follow the scoring directions found on page 154 and in Figure 1. Complete the after-practice assessment column for the OCBQ and compare your before- and after-practice scores. You will also need to plot your after-practice scores in Figure 2. In which categories did your scores improve? Think about what has made your progress possible. Perhaps you can apply your insights to categories where your performance has lagged.

The Oral Communication Awareness Scale (OCAS)

A second method to assess change in your oral communication skills is the Oral Communication Awareness Scale (OCAS). In the OCAS, you assume the role of a manager in several situations. You are asked to choose the most appropriate behavior from among several possible responses given the information available. This instrument helps you see how you actually behave in situations where your oral communication skills are needed. It will give you more insight into your oral communication behaviors and their impact on the messages you wish to convey to your listeners.

Described on the following pages are ten situations in which oral communication skills are required. Select the response that demonstrates the highest level of oral communication skills in the situation described. Check the appropriate space at the left of the responses. Please choose only one response for each situation.

1. You are the manager of the purchasing department at Lake Tool and Die, Inc. You are giving a formal briefing to a group of other managers. Already you have been interrupted by several questions that have taken you away from the main thrust of your presentation. The time for the briefing is limited, and you have planned for a short question period at the end of your presentation. You have just been asked another question on a matter that fits most logically into a later portion of your presentation. You decide that in order to communicate with your listeners in the most effective way you will:

_____ a) Answer the question now.

_____ b) State that you will respond to the question later since it will be clearer after you've presented some additional information.

_____ c) Tell the group that because time is limited you cannot respond to further questions.

_____ d) Ignore the question. Proceed as if you had not been interrupted.

_____ e) Answer the question, but ask the group to hold all further questions until the end of your presentation.

2. You are the personnel manager of Real Good Restaurants. You have developed a new appraisal system for restaurant personnel including cooks, servers, and cashiers. Last week, in an hour-long presentation, you explained the new appraisal system to the district managers and the administrative staff. Your talk received many positive comments, both on the new system itself and your skill in presenting it. Now you must brief employees at each of the ten restaurants operated by Real Good. The purpose of this briefing is to make certain that the employees understand the new system. You are most likely to accomplish this if you:

_____ a) Use the same presentation for the employees that you used for management.

_____ b) Shorten your presentation and ask for questions.

_____ c) Explain why the new system will work better than the old.

_____ d) Use visual aids.

_____ e) Brief each employee separately.

3. You are the manager of the testing department at Anzar, Inc. You are talking to your employees, enthusiastically describing a new circuit design they will be testing. You emphasize what you are saying with arm movements. As you talk, you notice that Toni, one of the employees, is watching your arms. Toni's eyes dart back and forth, following the movements of your arms. Under the circumstances, it would be advisable for you to:

_____ a) Continue talking, and ignore what you have noticed.

_____ b) Put your hands at your sides.

_____ c) Get a pad and draw a sketch.

_____ d) Smile and ask Toni what she is thinking about.

_____ e) Speak more slowly.

4. You are an account executive for Woodline Advertising Company. Rhone Airlines is one of your accounts. The time for contract renewal is approaching, and a contact at Rhone has informed you that Sam Holt, Rhone's marketing manager, has been looking around for a new ad agency. You phone Sam and make a luncheon appointment. You are not sure that Sam is thinking of changing agencies, but if he is, you want to persuade him to remain with Woodline. At your luncheon, you will have a better chance of getting your message across if you:

_____ a) Make a carefully thought out, structured presentation.

_____ b) Maintain a friendly, informal interchange.

_____ c) Encourage Sam to express his thoughts about Woodline.

_____ d) Clearly state the purpose of your meeting.

_____ e) All of the above.

5. You are the production manager for Todd Frozen Foods, Inc. Todd is starting a Quality Circle system. You have just returned from a seminar on Quality Circles. Now the plant manager has asked you to meet with the production employees, including line workers and supervisors, to talk about Quality Circles. Already some of the supervisors have said that Quality Circles will upset production because they will interfere with the supervisors' authority. The objective of your meeting is to explain the Quality Circles to your employees. At your meeting, you are most likely to get your message across if you:

_____ a) Talk separately with the supervisors and line workers.

_____ b) Involve your audience in a sample circle.

_____ c) Assume your supervisors feel that nothing will really change as far as they are concerned.

_____ d) Explain the reasons for Quality Circles.

_____ e) Ask the employees to express their feelings.

6. You are the project manager for the Cannoe project at Ames Aerospace, Inc. You have arranged for the engineering and manufacturing managers to meet together to see if interface problems that have arisen recently can be resolved. You will best promote good oral communication skills at this meeting if you:

_____ a) Begin the meeting by stating its purpose in a pleasant, full voice.

_____ b) Request each manager, in turn, to present the problem from his or her own perspective.

_____ c) Use a flip chart to emphasize the objectives of the meeting.

_____ d) Make eye contact with each of the managers as you make your introductory remarks.

_____ e) Encourage spontaneous questions and comments.

7. You are the supervisor of the Risk Management department of the Carter Grant Medical Center. Today you will be meeting with Don Smith, one of the department employees, in order to discuss Don's performance appraisal. Last week you received Don's written self-appraisal. It was filled with superlatives that represented a gross overestimation of Don's job performance. It is hard to believe that Don took his self-appraisal seriously. In actuality, Don's performance is barely adequate. You want to communicate to Don that the performance appraisal process is a serious one and that his apparent view of his performance is unrealistic. You can get your message across best if you:

_____ a) Summarize Don's self-appraisal and ask him for supporting data.

_____ b) Tell Don with a smile that you appreciate his positive outlook but that he must appraise himself more factually. Then ask him to do the self-appraisal again.

_____ c) In a pleasant voice, explain to Don that the purpose of your meeting is both to iron out any misconceptions he may have about the requirements of his job and to encourage his growth with the organization.

_____ d) Tap your fingers on the desk while staring at Don and frowning.

_____ e) Start off the interview by graphically showing Don the results of his poor performance.

8. You are the district sales manager for the Yergi Book Publishing Company. You have finally managed to arrange for a briefing before the book committee of the Kato County School Board. You have been told that you will be allowed 45 minutes for the briefing and that it will begin at 8:00 A.M. tomorrow morning in the boardroom of the county offices. The county offices are a one-hour drive from your home.

You have all your visual aids assembled. Also, you have written out the key points of your presentation. However, you have not had time to practice it or time it. You have an important business engagement later this evening that you expect will last for several hours. It is now 5:00 P.M. You have just received a phone call from a friend reminding you of a tennis engagement at 5:30 P.M. To ensure that you will communicate effectively in the meeting tomorrow morning you should:

_____ a) Check over your materials before leaving the office; then go home and take a nap. Cancel your tennis appointment.

_____ b) Keep your tennis engagement, counting on the physical activity to relax you so that you will be more at ease during your presentation tomorrow.

_____ c) Make an excuse to skip the tennis; then go home and time and rehearse your presentation.

_____ d) Practice your presentation in the morning before you leave for the briefing.

_____ e) Cancel your tennis engagement and write out your speech so that you may read it the next morning.

9. You are the warehouse manager for the Biscay Softgoods Company. At a meeting of the warehouse supervisors, you are explaining the company's new inventory control plans. You notice that two people are whispering to each other and laughing. Nearby you can see two others doodling on their notepads. You want to make sure that what you are saying is being heard by your audience, so you should:

_____ a) Ask the people who are laughing to share their joke.

_____ b) Raise your voice so that you are talking louder.

_____ c) Ask a pointed question, such as "Who is responsible when inventory disappears?" Then call on people at random to respond.

_____ d) Establish eye contact with the whisperers by staring at them until they look your way.

_____ e) Stop talking until there is complete silence.

10. You have just been promoted from teller at the drive-in window of Central Bank to assistant manager. Prior to your promotion, your conversations with customers had been limited to only a few words spoken through the intercom at the glass window of your station. However, in your new position, you must talk at length to persons seated at your desk. You are with a customer now, explaining the new computerized bill-paying service the bank is offering. You are aware that your voice is strained and that you are stumbling over your words. To improve your oral communication skills, you should:

_____ a) Keep talking and ignore the strain so that you do not interrupt your communication with the customer.

_____ b) Hand your customer a pamphlet that explains the service and suggest that your customer read it for fuller explanation.

_____ c) Pause for a moment. Breathe deeply, smile, and ask the customer to talk about his or her bill-paying requirements.

_____ d) Apologize for your nervousness, explaining that you are new at the job.

_____ e) Tell the customer that you will be back in a moment; then leave and get a drink of water.

OCAS Scoring and Evaluation

Complete the OCAS scoring form in Figure 5. Compare your responses with the feedback your instructor will provide about the most appropriate responses for the ten situations.

SUMMARY

A manager skilled in oral communication will use the spoken word to transmit information and ideas clearly and easily. In this process, the manager must fine-tune the presentation of information to the specific audience and the specific situation involved. These situations may range from informal one-on-one discussions, to team meetings of all types and sizes, to formal briefings for customers or higher-level management.

In this module you learned that oral communication requires managers to demonstrate skills in five categories: (1) using the voice effectively, (2) employing nonverbal accompaniments, (3) structuring the message, (4) eliminating random noise, and (5) developing audience rapport.

Question	a	b	c	d	e	Response
1						
2						
3						
4						
5						
6						
7						
8						
9						
10						

FIGURE 5
Oral Communication Awareness Scale (OCAS) Scoring

FIGURE 6
Oral Communication Skills
Action Guide

You Show Oral Communication Skills When You:
■ Establish the goals of your communication
■ Analyze the audience
■ Diagnose the environmental conditions
■ Outline the content and structure of the communication
■ Practice
■ Deliver and respond to feedback

You Show Effective Oral Communication Skills When:
■ Your voice is used properly
■ Nonverbal accompaniments are employed
■ Your message is appropriately structured
■ Random noise is eliminated
■ Audience rapport is developed

Throughout this module, you have taken part in exercises that have helped improve your oral communication skills. The module provided you with a structured approach to oral communication skills that will help you deal with many situations in which your ability to communicate orally is essential. A note of caution is in order, however. The rules given here should be used loosely. As you develop your oral communication skills, you may discover your own insights that help you communicate effectively. Remember, though, that the process and elements defined here have been found effective by those experienced in the field.

As you have seen, effective oral communication skills depend on other skills such as perception, organizing and planning, flexibility, decisiveness, judgment, and leadership. To be an effective oral communicator, one must use all skills critical to management. Perhaps this is why oral communication skills are considered so heavily in determining management potential.

With luck, you are now applying the experience gained in this module to your work, home, or school situation. If so, you already may have had the pleasure of hearing positive feedback from others. Feedback from persons with whom you work will keep you informed about how effectively you are using your oral communication skills.

To remember key steps in practicing oral communication skills and to identify situations in which the skills are needed, use the action guide shown in Figure 6. Frequent review of the information will help you become a better manager.

SKILL-BUILDING EXERCISES

EXERCISE 1 ■ USING YOUR VOICE EFFECTIVELY

Take a short nursery tale or a passage from it (about half a page in length). Underline the key words in each sentence. Then read the passage to the class, emphasizing the key words. Read the passage a second time and vary your rate, inflection, volume, and voice tone to change the meaning of the material. Record your speech, if possible.

EXERCISE 2 ■ ORGANIZING AND PRESENTING EFFECTIVELY

Select one of the following topics, determine a theme, and select two different ways of organizing the material. Then develop two speeches by preparing an opening, a preview of the main points, clearly demarcated main points, and a closing for each method of organization. Be prepared to give both speeches in front of the class. Ask others in class to critique your organization, your delivery, and audience awareness. Suggested topics: (1) What college graduates want in a job, (2) How to redesign the college classroom, (3) How to dress for business success, or (4) Why we need to recycle.

EXERCISE 3 ■ THINKING ON YOUR FEET

Write a lighthearted topic on a slip of paper that will be collected along with slips from other students. Draw a slip and give a one-minute impromptu talk on the topic selected. Have the class provide feedback to you about your presentation.

■ Use Exhibits 1–2 with In-Basket Exercise 1,
Exhibits 3–7 with In-Basket Exercise 3,
Exhibits 8–11 with In-Basket Exercise 4,
Exhibit 12 with In-Basket Exercise 5.

EXHIBIT 1
Natori Sound Systems, Inc.,
Corporate Structure

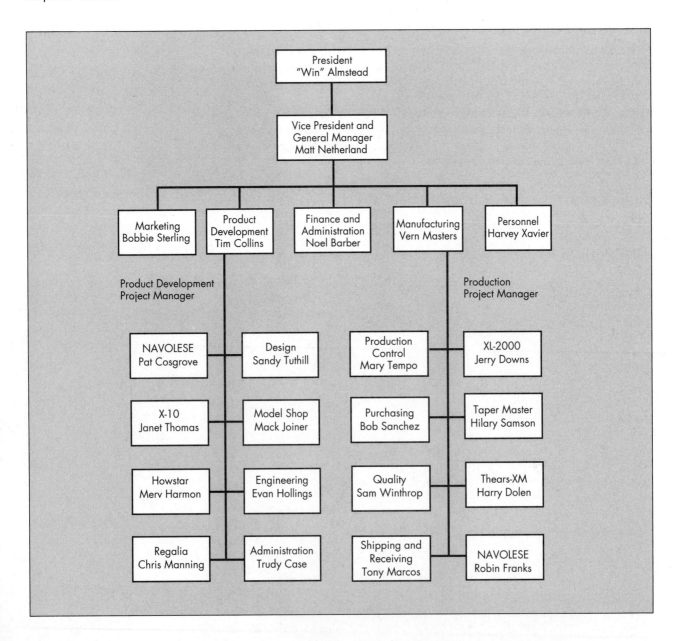

NATORI SOUND SYSTEMS, INC.

MEMORANDUM

TO: Tim Collins, Director, Product Development
FROM: Pat Cosgrove, Manager, NAVOLESE Product Development
DATE: December 21
RE: Talking to Purchasing Agents

Since you're sending me out of town tomorrow, you know I will not be able to talk to the purchasing agents. Attached is what I'd planned to say. Why not give Sandy a chance at it?

Speech on NAVOLESE

The NAVOLESE Sound System is a revolutionary advance in compact disc, cassette and record players for the home. The user will merely punch in the name of a particular selection, or a desired composer, or even just a type of music, and the desired music will be played automatically.

How can this work? Our design team has come up with a concept that permits CDs, records and tapes to be stored in a contamination-free storage bin that rests behind the controls and playing mechanism. This storage bin, combined with a normal stereo system and a new computer control, creates ease of use for the listener. The mechanism, developed by the engineering division at Natori, accepts the new item, files it, and then retrieves it on command from the computer whenever it fits the category or specific music selected by the listener.

Key to the system is the new computer control, which permits hours of music to be programmed for automatic play in just a few seconds. The operator does not need to refer to code numbers, all of which are filed in computer memory. The operator merely punches in the name of the composer, selection title, or type of music; the computer does the rest.

The NAVOLESE System has been in development for two years and is now moving into production. It will be on the market by next September. We are anticipating a large response for Christmas next year at this time. (BRING ALONG OPERATIONAL MODEL AND DEMONSTRATE IT TO THE GROUP AT THIS POINT.)

EXHIBIT 2
Natori Sound Systems, Inc.
Memorandum

EXHIBIT 3
Natori Sound Systems, Inc.
Memorandum

NATORI SOUND SYSTEMS, INC.

MEMORANDUM

TO: Terry Johnson, Purchasing – NAVOLESE
FROM: Pat Cosgrove, Project Development Manager – NAVOLESE
DATE: August 2
RE: NAVOLESE DESIGN – Purchasing Requirements

Until a production manager is named for NAVOLESE, I will be acting in that position. I have attached a sketch of the NAVOLESE System showing the key sections. Some of these will be made in-house; others will be purchased through your department. You are the only team member to be assigned to the production program this early. It is important that we look into the purchasing situation in case we face some unanticipated "make" decisions instead of "buy." We'd need lead time for that. All subcontracts *must* be firm by December 31.

Preliminary Planning by Key Sections

Section	Planned Make/Buy Strategy
• AM/FM Unit and Master	Components used will be the same as those in the System Control Unit company's THEARS-XM system. Probably, we'll want to use the same supplier unless problems have arisen. For our system, only the cabinet and layout will differ from the THEARS-XM Master System Control Unit.
• Turntable	We will use the same component as the THEARS-XM. Only the cabinet and layout will be different in the NAVOLESE.
• Computerized-Selection Control Unit	All new design for external cabinet only (major purchasing effort involved here).
• Speaker Units	New design for external cabinet only. Will use same suppliers for all other NATORI Systems.
• CD/Record/Tape File/ Storage Cabinet	New design. Past policy would dictate our shop build this (i.e., we will not subcontract it).

NATORI SOUND SYSTEMS, INC.

MEMORANDUM

TO: Terry Johnson, Manager of Purchasing – NAVOLESE
FROM: Helene Toole, Manager of Purchasing – THEARS-XM
DATE: November 11
RE: Supplier Problems

Since you have been planning to use the same suppliers on the Master unit for NAVOLESE as we use on THEARS-XM, I thought you'd like to know that Mishalt Company has been running into trouble providing parts that meet specifications.

We're also having quality problems. We're thinking of changing suppliers. You might want to put out a request for new bids, too.

EXHIBIT 4
Natori Sound Systems, Inc.
Memorandum

EXHIBIT 5
Natori Sound Systems, Inc.
Memorandum

Natori Sound Systems, Inc.

MEMORANDUM

TO: Terry Johnson, Manager of Purchasing — NAVOLESE
FROM: Marilyn Boley, Buyer
DATE: November 13
RE: Purchasing Status — Speakers (NAVOLESE)

The woofers for the speaker unit from Hillyer do not exactly match our requirements. However, Hillyer would be able to supply them right away if we could use them. You said we have to have firm commitments by December 31. Did you mean contract in hand—or just word-of-mouth commitment?

I will be out of town all next week on vacation. Do you remember that my husband and I are going on our long-planned trip to Mexico? I think I have everything under control so that nothing will slip through the cracks while I'm gone.

About the woofers: I have three other companies to explore if Hillyer doesn't come around. I don't see any problem.

All my parts, I'm sure, will be under contract by December 31, to Engineering specs.

NATORI SOUND SYSTEMS, INC.

MEMORANDUM

TO: Terry Johnson, Manager of Purchasing – NAVOLESE
FROM: Tony Casto, Buyer
DATE: November 15
RE: Problem—Component XM2R, Computerized Selection Control Unit

---

I have not been able to find any suppliers willing to bid for this part for the time schedule we are aiming for. We need to have a make-or-buy committee meeting; looks like we'll have to make it ourselves if we want to meet our schedule.

Attached is a complete listing of current status for my area. It shows the date we released requests for proposal (RFP), how many bids we received, and anticipated selection date (including suppliers if we've already selected one). It highlights the XM2R as a potential problem.

EXHIBIT 6
Natori Sound Systems, Inc.
Memorandum

EXHIBIT 7
Natori Sound Systems, Inc. Computer
Selection Module

NATORI SOUND SYSTEMS, INC.

PURCHASING DEPARTMENT

NAVOLESE PROJECT

COMPUTER SELECTION MODULE

Current Status	Source Selection for All Components			Date
Part	Potential Sources	Date RFP Out	No. of Bids in	Anticipated Firm Source Selection Date
Input Section				
Keyboard Unit	4	8–23	3	Complete – Marjam Co.
Control Unit 1	3	11–10	Due 11–29	December 15
Control Unit 2	3	11–10	Due 11–29	December 15
Control Unit 3	3	11–10	Due 11–29	December 15
Control Unit 4	3	11–10	Due 11–29	December 15
Computerized Selection Control Unit				
RYX1	10	10–4	8	Complete – Sandro, Inc.
TL40	5	10–18	4	Complete – Sandro, Inc.
ZMOO	3	10–18	3	Complete – Torey Co.
XM2R*	**None Yet**	**None**	—	**Must by 12–31***
XM5T	open	Plan 11–29	0	12–24
RT2L	2 open	Plan 11–29	0	12–24
Selection Mechanism				
Electronics	open	Plan 11–29	0	12–24
Mechanical	open	Plan 11–29	0	12–24

*Potential problem (make?)

NATORI SOUND SYSTEMS, INC.

MEMORANDUM

TO: Robin Franks, Production Manager – NAVOLESE
FROM: Vern Masters, Director, Manufacturing
DATE: November 17
RE: Top Management Briefing on NAVOLESE System

On Friday, November 19, Matt Netherland, our general manager, wants to devote part of his staff meeting to a report on NAVOLESE.

In addition to his regular staff, Matt will be inviting other interested persons to sit in. These include several members of the board of directors who are in town.

They will be interested in the big picture.

I want you to give the briefing. Please be sure you cover the following key points:

- Current status
- Planned delivery dates
- Potential problems (such as recruiting and training employees)

I think you have all the information you need. Plan to be brief. Matt tells me that you have been allotted ten minutes for your presentation. More time will be allowed for questions after your talk.

EXHIBIT 8
Natori Sound Systems, Inc.
Memorandum

EXHIBIT 9
Natori Sound Systems, Inc.
Memorandum

NATORI SOUND SYSTEMS, INC.

MEMORANDUM

TO: Robin Franks, Production Manager – NAVOLESE
FROM: Judy Tarshall, NAVOLESE Production Control Manager
DATE: November 18
RE: Impact of "make" decision for XM2R (Part for Computerized
             Selection Control Unit)

You asked me to investigate potential impact on workforce and training if we get a "make" decision on the XM2R.

Workforce Requirements:	Fifty skilled workers (would have to be taken from the THEARS program or else hired and trained).
Training:	If training is required, it would take a minimum of 4 weeks.
Conclusion:	We need a decision (make or buy) no later than December 13. This would allow us time, if it's a "make" decision, to hire/train needed workers. For example:

12/13	"Make" Decision
1/3	Hiring Plan to Employment
3/1	Workers Hired
4/1	Training Ends/XM2R Production Begins
6/1	First XM2R units delivered to Selection Control Unit Assembly Line

Our schedule shows first completed units will be delivered to shipping by August 1 of the next year. These will be in dealer's hands by September 1 to tie in with ad campaigns, news releases, etc.

NATORI SOUND SYSTEMS, INC.

MEMORANDUM

TO: Robin Franks, Production Manager – NAVOLESE
FROM: Terry Johnson, Manager, Purchasing – NAVOLESE
DATE: November 17
RE: Status – major issues – NAVOLESE purchasing

As per your request for status report:

Key Issues

- We need a make-or-buy decision by December 31 on the XM2R component if we want to make sure our Computerized Selection Control Unit will meet delivery schedules.
- We may have to review the use of Mishalt Company as a supplier for the Master AM/FM Control Unit. This is the same unit as used in THEARS-XM, and Mishalt has quality problems in delivering the units for THEARS-XM.
- All other elements are on schedule.

I have attached a sketch of the overall system showing the major sections. You might want to use this at your briefing.

EXHIBIT 10
Natori Sound Systems, Inc.
Memorandum

EXHIBIT 11
Robin Frank's Notes on Attendees at Meeting

ROBIN FRANK'S NOTES ON ATTENDEES AT MEETING

Attendee	Title	Notes, Special Interests, etc.
Matt Netherland	Vice President & General Manager	
Bobbie Sterling	Marketing Director	Will we meet delivery dates to tie in with ad campaign?
Tim Collins	Product Development Director	His baby—they developed it. Are we taking care of it?
Noel Barber	Finance & Administration Director	Facts and Figures—cost controls.
Vern Masters	Manufacturing Director	My boss.
Harvey Xavier	Personnel Director	Work Force Plans/Hiring Plans/Training Needs?
Pat Cosgrove	Product Development Manager for NAVOLESE	I want to convey that Pat and I are working closely together and have a great working relationship.

NATORI SOUND SYSTEMS, INC.

MEMORANDUM

TO: Pat Cosgrove, Project Development Manager – NAVOLESE
FROM: Corey Blau, Secretary
DATE: November 18
RE: Team Meeting

The following is a brief rundown on the attendees of the NAVOLESE transition meeting:

Audience Profiles

Robin Franks – Production Manager for NAVOLESE – Robin is your counterpart in the Manufacturing Division, i.e., Production Manager for NAVOLESE. Robin has recently been promoted to the level of manager. You have not yet had the opportunity to meet Robin, but you will be working together closely during the transition and on an ongoing basis in the future.

Terry Johnson – Manager of Purchasing for NAVOLESE – Terry you have met briefly. Terry reports to Robin Franks and will be responsible for all purchasing for NAVOLESE.

Jill Ranks – Manager of Quality for NAVOLESE – You have worked with Jill before on another project. Jill also reports to Robin. Jill tends to stir up dissension in a group. You have had problems with Jill.

Judy Tarshall – Manager of Production Control for NAVOLESE – Judy is new. She has been hired from a competitor to head Production Control for NAVOLESE. They say she's worth the price they paid for her; she'll earn it. Marketing says that scheduling and meeting shipments will be critical to match their advanced publicity schedule.

Trish Potter – Engineering Manager for NAVOLESE – Trish reports to you and is a top-notch engineer. As you know, Trish tends to get bogged down in engineering details instead of delegating.

Fred Summers – Design Manager for NAVOLESE – Fred also reports to you. Fred is a more effective manager than Trish. Fred was a key creative element in developing the concept of NAVOLESE.

EXHIBIT 12
Natori Sound Systems, Inc.
Memorandum

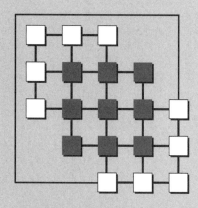

PART 3
PROBLEM-SOLVING SKILLS: FORMULATING AND EXECUTING CREATIVE SOLUTIONS TO PROBLEMS

MODULE 5
Perception Skills: Identifying Information

MODULE 6
Organizing and Planning Skills: Establishing Courses of Action

MODULE 7
Decision-Making Skills: Reaching Conclusions

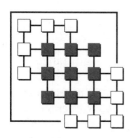

MODULE 5
PERCEPTION SKILLS:
IDENTIFYING INFORMATION

INTRODUCTION

Perception can be defined as the way people experience, process, define, and interpret the world around them. All kinds of messages exist in our world, but we take in or see only certain elements in any given situation. These messages, often referred to as sensations, are filtered, modified, or completely changed by our perception to provide meaning for us. The stimuli that we perceive may be in the form of data such as numbers on a chart or graph, or it may be our observations of an employee's job performance.

As a managerial skill, perception means to identify, interpret, and analyze information. Perception requires the ability to understand and interpret data, to identify the critical elements of a situation, to determine factors essential to a problem's solution, to perceive relationships among various types of information, and to be aware of interpersonal differences and similarities.

Good management is facilitated by good perception skills, which include the following categories of behaviors: (1) searching for information, (2) interpreting and comprehending information, (3) determining essential factors, (4) recognizing characteristics of people, and (5) identifying relationships.

The purpose of this module is to help you develop and strengthen your perception skills. You will assume the role of manager in a variety of situations. In each situation, you will be provided with information—samples of material that typically find their way to the manager's desk. As manager, you must use your perception skills to solve potential problems. By actually participating in situations, you can learn and practice perception skills.

The module is organized so that you will develop a before-practice assessment of your perception skills by completing the Perception Process Questionnaire (PPQ). This assessment instrument measures your skills of perception at the present time. We then present a brief discussion of the perception process and problems that arise in perception. Next, through in-basket exercises, you will practice various perceptual skill behaviors. Feedback from your instructor will help you judge the quality of your responses and provide guidance on improving specific behaviors.

After you complete the exercises, you will have an opportunity to retake the PPQ and compare your after-practice assessment results with your earlier results. You will also complete the Perception Behaviors Profile Questionnaire (PBPQ). This assessment instrument examines how you actually behave in situations where perception skills are needed. It will give you more insight into your behaviors in situations requiring perception skills.

ASSESSING YOUR PERCEPTION SKILLS

Complete the PPQ on the following pages before proceeding with the rest of the module. It is both a teaching tool and a means of evaluating your present perception skills level. Take time to complete the instrument carefully. Your answers should reflect your behaviors as they are now, not as you would like them to be. Be honest. This instrument is designed to help you discover where you are now so you can work to improve your perception skills.

The Perception Process Questionnaire (PPQ)

The Perception Process Questionnaire (PPQ) is designed to help you evaluate your current level of perception skills. If you do not have experience in a management level position, consider a project you have worked on either in the classroom or in an organization such as a fraternity, sorority, club, church, or service group. You will find that the questions are applicable to your own experience even if you are not yet a manager.

Use the following scale to rate the frequency with which you perform the behaviors described in each question. Place the corresponding number (1–7) in the blank space preceding the statement.

Rarely	Irregularly	Occasionally	Usually	Frequently	Almost Always	Consistently
1	2	3	4	5	6	7

_____ **1.** I search for verified facts and observations to support inferences or conclusions.

_____ **2.** I examine available information related to my area of job responsibility.

_____ **3.** I note organizational changes and policies that might affect my information.

_____ **4.** I ask others for their opinions and observations to get access to more information.

_____ **5.** I note inconsistencies and seek explanations for them.

_____ **6.** I look at information in terms of similarities and differences.

_____ **7.** I generate possible explanations for available information.

_____ 8. I check for omissions, distortions, or exaggerations in available information.

_____ 9. I verbally summarize data that are not completely quantified (e.g., trends).

_____ 10. I distinguish facts from opinions.

_____ 11. I am aware of my own style of approaching problems and how this might affect the way I process information.

_____ 12. I put quantitative information in tables, charts, and graphs.

_____ 13. I am aware of the personality characteristics of my peers, colleagues, subordinates, and superiors.

_____ 14. I am aware of my own biases and value systems that influence the way I see people.

_____ 15. I am aware of patterns of people's performance and how these patterns might indicate characteristics.

_____ 16. I recognize differences and similarities among people.

_____ 17. I actively seek to determine how pieces of information might be related.

_____ 18. I relate current information to past experience.

_____ 19. I relate my own attitudes and feelings and those of others to job performance.

_____ 20. I relate work methods to outcomes.

PPQ Scoring

The scoring sheet in Figure 1 summarizes your responses for the PPQ. It will help you identify your existing strengths and pinpoint areas that need improvement. Right now, fill in the before-practice assessment column for each skill area by adding your scores for each item. Add the five category scores to obtain a total score. Enter that total score in the space indicated. After completing the module, you will take the PPQ again and fill in the after-practice assessment column.

PPQ Evaluation

Figure 2 shows score lines for your total score and for each category measured on the PPQ. Each line shows a continuum from the lowest possible score to the highest. Place a B (before-practice) where your personal score falls on each of these lines. The score lines in Figure 2 show graphically where you stand with regard to five areas of perception. If you have been honest with yourself, you now have a better idea of your relative strengths and weaknesses in the categories of behavior that make up perception skills.

FIGURE 1

The Perception Process Questionnaire (PPQ) Scoring

Skill Area	Items	Assessment	
		Before Practice	After Practice
Searching for information	1,2,3,4		
Intepreting and comprehending information	5,6,7,8		
Determining essential factors	9,10,11,12		
Recognizing characteristics of people	13,14,15,16		
Identifying relationships	17,18,19,20		
TOTAL SCORE			

Learning to Use the PPQ Skills

You have now completed the initial evaluation of your perception skills. This questionnaire provides a baseline against which you will assess improvements that have taken place after you have completed this module.

Before moving on, think about what you have discovered about yourself in this evaluation. What areas of your perception skills are least developed? These will require most of your attention during the remainder of this module. What areas of perception behaviors are your strongest? Use this module to fine-tune these even further so that you may take full advantage of them. In these stronger areas, learning only one or two new things may be all you need for significant improvement in your perception skills.

The PPQ will help you identify perception behaviors that are appropriate for the management situations described in this module. After you have completed the module and have had an opportunity to put into practice what you have learned, retake the PPQ. Then, compare your after-practice scores with your before-practice scores. This comparison will show you where you have progressed and where you need further work.

UNDERSTANDING PERCEPTION

Perception is complex. It involves selecting, organizing, and interpreting environmental stimuli. Everything in our environment represents potential stimulation. Of course, we don't notice everything because there is simply too much to take in.

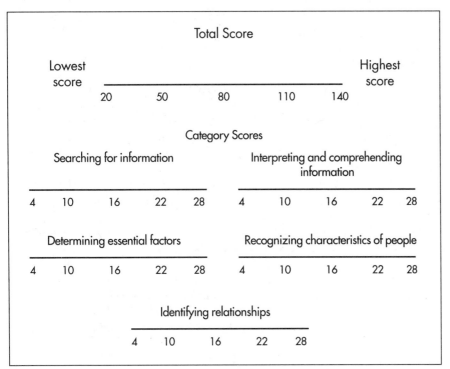

FIGURE 2
The Perception Process Questionnaire
(PPQ) Evaluation

We pay attention to some information and ignore other information, often without consciously realizing that we are doing so. For example, a hungry person is likely to focus on the food pictured in an advertisement for china, whereas a person who is not hungry may focus on the color and pattern of the china.

Once we have selected something, we organize it into a pattern. This process is affected by internal factors such as an individual's learning, motivation, and personality. As a result, our perceptions are not necessarily accurate. But they are unique and explain why two individuals may look at the same situation or message and perceive it differently. For example, in a company, sales managers and production managers may perceive the weekly sales data differently. Would you expect the presidents of General Motors and the United Auto Workers union to agree on the distribution of corporate profits?

How we interpret the information we have selected and organized also varies considerably. Depending on the circumstances and our state of mind, we may interpret a wave of the hand as a friendly gesture or a threat.

The Perception Process

In the perception process, you will attend to some things more than to others. For example, when you receive a memo from the president of your organization, chances are that you will pay attention to it. A variety of factors affect whether or not you pay attention to something. These factors, called attention-getters, are external to the individual and include the intensity of the message, its size, repetition, and contrast. Let's look at selection and some attention-getters that influence this aspect of perception.

Selection

Several external factors can influence the selection of stimuli. Intense or extreme messages, such as a loud siren or a flashy dresser, tend to get attention. Intense language in a memo can draw attention. In face-to-face situations, an extreme tone of voice or facial expression can be used to create a noticeable message. In a meeting, very soft-spoken people can send an intense message by raising their voices to demand answers to their questions.

Size is another influence on selection. Large stimuli get attention. For example, an expense report of $761 plus airfare for a one-night business trip would probably get some attention.

Repetition influences selection. Repeating, summarizing, or restating a concept increases the likelihood that the message will be noticed.

Another external influence is contrast. Messages that are novel or unusual tend to attract attention. For example, you may grow accustomed to seeing competent performance on the part of your employees. When you see poor performance, it stands out. Changing jobs (such as in a job rotation program) may create a novel situation and actually may increase an employee's attention level.

Organization

We seek to organize our world—to structure sensations that provide consistent messages. We do this by attempting to determine what is important versus what is in the background. You are now reading dark letters printed on a light background. The letters represent "figures," and the lighter page is the "ground."

In some cases, camouflage makes it difficult to distinguish the figure from the ground. For example, when an unfavorable clause is placed among unimportant items in a contract, it is camouflaged.

There are at least three things that people do in the perception of figure–ground relationships. The first, closure, is the tendency for people to see a whole picture when one doesn't exist. Take a look at the sales graph shown in Figure 3. Some people would perceive that sales have increased from month to month. While this is generally true, there is no information for the month of May. This is an example of how closure may occur. The gap may be filled in to complete the line. Closure operates in important ways in organizations. For example, managers may perceptually close gaps of disagreement between workers and have an erroneous perception of high morale.

Proximity is another aspect that affects perceptual organization. Separate stimuli that are physically close may be seen as belonging to each other. For example, people having lunch together in the employee lunchroom may be perceived to be a single group. Upper management often perceives groups of workers as single entities and labels them inefficient or efficient, even though within the groups there may be a wide range of performance.

Similarity is a third factor that influences organization. Messages that are similar are seen as belonging to each other. Similarity is a key concept in

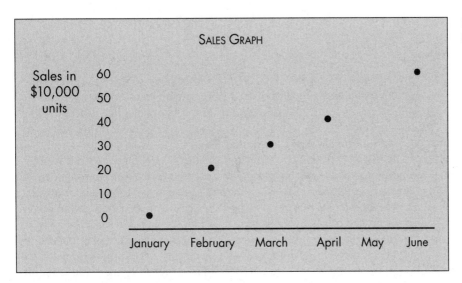

FIGURE 3
Sales Graph

understanding stereotypes. Stereotyping is nothing more than grouping similar stimuli (e.g., skin color, body shape, gender) while ignoring less observable differences among people.

Interpretation

Once we have sensed something and organized it, we add meaning. This process, called interpretation, is initially affected by our perceptual set. A perceptual set is made up of internal factors like motivation, personality, and previous learning. For example, your motivation for listening to a speech or reading a contract might influence what you hear or see. Employees listening to the president of a corporation stating the reasons for layoffs might be motivated to hear evidence that they are being wronged.

Your personality, including beliefs, opinions, and values, can affect the way you interpret messages. For example, an argumentative or assertive individual participating in a discussion might look for points of disagreement to use in a rebuttal. An empathetic individual might avoid making value judgments about others.

Prior learning establishes certain expectations about information. People tend to pay attention to information that is familiar to them. Serious misinterpretations and perceptual errors may result. For example, a male manager may expect female employees to be physically weak and thus avoid giving them physically demanding assignments.

Problems in Perception

Perceptual biases, or errors, may hamper your competency as a manager as well as the competency of your organization or group. For example, overlooking a deadline on a memo or perceiving all subordinates as having identical career aspirations may not only detract from your managerial effectiveness but may damage the organization.

One step in becoming more perceptive is to recognize potential problems in the perception process. Identify what can go wrong. Here is a list of problem areas:

1. *Information isn't available.* This may be either because the necessary information doesn't reach you or because there are no sources of information.
2. *Information isn't analyzed correctly or thoroughly.* This could occur either because the data is contradictory and you don't realize it or because there are errors in the data that you don't catch.
3. *Characteristics of the data are overlooked.* For example, there are trends in the data but you miss them, facts are not distinguished from opinions, or the data are not expressed in a way that makes them easy to understand.
4. *Characteristics of people are misjudged.* Several common perceptual errors involve individuals. *Halo errors* occur when we form an impression of an individual based on just one trait or dimension, such as enthusiasm, gender, appearance, or intelligence. For example, you think your colleague is highly intelligent, so you also view her as well organized and highly motivated. In fact, she may not be. *Stereotyping* is the tendency to assign attributes to someone solely on the basis of a category or group to which that person belongs. We expect someone identified as a professor, surgeon, police officer, or janitor to have certain attributes, even if we have not met the individual. Judging an employee by such broad categories as age, sex, or race, which should not bring to mind any attributes beyond obvious physical characteristics, can lead to perceptual errors.
5. *Relationships between information, people, and things are overlooked.* Many relationships can be overlooked. The relationship between a problem occurring now and a solution to a related problem in the past may be missed. You may not relate a person's skills to those that are required in a new assignment. Or you may fail to recognize how a deadline for one project affects the assignment of people to another project.

Perception Skills and Their Relationships to Other Managerial Skills

Perception skills are important to many other management skills. In baseball, players say that you can't hit what you don't see. As a manager, you can't make sound decisions about problems you don't perceive correctly. Perception and interpersonal skills are intertwined, for example. You won't show sensitivity to individual differences and needs unless you first perceive these differences and needs. Whether you are organizing, planning, leading, adapting, controlling, writing, or speaking, perception influences your behavior. Many managers agree that perception is an important management skill.

Perception is closely tied to problem solving and decision making. When solving problems, the manager must be able to evaluate, interpret, and apply information. Perception is needed to identify a problem, analyze its elements, and recognize potential ways of dealing with it. Without strong perception skills, a manager may leave important questions unanswered and problems unresolved.

PRACTICING PERCEPTION

Perception skills consist of the following behaviors:

- *Searching for information*—This category includes identifying the sources of your information, seeking both facts and opinions, keeping up to date on information related to your job, and noting organizational changes and policies.
- *Interpreting and comprehending information*—Once you have gathered information, you must check it for inconsistencies, problems, omissions, distortions, similarities, differences, and exaggerations. Then you must generate possible explanations for your observations.
- *Determining essential factors*—In this category, you evaluate quantitative data and distinguish fact from opinion. You must be conscious of how your style of approaching problems affects the way you process information.
- *Recognizing characteristics of people*—This skill deals with your awareness of personality characteristics and patterns of performance of others. To be fully perceptive, you must also be candid about your own biases and value systems.
- *Identifying relationships*—This aspect of perception involves determining the relationship between separate pieces of information such as attitudes and feelings, work methods and outcomes, and past actions and current occurrences.

The next section of in-basket exercises focuses on each component of the perception skills we have been discussing. Before you begin the exercises, review your scores on the five parts of the PPQ that you completed earlier. Then, as you complete the exercises, think about the behaviors noted in the questionnaire. The questions in the PPQ deepen your understanding of basic perception skills.

Situation

You are Pat Crosby, production supervisor for the Pioneer Manufacturing Company at its Grafton plant. Pioneer is a medium-sized manufacturer of plastic eyeglass frames. Its market is nationwide. It operates two production plants and will soon open a third.

You have just arrived in your new job. Frank Bunwell, your predecessor, died suddenly of a heart attack Thursday evening. You were notified Friday at 10:00 A.M. of your new appointment, but because you needed to take care of some last-minute details at your old job, you could not begin your new job until today, Saturday, July 21.

Frank Bunwell was 54 years old and had 32 years of service with the company. Apparently he was in good health, and you have been informed that he did an adequate, though not outstanding, job. He had been production supervisor for 14 years.

Your new secretary, Jan Pinson, has worked as the production supervisor's secretary for seven years. Pinson has a reputation in the plant as being very efficient.

Now that you have a brief background of your new position, you are ready to go on with the in-basket exercises that follow. Remember, today is Saturday, July 21. You cannot reach anyone by phone, and you are alone in your new office. Your files are locked and your secretary has the key. You must work with the materials at hand.

The materials available to you are a July calendar, an organizational chart, and the information your secretary left for your attention (shown in Exhibits 1 through 34). Review the material and answer the questions after each in-basket exercise. When you answer the questions, take into consideration all of the information from previous exercises, and, if pertinent, use it in your answers.

IN-BASKET EXERCISE 1: SEARCHING FOR INFORMATION

When you search for information, you must know your sources and be able to locate both facts and opinions. Refer to the materials in Exhibits 1 through 6. Then respond to the questions about the materials.

Your perception skills focus:

- Determine what is needed.
- Identify your information sources.
- Examine available quantitative data.
- Review company records and files to confirm data.

Questions for In-Basket Exercise 1:

1. If you want reject and production information for the past two years, who might be a good source of information? Why?

2. If you need to find out more facts about the reasons for rejects on the shifts, whom will you ask? Explain.

3. With the information given so far, can you determine differences in shift production from month to month for each shift? How? Explain.

4. Does any of the information available give you an idea about the level of performance of some people?

5. What is the new organizational policy concerning maximum expenditure authorized without management approval?

IN-BASKET EXERCISE 2: INTERPRETING AND COMPREHENDING INFORMATION

Once you have identified sources of information and have actually obtained a body of data, it is necessary to spend some time analyzing it. In this important phase, you look for inconsistencies, cause–effect relationships, similarities and differences, and omissions or distortions. You might also generate hypotheses to explain the data. It is necessary to understand and interpret information so that the data you find are fully usable. Review the resource material once more. Now examine the tables and graphs in Exhibits 7 through 11. Then answer the questions that test your understanding of the information.

Your perception skills focus:

- Understand what the data include.
- Be aware of the form in which the data are given (for example, index numbers, numerical quantities, etc.).
- Clarify unfamiliar terminology.
- Make sure that the data are comparable before drawing comparisons.
- Identify inconsistencies and absurdities.
- Identify and evaluate your data sources.

Questions for In-Basket Exercise 2:

1. For the months of January through June, determine the ratio of the average number of rejects to the average number of production units for each shift. (Ratios compare number of units rejected to number of units produced; e.g., if two units were rejected out of five produced, the ratio would be 2:5 or 0.4.)

   Shift #1 ratio =

   Shift #2 ratio =

   Shift #3 ratio =

2. For Shift #3, what is the difference between the highest and lowest level of monthly rejects?

3. What do the ratios of rejects to production indicate? What are some possible explanations for the level and direction of these ratios over the six months covered for the three separate shifts?

4. What are the sources of the data in tables one and two (Exhibits 7 and 11)?

IN-BASKET EXERCISE 3: DETERMINING ESSENTIAL FACTORS

When determining essential factors in a situation, you are often required to look at quantitative data and to organize it into tables, charts, or graphs, You may also have to summarize the data in words. An important part of this aspect of perception is the ability to separate facts from opinions and to understand the personal style of others in your organization. Refer to Exhibits 12 through 17, as well as earlier information, to answer the questions that follow.

Your perception skills focus:

- Determine what information is needed to deal with the problem.
- Use tables presenting quantitative information.
- Summarize quantitative data verbally.
- Distinguish facts from opinions.

Questions for In-Basket Exercise 3:

1. In the period January through June, which of the three shifts produced the most units?

2. Which of the three shifts had the highest reject level? (Refer to Exhibit 4.)

3. Verbally summarize the data shown in Table Three.

4. In Jan Pinson's letter (Exhibit 12), the following is stated: Bunwell had a way of avoiding decisions; you (as Pat Crosby) will have a difficult job until things get straightened out; Bunwell left papers on his desk. Which of these statements are fact? Which are opinion?

5. In Connors' memo to Howell (Exhibit 13), Connors suggests two factual criteria on which to base the companywide special recognition award. What are they?

6. In the Howell memo to Crosby (Exhibit 15), Howell says he wants to discuss how to get along with maintenance. What opinion does he give about maintenance?

7. In Howell's memo to Bunwell (Exhibit 16), Howell suggests alternative criteria for selecting the person who will be recommended for the Special Recognition Award. What are these criteria? Which is the most factually based?

8. In Exhibit 17, Arden James has some things to say about the punch machine on production line #3. Which of these are fact? Which are opinion?

IN-BASKET EXERCISE 4: RECOGNIZING CHARACTERISTICS OF PEOPLE

Understanding people is an integral part of managing. When working with or directing others, your performance improves and your task is made easier when you are aware of their personality characteristics. Ask yourself how the people you work with operate. What are their values? What kinds of performance patterns have they shown? Refer to Exhibits 18 through 26, and then answer the questions that follow. Be sure to refer to previous exhibits when necessary.

Your perception skills focus:

■ Relate to others.
■ Review and analyze others' behaviors.
■ Identify others' value systems.
■ Understand your own value system.
■ Win others to your point of view.

Questions for In-Basket Exercise 4:

1. Identify some of the personal characteristics of Jan Pinson based on her letter of July 20 (Exhibit 12).

2. How can you describe Arden James? Support your description by citing relevant memos.

3. What may you conclude about the personal characteristics of C. Mondar based on the letter shown in Exhibit 18?

4. What can you say about the personal characteristics of Marty Densmore?

5. Based on his letter of July 16 (Exhibit 26), describe Joe Foster.

IN-BASKET EXERCISE 5: IDENTIFYING RELATIONSHIPS

After you have accurately noted the source of information, thoroughly analyzed data, and correctly perceived data and people, there is still one crucial step in perception. You need to recognize how the available information fits together. You must identify how pieces of information relate to one another. Your information for this in-basket exercise includes the material in all preceding sections as well as Exhibits 27 through 34. Review this information and respond to the questions that follow.

Your perception skills focus:

- Separate pieces of information that deal with the same or similar subjects.
- Explain facts.
- Identify underlying issues and conflicts.
- Examine how events influence or are influenced by one another.
- Group information according to subject matter or issue.

Questions for In-Basket Exercise 5:

1. What has been the relationship between your (Pat Crosby's) department and the maintenance department?

2. What pieces of information relate to the question of an extra lathe operator?

3. Marty Densmore has asked for money to purchase repair parts for machinery. What problem brought up in the exercise may relate to this request?

4. In what way does the complaint about the performance appraisal system referred to in Exhibit 22 relate to other material in the exhibits?

5. Review and examine all the material presented in the exhibits and indicate on each piece of information if and how it is related to other materials. List below at least ten examples of such interrelationships.

Item and
Information   **Related To**   **Explanation of Relationship**

ASSESSING CHANGE

The purpose of this module has been to help you develop more effective perception skills. You have worked through exercises that require accurate and thorough perceptions. A series of questions has helped you focus on the various facets of perception skills, which include:

- *Searching for information*—As Pat Crosby, production supervisor for Pioneer Manufacturing Company, you were required to seek sources of information and look for facts and opinions to form a base of information.
- *Interpreting and comprehending information*—As Pat Crosby, you had to carefully study available data. You were asked to look for inconsistencies, omissions, and cause and effect relationships and generate hypotheses and explanations.
- *Determining essential factors*—In your role as production supervisor, you determined essential factors by placing quantitative information into usable formats, summarizing data, distinguishing facts from opinions, and noting various characteristics of data.
- *Recognizing characteristics of people*—Your task was to become aware of patterns in others' behavior, recognize similarities and differences among people, and note styles or methods of operation.
- *Identifying relationships*—Finally, you were asked to look for relationships between various pieces of information presented in the exhibits.

At the beginning of this module, you completed the Perception Process Questionnaire, which provided a baseline against which you could measure improvements in your perception skills. Now it is time to assess some of these improvements.

First, retake the PPQ. When you have finished, compare your scores with those you had earlier to see how much you have strengthened your skills.

The Perception Process Questionnaire (PPQ)

Use the following scale to rate the frequency with which you perform the behaviors described in each question. Place the corresponding number (1–7) in the blank space preceding the statement.

Rarely	Irregularly	Occasionally	Usually	Frequently	Almost Always	Consistently
1	2	3	4	5	6	7

_____ **1.** I search for verified facts and observations to support inferences or conclusions.

_____ **2.** I examine available information related to my area of job responsibility.

_____ **3.** I note organizational changes and policies that might affect my information.

_____ **4.** I ask others for their opinions and observations to get access to more information.

_____ **5.** I note inconsistencies and seek explanations for them.

_____ **6.** I look at information in terms of similarities and differences.

_____ **7.** I generate possible explanations for available information.

_____ **8.** I check for omissions, distortions, or exaggerations in available information.

_____ **9.** I verbally summarize data that are not completely quantified (e.g., trends).

_____ **10.** I distinguish facts from opinions.

_____ **11.** I am aware of my own style of approaching problems and how this might affect the way I process information.

_____ **12.** I put quantitative information in tables, charts, and graphs.

_____ **13.** I am aware of the personality characteristics of my peers, colleagues, subordinates, and superiors.

_____ **14.** I am aware of my own biases and value systems that influence the way I see people.

_____ **15.** I am aware of patterns of people's performance and how these patterns might indicate characteristics.

_____ **16.** I recognize differences and similarities among people.

_____ **17.** I actively seek to determine how pieces of information might be related.

_____ **18.** I relate current information to past experience.

_____ **19.** I relate my own attitudes and feelings and those of others to job performance.

_____ **20.** I relate work methods to outcomes.

PPQ Scoring and Evaluation

Follow the scoring directions found on page 211 and in Figure 1. Complete the after-practice assessment column for the PPQ and compare your before- and after-practice scores. Plot your after-practice scores in Figure 2. In which categories did your scores improve? Think about what has made your progress possible. Perhaps you can apply your insights to categories where your performance has lagged.

The Perception Behaviors Profile Questionnaire (PBPQ)

In the Perception Behaviors Profile Questionnaire (PBPQ), you assume managerial responsibility in a variety of situations where you must exercise your perception skills.

Described on the following pages are ten situations. Following each paragraph is a list of five possible responses. Mark the response that, in your opinion, reflects the most effective use of perception skills. Please select only one response.

1. You are a relatively new manager (three months) in a branch office of a bank. The bank has grown rapidly and a new site for a larger building is being considered. Plans for the new office space are virtually complete. You have been asked to attend a meeting this evening to review and finalize the plans. Prior to this meeting you would:

_____ a) Carefully review the plans.

_____ b) Construct a questionnaire and survey others at the branch for their opinions.

_____ c) Find out who will be at the meeting so that you can predict the outcome.

_____ d) Identify the source of the plans.

_____ e) Visit other banks in the area to see what their office space looks like.

2. You are a general manager of a medium-sized electronics firm. You are now trying to plan for the upcoming quarter's production. Your sales manager has sent you a memo in which she says, "I think we ought to gear up production next quarter because we are beginning to turn the market around. During the last eight weeks, our sales percentages of projected sales were 91, 104, 97, 91, 89, 99, 92." Having read this, you would:

_____ a) Seek to identify the nature of these figures.

_____ b) Place the percentage figures in graph form for easy reference.

_____ c) Proceed with your original production plans.

_____ d) Seek information from production problem-solving groups.

_____ e) Seek to explain the apparent inconsistency in the memo.

3. You are a manager with a moderately anti-union view. Lately there has been some support for union organizing in your company. A recent survey indicates that 1) 54 percent of the workforce responded to the survey and 2) of these, 59 percent favored the union and 41 percent were against the union. In this situation, you would:

_____ a) Conclude that since 59 percent of 54 percent is only 32 percent, the majority of employees oppose the union.

_____ b) Conclude that the 46 percent of the employees who did not vote were pro-union but were afraid to put themselves on record.

_____ c) Conclude that the survey is useless.

_____ d) Conclude that some employees had grievances.

_____ e) Be careful not to let your personal views affect your processing of the data.

4. An employee who reports to you is not performing as well as she usually does. For four years her ratings have been excellent, but now they are just slightly above average. In demonstrating perception, you would:

_____ a) Dismiss past evaluations as inaccurate.

_____ b)   Conclude that the employee should be transferred to another job.

_____ c)   Ask someone else to evaluate the employee.

_____ d)   Develop a possible explanation for the decline.

_____ e)   All of the above.

5.   One of your employees has been dropping by your office recently just to "shoot the breeze." This seems unusual to you. What might be a perceptive move on your part?

_____ a)   Note whether this employee behaves the same way toward others in the organization.

_____ b)   Ask him if he has personal problems.

_____ c)   Make sure he understands his role in the organization.

_____ d)   Check out his job performance.

_____ e)   Look at his background interview information.

6.   Suppose you are being interviewed tomorrow by a local news team because your company has been charged with excessive pollution of a nearby river. You know that you will be asked sensitive questions about a lengthy report written by a local university professor on various indications of pollution in the river. Regarding perception behaviors you should:

_____ a)   Put quantitative information into visual charts.

_____ b)   Search for facts to support your own comments.

_____ c)   Note any inconsistencies in the professor's report.

_____ d)   Prepare to talk about possible biases the professor holds as author of the report.

_____ e)   Determine whether the professor's report is based on measurable relationships.

7.   You are a sales manager responsible for fifteen salespersons in a two-state area. Sales have recently declined, and two of your top performers have made two very different suggestions to change strategies in midstream in order to improve the situation. You are trying to decide which of the opposing strategies to use. To be perceptive you would:

_____ a)   Make a decision on the basis of your experience.

_____ b)   Relate current sales data to past decisions about strategies.

_____ c)   Attempt to determine probable outcomes for the two approaches.

_____ d)   Identify the similarities and differences between the two approaches.

_____ e)   Distinguish sales data from opinions about sales data.

8.   When presented with a fifteen-page summary report that includes ten graphs and two detailed tables of numbers, your approach to this data-based report would be to:

_____ a)   Look for possible cause-and-effect relationships.

_____ b)   Ask yourself questions about the author's background.

_____ c)   Search for its major points.

_____ d)   Evaluate the positions taken.

_____ e)   All of the above.

9. Suppose you need to fill a position in your organization that requires a great deal of leadership. You ask one of your colleagues to recommend someone, and he says, "I would strongly recommend Chris Bailey because he is well respected and a good leader." What would you do now?

_____ a)   Relate the job's functions to leadership skills.

_____ b)   Ask for data that would support the statement made.

_____ c)   Relate your own feelings about the job to performance.

_____ d)   Ask Bailey about his own interest in the position.

_____ e)   Seek an explanation for any inconsistencies in performance.

10. You must make a decision soon about the possible expansion of your branch office. This expansion would require at least three new people and a lot of effort on everyone's part. In selecting data to help you arrive at your decision, you would demonstrate your perception skill best if you:

_____ a)   Use quantitative data only.

_____ b)   Use all credible information, including opinions of others.

_____ c)   Evaluate your data sources.

_____ d)   Check for distortions in data.

_____ e)   Use in-house data only.

PBPQ Scoring and Evaluation

Complete the PBPQ scoring form in Figure 4. Compare your responses with the feedback your instructor will provide about the most appropriate responses for the ten situations.

SUMMARY

As a managerial skill, perception involves identifying, interpreting, and analyzing information. As we have discussed and practiced in this module, perception covers the ability to understand and interpret data, to identify the critical elements of a situation, to determine factors essential to a problem's solution, to perceive relationships among various types of information, and to be aware of interpersonal differences and similarities.

In working through this module, you have learned about the various aspects of perception, and you have practiced perception skills in a variety of exercises.

FIGURE 4
Perception Behaviors Profile
Questionnaire (PBPQ) Scoring

Question	a	b	c	d	e	Response
1						
2						
3						
4						
5						
6						
7						
8						
9						
10						

The skill-building exercises at the end of the chapter provide further practice. Perhaps you have already been able to apply these skills in a job or classroom situation. If so, you may well have experienced the pleasure of positive feedback from others. Feedback from persons with whom you work will help you gauge whether you are using your perception skills in an appropriate manner. Remember that successful and competent managers continually work to improve their perception skills.

To remember key steps in practicing effective perception and to identify situations in which the skills are needed, use the action guide shown in Figure 5. Frequent review of the information will help you become a better manager.

You Show Perception Skills When You:
- Search for information
- Interpret and comprehend information
- Determine essential factors
- Recognize characteristics of people
- Identify relationships

You Should Show Perception Skills When:
- Information is needed
- Information must be interpreted and understood
- Essential factors must be determined
- Personal characteristics must be recognized
- Relationships between various facts, data, or events must be identified

FIGURE 5
Perception Skills Action Guide

SKILL-BUILDING EXERCISES

EXERCISE 1 ■ CONFRONTING PERCEPTUAL BIAS

Think back to the first day of class (in this course) and your first impressions of the instructor, the course, and your peers. Make a list of all the adjectives that best describe your perceptions of that first day. For example, did the instructor seem strict, precise, friendly, helpful? Did your peers seem cordial, warm, distant? What was your perception of the course and course requirements? Now, working with several others in your class, compare your perceptions. How accurate were these perceptions? Were many of your perceptions the same? Different? What biases are evident? How can you work to correct these biases?

EXERCISE 2 ■ IDENTIFYING RELATIONSHIPS AND CHARACTERISTICS OF PEOPLE

Your instructor will show you a picture of a group of individuals engaged in an activity. After carefully observing the picture, write down what you think the people are doing and how each person's action may impact on the others. Describe what the individuals in the photo are like, their personalities, occupations, how they spend their leisure time, and their backgrounds. Now, form a small group and summarize your perceptions about the individuals in the picture. After you have completed your group discussion, present your information to the class. Your instructor will provide feedback about how accurate your perceptions were in this exercise. Did you fall victim to perceptual problems? How reliable were your own perceptions compared to the group's perceptions? Was there consensus on any issues? If not, what are the reasons that differences exist in the group?

EXERCISE 3 ■ PERCEPTION ANALYSIS REPORT

Working individually or in a small group, identify a common stereotype. What people or things belong to this stereotype? What characteristics are commonly assigned to members of the group? Give an example of a member of the group who does not fit the stereotype. As a manager, how might this stereotype affect your perception process?

■ Use Exhibits 1–6 with In-Basket Exercise 1,
Exhibits 7–11 with In-Basket Exercise 2,
Exhibits 12–17 with In-Basket Exercise 3,
Exhibits 18–26 with In-Basket Exercise 4,
Exhibits 27–39 with In-Basket Exercise 5.

EXHIBIT 1
Pioneer Manufacturing Company
July Calendar

JULY

Sunday	Monday	Tuesday	Wednesday	Thursday	Friday	Saturday
1	2	3	4	5	6	7
8	9	10	11	12	13	14
15	16	17	18	19	20	21
22	23	24	25	26	27	28
29	30	31				

EXHIBIT 2
Pioneer Manufacturing Company
Organization Chart

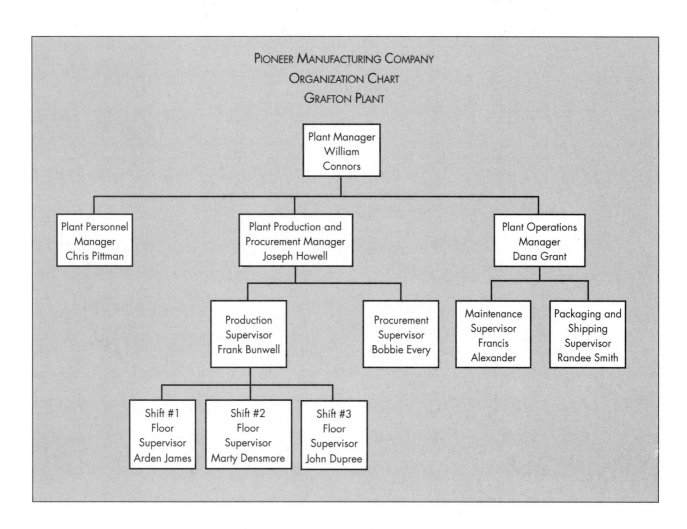

PIONEER MANUFACTURING COMPANY
ORGANIZATION CHART
GRAFTON PLANT

EXHIBIT 3
Chart One
Pioneer Manufacturing Company
Shift Productivity Chart

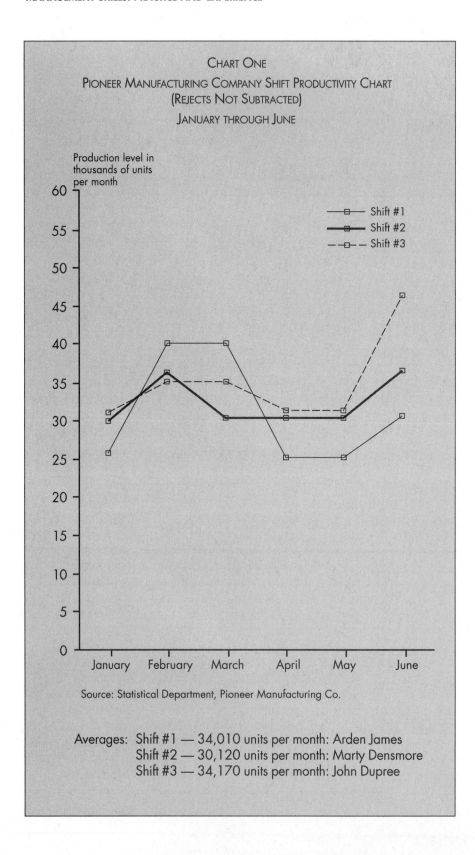

CHART ONE
PIONEER MANUFACTURING COMPANY SHIFT PRODUCTIVITY CHART
(REJECTS NOT SUBTRACTED)
JANUARY THROUGH JUNE

Source: Statistical Department, Pioneer Manufacturing Co.

Averages: Shift #1 — 34,010 units per month: Arden James
Shift #2 — 30,120 units per month: Marty Densmore
Shift #3 — 34,170 units per month: John Dupree

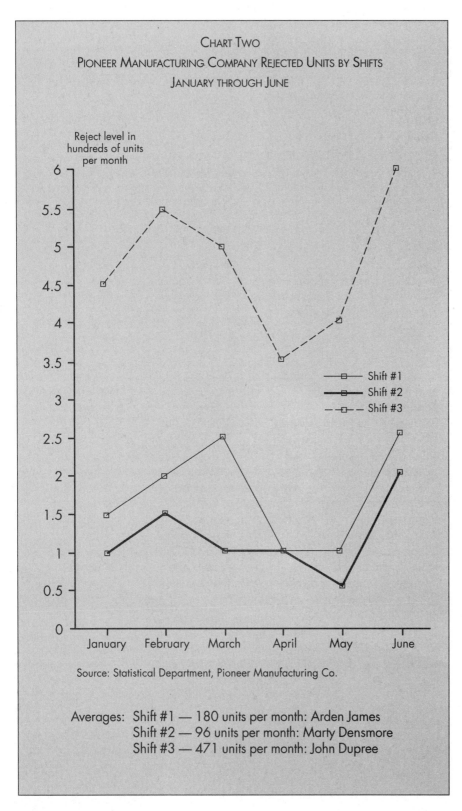

CHART TWO

PIONEER MANUFACTURING COMPANY REJECTED UNITS BY SHIFTS

JANUARY THROUGH JUNE

Reject level in
hundreds of units
per month

Shift #1
Shift #2
Shift #3

January February March April May June

Source: Statistical Department, Pioneer Manufacturing Co.

Averages: Shift #1 — 180 units per month: Arden James
Shift #2 — 96 units per month: Marty Densmore
Shift #3 — 471 units per month: John Dupree

EXHIBIT 4
Chart Two
Pioneer Manufacturing Company
Rejected Units by Shifts

EXHIBIT 5
Pioneer Manufacturing Company
Supervisor Performance Appraisal

PIONEER MANUFACTURING COMPANY
SUPERVISOR PERFORMANCE APPRAISAL
JANUARY THROUGH JUNE

Shift #1

Position	Name	Performance Rating
Production Line Floor Supervisor	Arden James	Excellent
Maintenance Floor Supervisor	William Tunney	Poor
Packaging & Shipping Floor Supervisor	Charles Stump	Good

Shift #2

Position	Name	Performance Rating
Production Line Floor Supervisor	Marty Densmore	Poor
Maintenance Floor Supervisor	Paul Johnston	Good
Packaging & Shipping Floor Supervisor	Thomas Reid	Excellent

Shift #3

Position	Name	Performance Rating
Production Line Floor Supervisor	John Dupree	Good
Maintenance Floor Supervisor	Nel Bangston	Good
Packaging & Shipping Floor Supervisor	Virginia Lenter	Poor

Supervisors	Name	Performance Rating
Production Supervisor	Frank Bunwell	Good
Maintenance Supervisor	Francis Alexander	Good
Procurement Supervisor	Bobbie Every	Excellent
Packaging & Shipping Supervisor	Randee Smith	Good

PIONEER MANUFACTURING COMPANY

MEMORANDUM

TO: Frank Bunwell, Production Supervisor
FROM: Dana Grant, Plant Operations Manager
DATE: July 6
SUBJECT: Expenditures

There will be no expenditures of over $50.00 for any purpose unless they have been authorized by Connors, Pittman, Howell, or me.

EXHIBIT 6
Pioneer Manufacturing Company
Memorandum

EXHIBIT 7
Pioneer Manufacturing Company
Production and Reject Units

TABLE ONE

PIONEER MANUFACTURING COMPANY PRODUCTION AND REJECT UNITS

Shift 1	Production	Rejects	Net Production	Ratio of Rejects to Production Unit
January	28,000	110	27,890	.004
February	44,000	215	43,785	.005
March	43,000	270	42,730	.006
April	28,000	110	27,890	.004
May	28,000	105	27,895	.004
June	33,000	270	32,730	.008
Average	34,010	180	33,830	.005
Shift 2				
January	29,000	80	28,920	.003
February	34,000	130	33,870	.004
March	29,000	90	28,910	.003
April	28,000	70	27,930	.003
May	27,000	30	26,970	.001
June	33,000	175	32,825	.005
Average	30,120	96	30,024	.003
Shift 3				
January	30,000	430	29,570	.014
February	38,000	550	37,450	.014
March	35,000	465	34,535	.013
April	30,000	360	29,640	.012
May	25,000	410	24,590	.016
June	47,000	610	45,390	.013
Average	34,170	471	33,699	.014
Overall				
Average	32,767	249	32,518	.008

Source: Statistical Department, Pioneer Manufacturing Company.

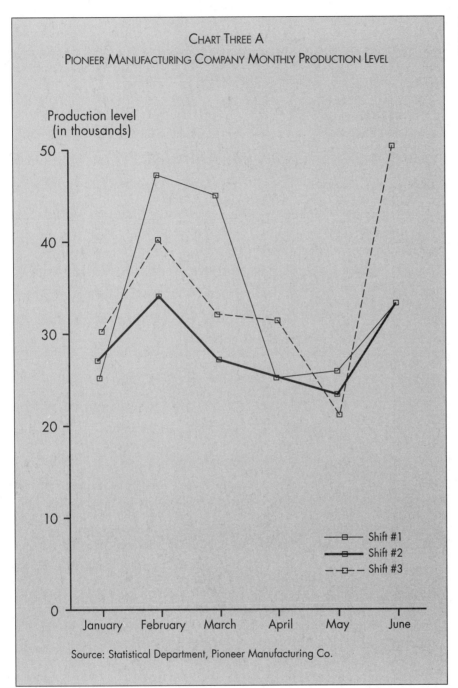

CHART THREE A
PIONEER MANUFACTURING COMPANY MONTHLY PRODUCTION LEVEL

Production level
(in thousands)

Shift #1
Shift #2
Shift #3

January February March April May June

Source: Statistical Department, Pioneer Manufacturing Co.

EXHIBIT 8
Pioneer Manufacturing Company
Monthly Production Level

EXHIBIT 9
Pioneer Manufacturing Company
Net Production Units

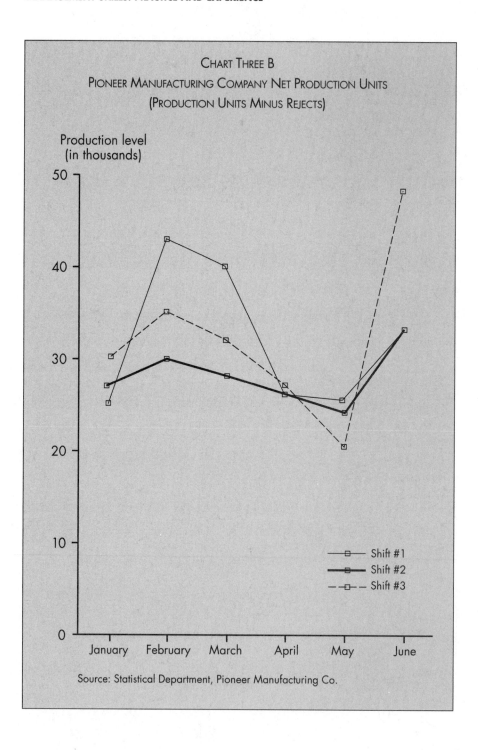

CHART THREE B
PIONEER MANUFACTURING COMPANY NET PRODUCTION UNITS
(PRODUCTION UNITS MINUS REJECTS)

Source: Statistical Department, Pioneer Manufacturing Co.

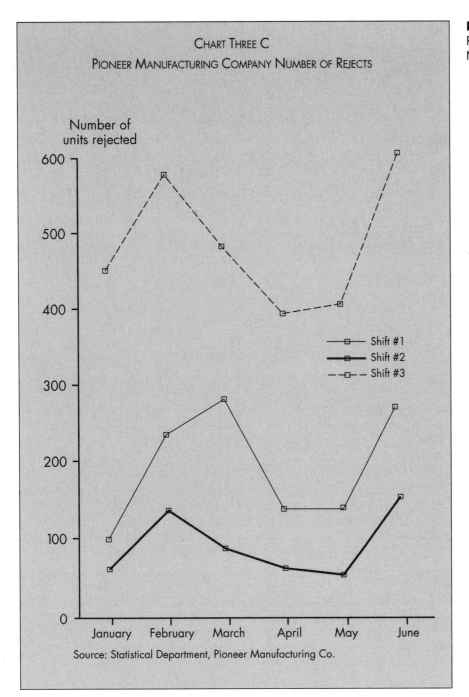

CHART THREE C

PIONEER MANUFACTURING COMPANY NUMBER OF REJECTS

Number of
units rejected

Shift #1
Shift #2
Shift #3

Source: Statistical Department, Pioneer Manufacturing Co.

EXHIBIT 10
Pioneer Manufacturing Company
Number of Rejects

EXHIBIT 11
Pioneer Manufacturing Company
Production Index

TABLE TWO

PIONEER MANUFACTURING COMPANY

PRODUCTION INDEX

(AVERAGE SEMIANNUAL PRODUCTION UNITS
FOR ALL SHIFTS COMBINED = 100)

	Shift 1	Shift 2	Shift 3
January	85	88	92
February	134	104	116
March	131	89	107
April	85	85	92
May	85	82	76
June	101	101	143
Shift Average	104	92	104

REJECT INDEX

(AVERAGE SEMIANNUAL NUMBER OF UNITS REJECTED
FOR ALL SHIFTS COMBINED = 100)

	Shift 1	Shift 2	Shift 3
January	44	32	173
February	86	52	221
March	108	36	187
April	44	28	145
May	42	12	165
June	108	70	245
Shift Average	72	39	189

Source: Zenith Management Consultants (based on data furnished by the
Pioneer Manufacturing Company).

PIONEER MANUFACTURING COMPANY

MEMORANDUM

Friday Evening, July 20
TO: Pat Crosby

As your secretary, I would like to welcome you to your new job.

I was very distressed to learn of Mr. Bunwell's passing away. The following is a group of papers that he left on his desk. He had a way of avoiding decisions, and I know that your job will be difficult until you get things straightened out.

I'm looking forward to meeting you.

EXHIBIT 12
Pioneer Manufacturing Company
Memorandum

PIONEER MANUFACTURING COMPANY

MEMORANDUM

TO: Joseph Howell, Production Manager
FROM: William Connors, Plant Manager
DATE: June 14
SUBJECT: Special Recognition Award

It is time for the annual companywide Special Recognition Award. The president has asked me to present this award to an employee from this plant because of our good production record this past year. I know that good production is a team effort, but I feel that the floor supervisors deserve much of the credit for our good record. The person we want to nominate for the award should have a good production record for his or her shift and have been shift floor supervisor throughout the past year. I need your recommendation by July 23.

EXHIBIT 13
Pioneer Manufacturing Company
Memorandum

EXHIBIT 14
Pioneer Manufacturing Company
Material Loss (Waste)

TABLE THREE

MATERIAL LOSS (WASTE)

	Units Produced	Material Loss in $	$ Loss per Thousand Units Produced
Shift 1			
January	28,000	$ 3,300	$118
February	44,000	$ 5,900	$134
March	43,000	$ 5,300	$123
April	28,000	$ 3,300	$118
May	28,000	$ 2,900	$104
June	33,000	$ 3,700	$112
Average	34,000	$ 4,067	$120
Shift 2			
January	29,000	$ 3,900	$134
February	34,000	$ 5,200	$153
March	29,000	$ 4,100	$141
April	28,000	$ 3,600	$129
May	27,000	$ 3,400	$126
June	33,000	$ 4,800	$145
Average	30,120	$ 4,167	$138
Shift 3			
January	30,000	$ 4,700	$156
February	38,000	$ 6,900	$182
March	35,000	$ 5,900	$169
April	30,000	$ 4,900	$163
May	25,000	$ 4,100	$164
June	47,000	$10,100	$215
Average	34,170	$ 6,100	$179

PIONEER MANUFACTURING COMPANY

MEMORANDUM

TO: Pat Crosby, Production Supervisor
FROM: Joseph Howell, Plant Production Manager
DATE: July 20
SUBJECT: Meeting

I would like to congratulate you on your new job! Why don't we get together on July 30th at 3 P.M. to discuss your new position and how to get along with maintenance and other headaches around the plant. Glad to have you aboard! I'll be looking for you in my office on the 30th of July at 3 P.M.

EXHIBIT 15
Pioneer Manufacturing Company Memorandum

PIONEER MANUFACTURING COMPANY

MEMORANDUM

TO: Frank Bunwell, Production Supervisor
FROM: Joseph Howell, Plant Production Manager
DATE: July 17
SUBJECT: Special Recognition Award

I really need that recommendation for the Special Recognition Award by July 25, at the latest. I know nothing about your floor supervisors, so you will have to make the decision yourself. Choose the floor supervisor with the best production record from January through June, or the one with the best performance appraisal, whichever you think is the better basis for the award.

EXHIBIT 16
Pioneer Manufacturing Company Memorandum

EXHIBIT 17
Arden James Letter

July 11

Mr. Bunwell,

Unless something is done to the punch machine on production line #3 soon, it is going to break down for good and will have to be replaced. It needs a new alignment arm, and it needs it soon. All maintenance does is tell me how they have more important things to do. The punches on #3 were made for metal, and the plastic clogs them up.

Arden James

EXHIBIT 18
C. Mondar Letter

2213 Leafy Way
Grafton

July 12

Dear Mr. Bunwell,

It is a pleasure to write to your distinguished company which has done so much for the town of Grafton. The topic of this letter, however, is rather unpleasant.

One of your employees, Frank Harrington, is a new neighbor of mine. Since he moved next door, a few weeks ago, his behavior has been impossible. He has had loud parties that last well past midnight, and he drinks and consorts with sleazy characters.

Such a man is a disgrace to your company. I'm sure you will do the right thing and fire him so that he will leave the area.

Sincerely yours,

C. Mondar

C. Mondar

PIONEER MANUFACTURING COMPANY

MEMORANDUM

TO: Frank Bunwell, Production Supervisor
FROM: Marty Densmore, Production Line Floor Supervisor, Shift #2
DATE: July 17
RE: Machine Breakdown

Frank,

We will need $45.00 to fix one of our machines that is down. Please sign the following authorization.

I authorize the expenditure of $45.00 for the machine parts on the #3 production line.

Signed_____

EXHIBIT 19
Pioneer Manufacturing Company Memorandum

PIONEER MANUFACTURING COMPANY

MEMORANDUM

TO: Pat Crosby, Production Supervisor
FROM: Dana Grant, Plant Operations Manager
DATE: July 20
RE: Welcome!

Welcome to your new position. I'm looking forward to meeting and working with you.

You may have a tough job taking over for Bunwell, but I will be happy to give you all the help I can. I'm sure that our departments can work together in the future much more than they have in the past.

I would like to see you in my office at your convenience to discuss an important maintenance matter concerning your #3 production line.

EXHIBIT 20
Pioneer Manufacturing Company Memorandum

EXHIBIT 21
Pioneer Manufacturing Company
Memorandum

PIONEER MANUFACTURING COMPANY

MEMORANDUM

TO: Frank Bunwell, Production Supervisor
FROM: Arden James, Floor Supervisor, Shift #1
DATE: July 12
SUBJECT: Lathe Operator

I still need a lathe operator. I only have one, and I've had to use someone from maintenance because none of the other workers know how to run the lathe. I've tried to get someone from the other shifts, but the other floor supervisors tell me that they can't spare anyone that can run a lathe.

I feel that I am getting no support in my present position and will be looking for a new position elsewhere if I cannot get a lathe operator by two weeks from today.

EXHIBIT 22
Pioneer Manufacturing Company
Memorandum

PIONEER MANUFACTURING COMPANY

MEMORANDUM

TO: Frank Bunwell, Production Supervisor
FROM: Chris Pittman, Plant Personnel Manager
DATE: July 9
SUBJECT: Supervisor Performance Appraisal System

It has come to my attention that many of the supervisory personnel in the plant feel that the present supervisor performance appraisal system is unfair. I am, therefore, asking you not to use the present appraisals for any important decisions until this matter is investigated further.

July 20

TO: Pat Crosby, Production Supervisor

The undersigned workers, as union stewards for the three shifts of production workers, would like to enter a formal complaint about a number of contract violations concerning non-union maintenance workers performing union production jobs. This is an unfair practice, and we are ready to strike on the 1st of August at 8:00 A.M. unless you meet with us to discuss this matter.

We have also heard rumors of production workers repairing their own machines, which is a maintenance worker's job. Although we, as yet, have no proof of this, we will not tolerate this breach of union contract.

We will be in your office with some higher union officials on July 30 at 3:00 P.M.

Frank Harrington   Tim Simmons   Harry Andrews

EXHIBIT 23
Union letter

PIONEER MANUFACTURING COMPANY

MEMORANDUM

TO: Frank Bunwell, Production Supervisor
FROM: Dana Grant, Plant Operations Manager
DATE: June 26
SUBJECT: Overtime

All overtime must be formally requested three days in advance. This procedure will become effective on July 1st.

EXHIBIT 24
Pioneer Manufacturing Company Memorandum

EXHIBIT 25
Pioneer Manufacturing Company
Supervisor Longevity Record – June

PIONEER MANUFACTURING COMPANY
SUPERVISOR LONGEVITY RECORD
JUNE

Name	Length of Employment	
	Years	Months
Francis Alexander	7	4
Nel Bangston	4	0
Frank Bunwell	14	0
Bobbie Every	21	7
Marty Densmore	17	10
John Dupree	6	8
Arden James	0	5
Paul Johnston	11	6
Virginia Lenter	16	2
Thomas Reid	12	1
Randee Smith	5	6
Charles Stump	26	11
William Tunney	1	0

EXHIBIT 26
Joe Foster letter

July 16

Mr. Bunwell,

I've been working on the third shift in production for ten years now, and I have a lot of ideas about how we could turn the #3 production line into a line that could produce metal frames without much cost by using the Rockerton punches and Linsey press that line has and just changing a few of the machines. It wouldn't cost much, and getting to work with metal from time to time might break the monotony of the job.

I would like to see you by July 27, or I will resign my position. I am tired of being told my ideas are worthless by those in the plant who don't know anything and not being able to talk to those who do.

Joe Foster

July 16

TO: Frank Bunwell, Production Supervisor

I'm sick and tired of working on the #4 punch. I'm a press operator, and I just don't care for running that punch machine. I've talked to James, the shift floor supervisor, about switching me, and he says that I will have to stay where I am for now. I used to work on production line #2, and now James has me on line #1, and I have to do extra work to keep line #3 supplied because one of their punches keeps clogging up.

I wish you'd talk to James and straighten this thing out and get me back on a press machine.

Frank Harrington

EXHIBIT 27
Frank Harrington letter

PIONEER MANUFACTURING COMPANY

MEMORANDUM

TO: Frank Bunwell, Production Supervisor
FROM: William Connors, Plant Manager
DATE: July 13
SUBJECT: Special Production Run

Kelly Distributors is one of our largest customers and has for years carried our #1304 frame, which we discontinued last year. Kelly Distributors has asked us to make a special lot of these frames to cover residual orders that they have outstanding.

It is imperative that we get these frames finished and packaged by July 26. In order to get the order packaged and shipped in time, it is imperative that you have the production phase finished by the end of shift #3 on the 25th.

The order calls for 8,000 #1304 frames. I know I can count on you to handle this important order.

EXHIBIT 28
Pioneer Manufacturing Company
Memorandum

EXHIBIT 29
Pioneer Manufacturing Company
Memorandum

PIONEER MANUFACTURING COMPANY

MEMORANDUM

TO: Frank Bunwell, Production Supervisor
FROM: Chris Pittman, Plant Personnel Manager
DATE: July 18
SUBJECT: Lathe Operator Replacement

I have not been able to find a qualified lathe operator for you as per your request last week. I have temporary help available for all other production line jobs except the lathe operators.

If you wish, I can begin training a new person for lathe work. As you know, this training will require one month, and I don't have any replacements until then.

Are you sure that you can't get a lathe operator from one of the other shifts until I can get someone trained?

Let me know if you want me to train some lathe operators.

EXHIBIT 30
Pioneer Manufacturing Company
Memorandum

PIONEER MANUFACTURING COMPANY

MEMORANDUM

TO: Frank Bunwell, Production Supervisor
FROM: Dana Grant, Plant Operations Manager
DATE: July 10
SUBJECT: Meeting of Maintenance Supervisory Personnel

I would like to invite you to state your complaints against the maintenance department at their meeting on the morning of July 26th at 10:00 A.M. I expect to see you there and to hear your complaints about that punch machine.

PIONEER MANUFACTURING COMPANY

MEMORANDUM

TO: Pat Crosby, Production Supervisor
FROM: Chris Pittman, Plant Personnel Manager
DATE: July 20
SUBJECT: Frank Harrington

Congratulations on your new position. I'm looking forward to meeting and working with you soon.

One of your men, Frank Harrington, has been recommended for a promotion to a supervisory slot by your predecessor. This job needs someone with outstanding moral character, common sense, and care for quality and detail. I need your O.K. for his promotion so that I can send his recommended pay raise, along with others, to the operating department on the 25th of this month.

Please contact me with your decision on this matter.

EXHIBIT 31
Pioneer Manufacturing Company Memorandum

PIONEER MANUFACTURING COMPANY

MEMORANDUM

TO: Frank Bunwell, Production Supervisor
FROM: Jane Boswell, Quality Control Clerk
DATE: July 12
SUBJECT: Quality Control

In checking my records, I have come across a problem that I think you should be aware of. The quality control of shift #1, which usually has a low level of rejects, has gone steadily down in recent weeks. The rejects seem to mostly be coming off the #4 punch on shift #1 first production line. I hope that you can find a solution to this problem. Someone is turning out some very sloppy work.

EXHIBIT 32
Pioneer Manufacturing Company Memorandum

EXHIBIT 33
Pioneer Manufacturing Company
Memorandum

PIONEER MANUFACTURING COMPANY

MEMORANDUM

TO: Frank Bunwell, Production Supervisor
FROM: John Dupree, Shift #3 Floor Supervisor
DATE: July 18
RE: Special-Order Production

I have completed the estimates you asked me to make on the special-order production run next week. With all three lines running smoothly, we can complete the order in the required two days after receiving the special supplies on the afternoon of the 23rd, if we can keep the machines running constantly.

The setup of the machines Monday night for the special run starting on Tuesday will require six men that I can get from my shift. We will need a total of 21 hours of overtime Monday night to reset the machines for that order and get ready for the first shift to take over.

I've told the men about the overtime, and I'll just plan on staying late with them Monday night. I am also planning on eighteen to twenty hours of overtime on the night of the 25th to get the normal production line set up for shift #1 on the 26th.

EXHIBIT 34
Pioneer Manufacturing Company
Memorandum

PIONEER MANUFACTURING COMPANY

MEMORANDUM

TO: Mr. Frank Bunwell, Production Supervisor
FROM: Joseph Howell, Plant Production and Procurement Manager
DATE: July 16
SUBJECT: Meeting

There will be a meeting on July 26th at 9:30 A.M. for all production supervisory personnel with the plant manager to discuss the new procedures that are planned for implementation this fall. All production floor supervisors must attend. Tell your personnel to please be there. The meeting will take about one hour.

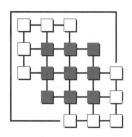

MODULE 6
ORGANIZING AND PLANNING SKILLS: ESTABLISHING COURSES OF ACTION

INTRODUCTION

Organizing and planning skills enable you to establish a course of action for yourself and others in order to accomplish a specific result. These skills include coordinating resources, clarifying objectives, setting priorities, managing personal and staff time, and organizing information so that it can be retrieved and used.

The terms *organizing* and *planning* are not synonymous: you can plan without organizing and organize without planning. Therefore, attention must be paid to both organizing and planning skills in order to be a successful manager.

Planning is a process that works out in advance a certain way to do things. It requires consideration of the future and envisioning the task as a whole. Organizing means arranging the activities required to complete a task and assigning the necessary resources. When more than two people are working toward an objective, organizing coordinates their efforts and keeps their activities focused on the task.

Organizing and planning skills consider whole tasks, how tasks may be divided, what is needed to accomplish the tasks, and how to arrange activities for the most effective results. In a managerial context, organizing and planning skills can be divided into the following categories of behavior: (1) clarifying goals and objectives, (2) establishing priorities, (3) developing work strategies, (4) scheduling activities, and (5) establishing systems for handling information.

The purpose of this module is to help you develop your organizing and planning skills or increase those you already have. You will assume the role of a manager in a variety of situations. In each situation, you will be provided with information—samples of material that typically find their way to the manager's desk. As a manager, you must use your organizing and planning skills to solve a potential problem. By actually participating in situations, you will learn and practice these skills.

The module is organized so that you will develop a before-practice assessment of your organizing and planning skills by completing the Organizing and Planning Process Questionnaire (OPPQ). This assessment instrument measures your organizing and planning skills at the present time. We then present a brief discussion of organizing and planning skills. Next, through in-basket exercises, you will have an opportunity to practice these skills. Feedback from your instructor will help you judge the quality of your own responses and provide guidance on improving specific behaviors.

After a review and summary, you will retake the OPPQ and compare your after-practice assessment results with your earlier results. You will also complete the Organizing and Planning Behaviors Choice Questionnaire (OPBC). This assessment instrument examines how you actually behave in situations where organizing and planning skills are needed. It will give you more insight into your behaviors in situations requiring these skills.

After completing this module, you may find that your practice will result in immediate improvement, or you may find that improvement is more noticeable after you have had opportunities to perform on the job or in a classroom situation.

ASSESSING ORGANIZING AND PLANNING SKILLS

Complete the OPPQ on the following pages before proceeding with the rest of the module. It is both a teaching tool and a means of evaluating your present organizing and planning skills. Take time to complete the instrument carefully. Your answers should reflect your behaviors as they are now, not as you would like them to be. Be honest. This instrument is designed to help you discover where you are now so you can work to improve your organizing and planning skills.

The Organizing and Planning Process Questionnaire (OPPQ)

The Organizing and Planning Process Questionnaire (OPPQ) is an assessment tool that measures your present level of organizing and planning skills. You will rate yourself according to the frequency of behaviors in the five categories that make up organizing and planning skills. Even if you do not have experience in a management position, consider a project you have worked on in an organization such as a fraternity, sorority, club, church, or service group.

Use the scale shown below to rate the frequency with which you perform the behaviors noted. Place the corresponding number (1–7) in the blank preceding the statements.

Rarely	Irregularly	Occasionally	Usually	Frequently	Almost Always	Consistently
1	2	3	4	5	6	7

_____ **1.** I identify long-range goals and objectives.

_____ **2.** I review the important elements of projects to be undertaken.

_____ **3.** I consider the goals and objectives of my organization or group when setting my own goals and objectives.

_____ **4.** I establish short-term, successive goals and objectives that lead to the attainment of long-range goals and objectives.

_____ **5.** I establish the priority of projects, tasks, or assignments before committing time to their completion.

_____ **6.** I compare projects to determine their urgency before committing time to their completion.

_____ **7.** I compare projects to evaluate the potential outcomes before committing time to their completion.

_____ **8.** I estimate the amount of time required to complete projects before committing time to their completion.

_____ **9.** I organize my activities by dividing long-term, complex projects into smaller, doable activities.

_____ **10.** I establish procedures that will control possible interruptions.

_____ **11.** I complete the important elements of projects before spending time on less essential elements.

_____ **12.** I get information and instructions from knowledgeable sources before starting on an unfamiliar task.

_____ **13.** I make realistic time commitments for working on long-term or complex projects.

_____ **14.** I coordinate activities so that short-term goals and objectives support long-term goals and objectives.

_____ **15.** I establish a schedule of intermediate deadlines that leads to the completion of long-term projects.

_____ **16.** I establish deadlines for the completion of long-term projects.

_____ **17.** I review relevant information before determining a course of action.

_____ **18.** I underline important information in memos or letters, and I make notes on letters and memos indicating other related materials.

_____ **19.** I mark my calendar as a reference when making appointments.

_____ **20.** I group related materials together for easier reference at later dates.

FIGURE 1

Organizing and Planning Process
Questionnaire (OPPQ) Scoring

Skill Area	Items	Assessment	
		Before Practice	After Practice
Clarifying goals and objectives	1,2,3,4		
Establishing priorities	5,6,7,8		
Developing work strategies	9,10,11,12		
Scheduling activities	13,14,15,16		
Establishing systems for handling information	17,18,19,20		
TOTAL SCORE			

OPPQ Scoring

The scoring sheet shown in Figure 1 summarizes your scores for the OPPQ. It will help you identify your existing strengths and pinpoint areas that need improvement. Right now, fill in the before-practice assessment score column for each skill area by adding your scores for each item. Add the five category scores to obtain a total score. Enter that score in the space indicated. After completing the module, you will take the OPPQ again and fill in the after-practice assessment column.

OPPQ Evaluation

Figure 2 shows score lines for your total score and for each category measured on the OPPQ. Each line shows a continuum from the lowest possible score to the highest. Place a B (before-practice) where your personal score falls on each of these lines. The score lines in Figure 2 show graphically where you stand with regard to five organizing and planning behaviors. If you have been honest with yourself, you now have a better idea of your relative strengths and weaknesses in the categories of behavior that make up organizing and planning skills.

Learning to Use the OPPQ Skills

You have now completed the initial evaluation of your organizing and planning skills. In the OPPQ, you rated the frequency with which you demonstrated organizing and planning behaviors in five skill categories. This questionnaire provides a baseline against which you will assess improvements that have taken place after you have completed this module.

Before moving on, think about what you have discovered about yourself in this assessment. Which categories of organizing and planning skills are least

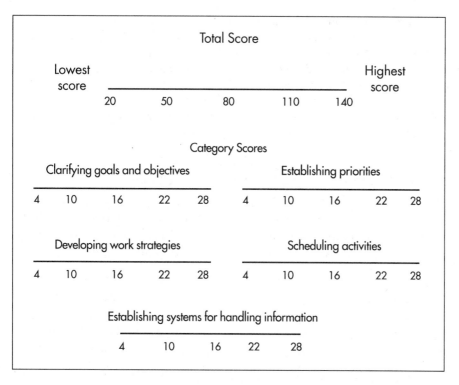

developed? These will require most of your attention during the remainder of the module. Which categories of organizing and planning are your strongest? Use this module to fine-tune these even further so that you may take full advantage of them. In these areas, learning a few new behaviors can lead to even greater accomplishment.

The OPPQ will help you identify organizing and planning behaviors that are appropriate for the management situations described in this module. After you have completed the module and have had an opportunity to put into practice what you have learned, retake the OPPQ. Then, compare your after-practice assessment scores with your before-practice scores. This comparison will show you where you have progressed and where further work is needed. Keep your own needs in mind as you proceed. The items in the OPPQ should be reviewed frequently and used as guides while you work through the material presented in this module.

UNDERSTANDING ORGANIZING AND PLANNING

Organizing and planning skills enable managers to consider the whole task, how to divide tasks, what they need to accomplish these tasks, and how to arrange activities for the most effective results. Organizing and planning skills are necessary in any organization. Managers use these skills to start projects, to make changes, and in the daily management of their units.

Resources are a valuable commodity in any organization. At times managers must compete with others for the resources they need. Managers with good organizing and planning skills will work out in advance a list of specific tasks needed to accomplish their objectives and the resources needed to accomplish these tasks. A clear mapping of tasks and resources makes it possible for managers to use all available resources in the most efficient way. It helps them compete for the resources they need to carry out the work of their department and allows for coordination of various departments or divisions.

Organizing and Planning Skills Required of Managers

Effective managers demonstrate organizing and planning skills in five categories: (1) clarifying goals and objectives, (2) establishing priorities, (3) developing work strategies, (4) scheduling activities, and (5) establishing systems for handling information. In the next section we will briefly discuss each of these categories.

Clarifying Goals and Objectives

Every organization has goals and objectives. Explanations of these goals and objectives may range from the vague, such as "our goal is to make a profit," to clear statements of the organization's function and all the groups that are involved. The focus, purpose, and kinds of activities that take place as part of the process vary with the level of the organization.

Overall organizational goals and objectives are often too general to guide individual units or departments. In order to be meaningful, these general goals and objectives must be translated into specific objectives for each unit. While managers do not necessarily set the goals for their own departments, they are responsible for making their departmental goals clear to everyone who works in their units.

At the CEO or vice president level, goal setting is strategic or directional. It involves an organization's most basic fundamental decisions, such as what markets do we pursue. At the middle management and supervisory levels, goals are more tactical, with a primary emphasis on implementing and carrying out decisions made by senior officers. For example, a tactical goal would involve how specific markets would be developed.

At the management level, goals must be specific and challenging. Specific goals result in better performance than do vague, easily attained goals. Goal setting is most effective when goals are clearly defined in terms of what needs to happen, how often, in what quantity, and by when.

Goals and objectives must be stated in clear terms. Clear language reduces the possibility of miscommunication or misunderstanding and provides a clear target to work toward. An example of a clearly worded company goal would be "increase gross sales by 12 percent and net profits by 4 percent, with no more than a 1 percent increase in sales staff turnover within the next 12 months." If the goal is vague, as in "increase profits over last year," each person in the unit may interpret what that means differently.

Failure to clarify goals can be detrimental to a manager. People in the unit may work at cross-purposes because each one interpreted the goal differently. This can result in work that is inconsistent and a department filled with disagreements. Similarly, if a manager fails to clarify his or her own goals, that manager will likely waste both time and effort.

The goals and objectives of various tasks must be clearly set forth to encourage uniform performance. For example, managers frequently call meetings. These meetings have a purpose, and that purpose must be made clear to the participants. Also, reports are written by managers for a reason. That reason should be noted at the beginning of the report. Stating the goals or objectives of a meeting, a report, or a task focuses attention on these goals or objectives and helps achieve the desired results.

Establishing Priorities

Plans are put into action by establishing priorities, assigning responsibilities, and developing time schedules. Once goals have been clarified, managers must determine which of these goals take precedence. Managers assign a value to each goal and determine what kind of attention it will receive. They assign priorities to the goals because each goal must compete for resources. By establishing priorities, managers provide a framework for making choices. This system allows for consistent and efficient decision making in the future.

For example, let's assume you are in a management position and you have to determine which orders should be filled first and which can wait. After identifying the primary goal—providing service to customers—you have to set priorities according to your interpretation of "service." A priority system is based on the importance of the customer and the urgency of each order. This combination allows you to provide the best service.

Once the priority (or value) system is determined, you can make efficient and consistent scheduling decisions. Establishing priorities provides an important framework for the orderly functioning of your unit.

If a manager has not established priorities to guide people within the unit, important activities may be delayed while less crucial tasks are performed. With no clear guidelines from the manager, each person may assign priorities to activities according to his or her own personal scheme. The result will be a department in disarray.

It is just as important for a manager to assign priorities to the tasks and activities involved in his or her own job. For example, it is often tempting for a manager to spend a great deal of time working with subordinates, even doing some of their work, and ignoring the job of managing. If the manager assigns priorities to his or her own tasks, this pitfall can be avoided. This is where good time management skills are needed.

From a personal perspective, time management is nothing more than the act of controlling events. Time is a scarce resource that must be controlled if a manager is to be effective. Time management reduces the frustrations and stress resulting from being overloaded with work. While it is not possible to create more time, most people can learn to make better and more efficient use of existing time. Time is wasted when it is used for things that are less important than others. The most difficult aspects of good time management are knowing what things are important enough to do and how to establish a system of priorities.

Effective use of time does not mean doing everything faster and better. Instead, time management means doing fewer things but doing them well. There are several techniques to become more effective at managing your time. First, learn to recognize common time wasters.

Studies of managerial activities find some common time wasters include drop-in visitors, telephone interruptions, a cluttered office, unessential tasks, and unnecessary or over-long meetings. Some possible remedies of these time wasters are shown in Figure 3.

Next, you need to learn to distinguish between things that are vital (have a high payoff and are important), things that are trivial (have a low payoff and are unimportant), and things that are urgent (things that move us to take action). You do this by carefully planning your daily, weekly, and monthly activities.

Start each day by determining what you need to accomplish, what meetings and appointments are scheduled, and other activities that are pending. This is essentially your daily action guide. It starts with a "to do" list and assigns priorities to each activity using a system of symbols. For example, priority A means an activity is vital and urgent. Priority B means an activity is vital but not

FIGURE 3
Time Wasters and Possible Remedies

Time Waster	Possible Remedy
Drop-in Visitor	■ Meet with people in their offices instead of yours. ■ Prepare polite excuses to discourage or shorten visits. ■ Make yourself inaccessible during particular times of the week by closing your door or working in a private location. ■ Remain standing when an unannounced visitor comes to your door.
Telephone Interruptions	■ Delegate responsibility for screening calls or answering particular types of telephone inquires to a secretary or subordinate. ■ Prepare polite excuses to shorten calls. ■ Ask the caller specifically "How can I help you?" ■ Have materials and information ready for calls that you expect to receive so you are prepared for them and do not need to waste time or call back. ■ Make telephone appointments to avoid call backs. ■ Use electronic mail messages whenever possible to receive or relay routine information.
Cluttered Office	■ Set priorities on incoming correspondence and paperwork before you deal with any items; discard or redirect unimportant items. ■ Develop an efficient file system with categories that are easy to remember and files that are easy to find. ■ Periodically discard old records and files that are no longer relevant or store them elsewhere.

urgent. Priority C means an activity is neither vital nor urgent. Priority D is a trivial activity. Discretionary time should be used to carry out a mix of priority A and priority B activities in appropriate time periods. Some priority C activities are handled at odd times or delegated to others.

In planning activities, you should consider that it is more efficient to do a series of similar tasks than to keep switching from one type of task to another. Learn to schedule similar activities, such as making telephone calls or writing letters, for the same time during the day. A quick glance at your day will help you decide where to place your efforts. It will also provide a guideline for delegating responsibilities to others.

Finally, get in the habit of writing information down. When you attend or conduct meetings, write down brief summaries of what has taken place. When you make an appointment or set a deadline, note it in your calendar. When you are beginning a project, write down important information, resource needs, and possible constraints.

Effective managers understand the value of using time wisely. To develop an understanding of time management you need to (1) learn where your time

Time Waster	Possible Remedy
Cluttered Office (Cont.)	■ Whenever appropriate, respond to memos or letters when you receive them by writing a short answer on the original document rather than waiting to prepare another memo or letter of your own.
	■ Try to handle items only once; develop a set of rules about how to handle recurrent types of correspondence.
	■ Clear your work space of all materials except for information that involves the task you are working on currently.
	■ Schedule time each day to file paperwork and put items not currently being used in their proper place.
Unnecessary Tasks	■ Prepare tactful ways to say no and use them.
	■ Identify unessential tasks that can be eliminated.
	■ Put off any unessential tasks that cannot be delegated or eliminated and do them in slack time or when you are waiting for someone.
Unnecessary or Over-Long Meetings	■ Prepare an agenda and distribute it in advance. Include starting time, location, and approximate length of the meeting.
	■ Follow the agenda and discourage attempts to bring up issues not relevant or scheduled.
	■ Inform people about what they need to do to prepare for a meeting.
	■ Consistently start meetings on time. Set a good example by arriving at the meeting on time.
	■ Hold meetings in quiet locations and take steps to avoid interruptions.
	■ Before ending a meeting, decide if and when a follow-up meeting should be scheduled. Assign responsibility to individuals for implementing decisions.

wasters are and eliminate them, (2) develop a sense of which tasks are vital, not vital, and urgent, (3) plan your daily, weekly, and monthly activities, (4) write down important dates, meetings, and facts that you know you won't remember, and (5) learn to prioritize your tasks.

Developing Work Strategies

Clarifying objectives, setting priorities, and managing your time are only part of organizing and planning. To accomplish these objectives, you must develop specific plans and work strategies. In order to do this, a manager must determine the necessary activities and the resources needed for their completion. These resources include people, time, money, and materials.

It is important to keep in mind that each strategy is developed to accomplish an objective and requires a manager to foresee the future of a task and determine the requirements at each stage of its development. It requires the manager to specify actions to accomplish the task or strategies. Developing work strategies helps the manager achieve his or her goals with optimum efficiency. By advance planning, the manager makes certain that all resources are used effectively. Gaps and duplications in jobs are avoided through proper planning.

In addition to developing work strategies for the department, the manager cannot overlook developing personal work strategies to meet his or her individual goals and objectives. In establishing these self-strategies, the manager can receive guidance and assistance from his or her own manager.

Developing work strategies provides structure and scheduling for your own and others' activities. They allow you to attend to requirements for personnel, facilities, and materials. They help avoid the duplication of effort as well as use time effectively.

Scheduling Activities

The manager must plan not only work strategies, but also the appropriate time and sequence of the activities involved. Managers are expected to see that the regular activities of their departments are scheduled. They also are expected to reschedule activities if necessary. A manager must schedule tasks, people, and other resources for the tasks, and his or her own time and activities as well as the time and activities of those who are managed.

In scheduling, the manager establishes a sequence of tasks and identifies initiation dates and target completion dates. Sequencing means prioritizing activities in terms of the tasks and in terms of the objectives. A manager needs to look at each task and ask, "What does this task demand of my time? Others' time? Will that time be available?" Effective scheduling is a vital part of organizing and planning. Without good scheduling, work may come in waves with people too busy at one time and idle at another. Even worse is a situation in which one employee is given too much work and another is not given enough.

Establishing Systems for Handling Information

Information from a wide variety of sources about a number of topics may be presented to a manager in both oral and written forms. The manager must determine what needs to be done with the information. Often this must be done quickly. Therefore, managers must have effective methods for handling the information. They must consider the future use of information and must have a way to store information and identify it for retrieval when it is needed. They must also take information and present it to others in a way that can be readily grasped. This includes presenting information in graphic form, when appropriate, and labeling, titling, and summarizing information. While the actual writing of a report falls under the skill of written communication, the arrangement of the information requires the skills of organizing and planning.

Organizing and Planning Behavior Time Sequence

The chart shown in Figure 4 summarizes the flow of activities that comprise the organizing and planning process. It demonstrates the required sequence of the various categories of behaviors that make up organizing and planning skills. You will find it helpful to refer to this chart frequently.

FIGURE 4
Organizing and Planning
Behavior Time Sequence

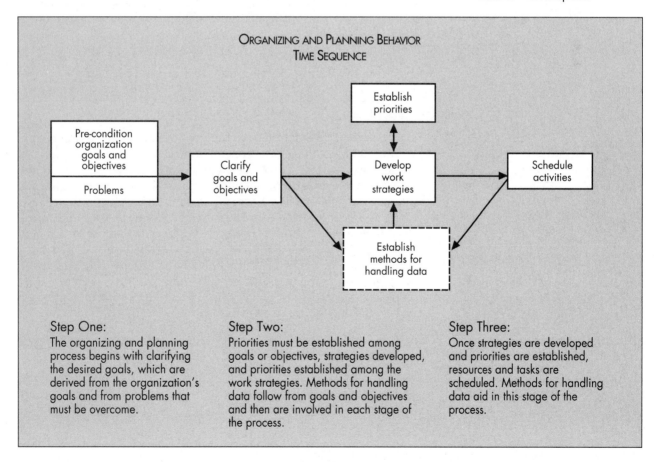

Organizing and Planning Skills and Their Relationships to Other Managerial Skills

The skills of organizing and planning are most closely associated with three other managerial skills—decision making, leadership, and flexibility. Decision making is involved in each of the five categories of organizing and planning. Organizing and planning aids the manager in making decisions by clarifying what needs to be done, dividing the work, setting deadlines, and scheduling activities. It is then a function of the manager's leadership to see that tasks are accomplished. The framework provided by organizing and planning skills helps the manager exercise leadership by setting the direction and boundaries of the work to be accomplished.

Although organizing and planning seems to be the opposite of flexibility, it is this skill that makes flexibility possible. If a manager has considered the objective of a task, has looked at it as a whole, and has developed strategies to complete it, he or she will be better prepared to respond effectively to unexpected problems. A response may include adjusting present plans or coming up with a completely new plan. The flexibility would not be possible if tasks had not been handled systematically in the first place.

Organizing and planning is also interwoven in the process of decision making. The objective of decision making is stated in terms of a satisfactory solution to a problem. The manager determines a plan using the necessary resources and activities for implementing that solution. Evaluation of the solution then takes place.

Guidelines for Increasing Organizing and Planning Skills

The following guidelines offer suggestions for you to increase your organizing and planning skills.

- *Take the time*—This is the first requirement of organizing and planning behavior. Before starting a task or project, you as manager need to take time to clarify goals and think the project through. Whatever the amount of time you are given, allocate time to the project before it begins, no matter how urgent it is. Remember to allow time for evaluating outcomes.
- *Get it straight*—Organizing and planning behaviors are not an end in themselves; they have a purpose. You need to determine that purpose. If you are trying to clarify the objectives of your own department, put those objectives in your own words. It will help you understand them. Meet with your own manager and be sure that you have correctly and completely interpreted these objectives. Then go back to your employees and help them restate the goals in their own words.
- *Write it down*—As a manager, you handle too much information to keep in your head. Get in the habit of writing information down. When you attend or conduct meetings, write down brief summaries of what has taken place. When you make an appointment or set a deadline, note it on your calendar. When establishing your goals, write them down. When you are facing a project, write down the facts, any limitations, and the requirements. There are many ways to do each task. With all the information in

front of you, some ways will appear clearly impractical and other ways may come to mind.

- *Use aids that are available to you*—Get in the habit of reading memos and reports with a highlighter in your hand and mark important information. This will save you the trouble of rereading the entire report later. Assemble related items in folders and label the folders so that their contents are clear. Use these files for saving relevant articles from magazines, trade publications, newspapers, etc., and for keeping policy and procedural guidelines, contracts, and technical information.
- *Learn to scan information*—Much of the written material that you receive does not need to be read word for word or can be saved for future reference. Scan written information to determine what you are dealing with so that you can act on high priority items and delay low priority items.
- *Use your plans and strategies*—It is not enough to develop plans and organize strategies. You must use them. Determining the priorities of tasks is just an empty activity if the tasks are not treated according to that priority. Noting only some meetings on your calendar and omitting others will not be of much help in organizing your time. Nor will it benefit you to note meetings on your calendar and then not look at it when planning each day.

PRACTICING ORGANIZING AND PLANNING

Organizing and planning skills consist of the following component behaviors:

- *Clarifying goals and objectives*—You identify long-term goals and objectives and also short-term objectives that lead to the long-term objectives.
- *Establishing priorities*—Ranking your tasks in the order of their importance before committing time to them is part of the skills of organizing and planning.
- *Developing work strategies*—Efficient work strategies include gathering the information you need before you actually begin a job; dividing complex projects into smaller, more doable parts; finishing the most important tasks first; and avoiding minor issues and unnecessary interruptions.
- *Scheduling activities*—Establishing the order in which tasks and parts of tasks must be completed and establishing their time frames is basic to organizing and planning skills.
- *Establishing systems for handling information*—Simple techniques such as underlining the essential information on memos, noting appointments on a calendar, and grouping related information together can help the manager handle information more effectively.

The next section of in-basket exercises focuses on each component of the organizing and planning skills we have been discussing. Each exercise is followed by questions that direct your attention to the appropriate behaviors.

Before you begin the exercises, take time to review your scores on the five parts of the OPPQ that you completed earlier. Then as you work to complete the exercises, keep in mind the behaviors noted in this questionnaire. The questions in the OPPQ deepen your understanding of basic organizing and planning skills.

Situation

You are Chris Nelson, sales manager, Area S III, for Guerin-Fiedler, Inc., a small pharmaceutical company that has built its reputation on a variety of staple drugs. Guerin-Fiedler has not increased its market share in a number of years, but it is planning to do so this year.

The company's hopes for increased sales are based on a revolutionary new drug, presently called THI. The Food and Drug Administration's approval is certain, and most of the company's efforts will be directed toward selling THI. As Chris Nelson, you will be dealing with some routine problems as well as some larger problems associated with the preparations to sell THI.

You are located in Charleston, South Carolina; your regional manager, Pat Ryan, is in Richmond, Virginia. You have just spent two weeks at the home office, a requirement for all area managers. Today is June 16. On your desk is a file of materials (Exhibits 1 through 20). Read the information and answer the questions in each in-basket exercise. When answering the questions, take all of the information from previous exercises into consideration and, if pertinent, use it in your answers.

IN-BASKET EXERCISE 1: CLARIFYING GOALS AND OBJECTIVES

It is the manager's job to clarify the goals and objectives of his or her unit or department. This exercise will help you clarify goals and objectives that relate to your job as an area sales manager for Guerin-Fiedler, Inc. Refer to Exhibits 1 through 5, and then respond to the questions that follow.

Your organizing and planning skills focus:

- Note the goals and objectives of your organization.
- State the goals and objectives of your position.
- Form subgoals that lead to principal goals.
- Explain objectives of scheduled activities.

Questions for In-Basket Exercise 1:

1. Before you begin on the work that you, as Chris Nelson, must deal with, you need to orient yourself and do what Chris did in the first days on the job. Look at the company's goals, as stated in the policy manual, and state them in your own terms.

2. As Chris Nelson, identify the main objective in the area sales manager's job description and state it in your own words.

3. Now that you have stated the major goal of the area sales manager's job, look for subgoals that lead to the attainment of the overall goal. Put them into clear, simple terms.

4. You have been asked to set up a meeting for the sales representatives in Area S III prior to the introduction of a new drug. Tell the sales reps the goal of the meeting. Be complete in your statement.

5. Six medical students have been assigned to Area S III. What objectives are there for assigning medical students to sales representatives?

IN-BASKET EXERCISE 2: ESTABLISHING PRIORITIES

In organizing and planning your work and that of others, you must assign priorities to different activities because activities often compete for limited resources. In this next exercise, you will be required to assign priorities to different activities based on the outcome and the urgency of each activity. Using the information in Exhibits 6 through 10, respond to the questions that follow.

Your organizing and planning skills focus:

- Note the importance of organizational and departmental goals.
- Understand the urgency of tasks.
- Determine the effect of tasks and assignments on subsequent tasks.
- Determine the impact of individual goals and responsibilities (your own as well as those of the employees you manage).

Questions for In-Basket Exercise 2:

1. You, as Chris Nelson, have a number of activities that require your time and attention, and a number of activities compete for your sales reps' time. You need to determine priorities to resolve the demands on everyone's time. What activity would you set as your highest priority? Why?

2. Does this priority system hold for everyone in your area? What about George Brown who has been slated to go to a management training session next week when the THI training is to occur in your area?

3. You have received some information on how to answer doctors' questions on HSP. You have also been asked for help on this problem. You can schedule this information into the area meeting. Should you spend any time on this issue prior to the area meeting? Explain your answer in terms of organizing and planning behaviors.

4. How should you consider the training situation with Paul Cooke? Paul is expecting your presence and already has set up three appointments. Should you find the time for them in this month's schedule?

IN-BASKET EXERCISE 3: DEVELOPING WORK STRATEGIES

Your job as manager requires you to determine how goals and objectives will be reached. That is, you must develop specific strategies for achieving outcomes. This activity requires you to consider the best use of the resources available to you. You have clarified your goals and established your priorities. Now you need to set up the activities that are necessary to reach these goals.

Use all of the information you have been given so far in the previous in-basket exercises and the information shown in Exhibits 11 through 17 to answer the questions below.

Your organizing and planning skills focus:

- Provide structure for your own and others' activities.
- Attend to requirements for personnel, facilities, and materials.
- Avoid duplication of effort.
- Use time effectively.

Questions for In-Basket Exercise 3:

1. In the previous section on priorities, you recognized that the THI meeting would need to be held before July 1 since that requirement was given top priority. The meeting will need to be held June 23 or 24 since those are the only days with enough time to prepare for the meeting. What steps must you take to have this meeting next week?

2. The regular bimonthly meeting is scheduled to take place the week after the THI meeting. Your regional manager has suggested that the meeting not be canceled. How can you arrange for the most effective use of the sales reps' time?

3. Now you must notify your sales representatives about the meetings. What will you include in your notification to prepare the sales reps for the sessions they must attend?

4. You have a job vacancy in the area and a possible vacancy coming up if George Brown is promoted. What activities should you plan to alleviate the vacancy problem?

5. You have received a request to miss the bimonthly meeting from Donna Atkinson. Should you take the time from your other activities to reply to Atkinson?

6. Six medical students have been assigned to your area, and they will be arriving in three weeks. What activities will you need to plan in preparation for the students?

IN-BASKET EXERCISE 4: SCHEDULING ACTIVITIES

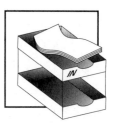

You have determined what meetings you need to have in your area. Now they must be scheduled. You also will need to schedule the medical students who are coming to your area. In this next in-basket exercise, these two scheduling tasks must be accomplished. Schedules for other activities will need to be worked out for the smooth functioning of your unit.

Use Exhibits 18 and 19 and the information from all the preceding exercises to develop the schedules asked for in the following questions.

Your organizing and planning skills focus:

- Identify tasks and objectives.
- Coordinate activities.
- Attend to time requirements.
- Consider human factors.

Questions for In-Basket Exercise 4:

1. You already have scheduled a meeting on THI, along with an area meeting. Now you find that the THI meeting must be rescheduled. This may or may not require rescheduling your area meeting. Below, list the options that you have for scheduling the THI meeting, listing special resource considerations with each.

2. On the abbreviated calendar shown in Exhibit 1, indicate your schedule for the next three weeks. You will need to review all the information presented in the exhibits. Include everything that you would do. First, think about what you need to schedule in the next three weeks. Then write out your schedule for the next three weeks.

3. You know that you must schedule a meeting on THI, an area meeting, medical students, and other activities. List each activity and the specific scheduling tasks each requires.

4. You are going to have six medical students in the area as a resource. Their scheduling is your responsibility. Some information is provided that gives you ideas about how to set up the scheduling. List the constraints or considerations to be made in scheduling so that you will be able to start the task.

IN-BASKET EXERCISE 5: ESTABLISHING SYSTEMS FOR HANDLING INFORMATION

A manager must deal with information from a variety of sources with a number of potential uses. You have just worked through a number of items in the preceding in-basket exercises. If you had been in this situation, you would have had to dispose of each item of information in some logical way. Otherwise, within a month or two, your desk would be covered with an insurmountable mass of paper.

This exercise presents you with one new item of information (Exhibit 20) and then asks you to go back through all the data presented to you and establish a system that will enable you to preserve and retrieve information.

Your organizing and planning skills focus:

- Collect and record information.
- Assure that information is accurate.
- Establish identifiable information files.
- Condense and hold information for future as well as present use.
- Discard information not useful.

Questions for In-Basket Exercise 5:

1. You have been sent a request for information from Fran Lee in personnel records. You will need to send this request on to your sales reps. Rewrite it so that it is simple for them to handle. First, state the purpose. Next, list the information requested so that it will be easy to supply. Include in your memo a due date and any other information you think is required.

2. In the preceding pages of this exercise, you received a number of separate pieces of information. Consider the different ways you might handle this information.

3. Now, go back to the beginning of this section and indicate the important items of information and the classification system that you would use. That is, where or how you would physically place each separate item?

Item of Information   **Classification**

ASSESSING CHANGE

The purpose of this module has been to help you develop and improve your organizing and planning skills through practice and experience. You have been placed in different managerial roles, and have used the types of behaviors that managers need to use when they plan and organize their activities. You have seen that skills in organizing and planning require the following:

- *Clarifying goals and objectives*—As Chris Nelson of Guerin-Fiedler, Inc., you made the goals and objectives of your company and department specific and understandable for yourself and the people you supervise.
- *Establishing priorities*—You had to resolve demands on your own time and on staff time by establishing the order in which your activities would be performed.
- *Developing work strategies*—You worked out methods for handling your tasks as an area sales manager for Guerin-Fiedler.
- *Scheduling activities*—As an area sales manager, you set the sequence and time for the performance of your own activities.
- *Establishing systems for handling information*—Finally, you established ways to identify, store, and retrieve important information.

To assess improvements in your organizing and planning skills, retake the OPPQ. A comparison of your before- and after-practice scores will demonstrate the extent to which you have increased the frequency and appropriateness of your organizing and planning behaviors. When you have retaken this questionnaire, compare your answers with those you gave earlier to see how much you have strengthened your organizing and planning skills.

The Organizing and Planning Process Questionnaire (OPPQ)

Use the following scale to rate the frequency with which you perform the behaviors described in each question. Place the corresponding number (1–7) in the blank space preceding the statement.

Rarely	Irregularly	Occasionally	Usually	Frequently	Almost Always	Consistently
1	2	3	4	5	6	7

_____ 1.   I identify long-range goals and objectives.

_____ 2.   I review the important elements of projects to be undertaken.

_____ 3.   I consider the goals and objectives of my organization or group when setting my own goals and objectives.

_____ 4.   I establish short-term, successive goals and objectives that lead to the attainment of long-range goals and objectives.

_____ 5.   I establish the priority of projects, tasks, or assignments before committing time to their completion.

_____ **6.** I compare projects to determine their urgency before committing time to their completion.

_____ **7.** I compare projects to evaluate the potential outcomes before committing time to their completion.

_____ **8.** I estimate the amount of time required to complete projects before committing time to their completion.

_____ **9.** I organize my activities by dividing long-term, complex projects into smaller, doable activities.

_____ **10.** I establish procedures that will control possible interruptions.

_____ **11.** I complete the important elements of projects before spending time on less essential elements.

_____ **12.** I get information and instructions from knowledgeable sources before starting on an unfamiliar task.

_____ **13.** I make realistic time commitments for working on long-term or complex projects.

_____ **14.** I coordinate activities so that short-term goals and objectives support long-term goals and objectives.

_____ **15.** I establish a schedule of intermediate deadlines that leads to the completion of long-term projects.

_____ **16.** I establish deadlines for the completion of long-term projects.

_____ **17.** I review relevant information before determining a course of action.

_____ **18.** I underline important information in memos or letters, and I make notes on letters and memos indicating other related materials.

_____ **19.** I mark my calendar as a reference when making appointments.

_____ **20.** I group related materials together for easier reference at later dates.

OPPQ Scoring and Evaluation

Follow the scoring directions found on page 268 and in Figure 1. Complete the after-practice assessment column for the OPPQ and compare your before- and after-practice assessment totals. Plot your after-practice scores in Figure 2. In which categories did your scores improve? Think about what has made your progress possible. Perhaps you can apply your insights to categories where your performance has lagged.

The Organizing and Planning Behaviors Choice Questionnaire (OPBC)

The Organizing and Planning Behaviors Choice Questionnaire (OPBC) asks you to identify behaviors that best demonstrate organizing and planning skills. Described on the following pages are ten situations. Following each paragraph is a list of five possible responses. Select the response that demonstrates the greatest degree of organizing and planning skills. Please select only one response.

1. You are a project manager for an industrial construction firm. Work on projects often must be handled independently by different people. However, it must be coordinated so that the various types of work are completed at the same time. Your employees display a wide array of work habits: some always complete their projects on time; others regularly ask for extensions. To plan so that deadlines in your department will be met, you should:

_____ a) Set up a system requiring weekly status reports.

_____ b) Establish a system of rewards for timely completion of projects and penalties for late completions.

_____ c) Before beginning a project, divide it into logical parts, and then establish deadlines for each part.

_____ d) Assign deadlines to employees according to their past performance.

_____ e) Assign people with similar work habits to the same project.

2. You are the manager of a large medical clinic. A new law requires government insurance payment forms to be filed within four days of a patient's visit. This means that doctors must dictate patient charts as soon as possible. In the past, this 15-minute task has taken as long as two weeks to complete because of other demands made on the doctors' time. You will help meet the four-day deadline by:

_____ a) Having the receptionist add 15 minutes to each appointment slot to give doctors time to dictate charts.

_____ b) Setting up a system that keeps track of patient charts so that if they are not dictated by the second day an automatic warning will be sent out.

_____ c) Placing a warning label reminding doctors of the four-day limit on the outside of every patient chart.

_____ d) Having dictaphones placed in examining rooms so that doctors can dictate the chart as soon as the examination is finished.

_____ e) Notifying the doctors of the new law and explaining that failure to comply could result in loss of fees.

3. As district sales manager for a national insurance company, you have been asked to submit a thorough report on sales projections for your area. Since your area has some problems common to a number of other areas, you also have been asked to make an oral presentation of your report to the home office planning board. In this situation you may demonstrate organizing and planning skills by:

_____ a) Copying your report for each member of the board.

_____ b) Preparing posters of the charts and graphs in the report to help clarify and illustrate the information.

_____ c) Preparing a summary of information and copying it to give to each listener.

_____ d) Preparing an outline for your speech.

_____ e)   Asking others to submit questions that are likely to be asked so that you can prepare to answer them.

4.   You are a district manager for Crown-King Products Inc. Crown-King manufactures a wide variety of kitchen gadgets that are sold through department stores. The company is adding a new line of products—pet supplies. These will be sold in pet shops and supermarkets. The present sales force will be increased to handle the new products. All salespersons will represent both the kitchen gadget and pet supply lines. Since each of these lines will have different outlets, sales areas must be restructured. You have been asked to head up a task force to suggest ways of restructuring the sales force in the Southwest. You can best demonstrate organizing and planning skills for this task by:

_____ a)   Establishing a date, time, and place for an initial meeting of the task force, then notifying the members of the agenda of this meeting.

_____ b)   Mailing each task force member a list of department stores, pet shops, and supermarkets for each sales area in the Southwest.

_____ c)   Assigning a member of the task force to draw up suggestions for restructuring prior to the meeting.

_____ d)   Writing to all task force members asking them to submit suggestions for restructuring before you set a meeting date.

_____ e)   Preparing estimates of the potential sales volume in each existing sales area.

5.   You are the manager of Oropesa Wines' champagne processing plant. Two different champagnes are processed at the plant, each on a different line. One step in the processing of champagne is ridding it of its sediment. This requires three specially trained people to keep the line moving at a rate that maintains the required daily quota. If only two people are engaged in this work, the line must slow to three-quarter speed. Beginning next month, you need to keep the lines moving at quota until the end of the year. But when any one of the six people trained for this task is absent, work is necessarily slowed. You would best demonstrate organizing and planning skills by initially:

_____ a)   Setting up a priority system, determining beforehand what line will be slowed in case of absence.

_____ b)   Making a roster of people who are willing to work overtime when the daily quota is not met.

_____ c)   Setting up a bonus system for workers who increase the line's speed.

_____ d)   Setting up a training program for people to learn this specialized work, and making a list of those eligible for training.

_____ e)   Checking to see if you have the resources to set up a training program for people who remove sediment from wine (trainer, equipment, time, etc.).

6.   You are an aircraft maintenance manager for a regional airline at a small Southeastern airport. You have noticed that safety procedures are not

being strictly followed during the de-icing procedure. Your skill in organizing and planning is best demonstrated by:

_____ a) Setting up a planning group to develop a test to determine employees' knowledge of safety procedures.

_____ b) Placing a warning label on all materials involved in de-icing.

_____ c) Both a and b.

_____ d) Posting a warning notice in the work area.

_____ e) Setting up a training session where safety procedures are stressed.

7. You are the manager of a real estate brokerage office. You have noticed that some new associates have difficulty making sales. They spend time calling "For Sale by Owner" newspaper ads and making door-to-door calls, trying to convince people to list their houses with them. The volume of their calls is low since they spend most of their time chatting with the people they contact. You would show organizing and planning skills by:

_____ a) Planning a quota system for all new associates with a minimum number of calls specified for each day or week.

_____ b) Devising a training session for all new associates designed to teach them how to make efficient calls.

_____ c) Devising an assignment system whereby each new associate is assigned to a more experienced associate to observe how he or she dispatches calls and meetings.

_____ d) Having all new associates keep logs of their calls (with duration of the calls and topics discussed noted) and using the logs for individualized training.

_____ e) Both a and c.

8. You are the manager of a rapidly growing catering firm, The Golden Pheasant. You have eight full-time employees and a large number of people who are trained and willing to work parties on call. You use a bakery for specialty items. An area florist supplies flowers for parties. The baker recently has complained that orders are sometimes drastically changed at the last minute, making them impossible to fill without upsetting his entire staff. The florist refused your most recent order because she said there was not enough time to handle it. You would display organizing and planning skills by:

_____ a) Arranging to subcontract some of your orders to another catering firm so your staff will not be overloaded.

_____ b) Setting firm limits on the size of orders that you will take.

_____ c) Asking the baker and florist to let you know their limitations and how much time they need for what type of orders.

_____ d) Carefully determining what is needed for each client and setting firm deadlines beyond which orders cannot be changed.

_____ e) Informing customers that there will be additional charges for order changes after an established cutoff date.

9. You are the plant manager for a men's clothing manufacturer. The company has just begun producing moderately priced suits in addition to sports coats and slacks. The supervisor of the cutting section and the supervisor of the assembly section (where the cut pieces are sewn together) have developed coordination problems because suits are expected to move through the construction process as a whole, but there is no storage space in either section. You would best demonstrate organizing and planning skills by:

_____ a) Working out a coordination plan for the two sections based on your knowledge of the plant.

_____ b) Setting up a meeting immediately with the two supervisors to work on a plan for coordination with them.

_____ c) Having an interior designer look over the area to see if storage space can be created.

_____ d) Clarifying for the supervisors the objectives of their sections.

_____ e) Both c and d.

10. You are an employee of Dumal County who has been promoted from supervisor of a section of seven people to department manager. The department is made up of 37 people. You have always been able to keep appointments and schedules in your head. Now that you have more demands on your time, you will show organizing and planning skills by:

_____ a) Using a notebook to keep track of your activities.

_____ b) Assigning your secretary the task of keeping track of your appointments.

_____ c) Working on methods to improve your memory.

_____ d) Using a calendar to keep track of dates.

_____ e) Developing a color-coded system, using different colored pens for marking appointments and deadlines (red for deadlines, green for meetings).

OPBC Scoring and Evaluation

Complete the OPBC scoring form in Figure 5. Compare your responses with the feedback your instructor will provide about the most appropriate responses for the ten situations.

Question	a	b	c	d	e	Response
1						
2						
3						
4						
5						
6						
7						
8						
9						
10						

FIGURE 5
Organization and Planning Behaviors
Choice Questionnaire (OPBC)
Scoring

SUMMARY

Organizing and planning skills enable managers to consider whole tasks, how tasks may be divided, what is needed to accomplish the tasks, and the arrangement of activities for the most effective results. These critical management skills are necessary to begin an organization, to start up projects, to make major changes, to manage the daily workings of a department, and to manage personal time.

Organizing and planning skills require a manager to demonstrate proficiency in five areas: (1) clarifying goals and objectives, (2) establishing priorities, (3) developing work strategies, (4) scheduling activities, and (5) establishing systems for handling information. In working through this module, you have taken part in exercises that have elicited your own organizing and planning skills. You had the opportunity to clarify goals, establish priorities, develop strategies, schedule work activities, and establish effective ways to handle information. The skill-building exercises at the end of the module will provide further opportunities for you to practice these skills.

Perhaps you are now ready to apply the experience gained in this module to a work situation or a group project in a class or an organization in which you are a

FIGURE 6
Organizing and Planning Skills
Action Guide

You Show Organizing and Planning Skills When You:
- Clarify goals and objectives
- Establish priorities
- Develop work strategies
- Schedule activities
- Establish systems for handling information

You Should Show Organizing and Planning Skills When:
- Goals and objectives must be established
- The setting of priorities is required
- Systematic approaches and methods for work need to be applied
- Multiple tasks and activities require coordination
- Quick and accurate retrieval of information is necessary

member. If so, you may well experience feedback from others about your use of these skills. Feedback from persons with whom you work will keep you informed about how effectively you are using your organizing and planning skills. Ask your manager or instructor to help guide you in the full development of your organizing and planning skills. Remember that successful and competent managers are continually working to improve their organizing and planning skills.

To remember key steps in effective planning and organizing skills and to identify situations in which the skills are needed, use the action guide shown in Figure 6. Frequent review of the information will help you become a better manager.

SKILL-BUILDING EXERCISES

EXERCISE 1 ■ TIME MANAGEMENT

The Time Management Profile below is a short quiz that helps you determine how well you manage your time. Place a T in the space indicated if the statement is mostly true for you. Place an F in the space indicated if the statement is mostly false for you. Be honest! This test will not provide any insight into your current behavior if you do not tell the truth.

_____ 1. I develop step-by-step plans to achieve outcomes.

_____ 2. I establish measurable goals and objectives for myself and, if required, for others.

_____ 3. I establish explicit time frames in which to achieve both short-term and long-term goals and objectives.

_____ 4. I meet the deadlines that have been set for completing specific tasks.

_____ 5. Before beginning a task, I identify the resources required for its completion.

_____ 6. I develop specific work procedures for achieving established goals and objectives.

_____ 7. I rank the importance of activities according to the demands of the situation.

_____ 8. I set up and use a standard system, method, and procedure for handling information.

_____ 9. If I find times during the day when I'm ahead of schedule, I take a break and relax before starting the next scheduled task or activity.

_____ 10. I prepare for meetings, presentations, and discussions by organizing information in a thorough and logical manner.

_____ 11. I complete all easy, routine tasks before beginning or returning to more complex tasks.

_____ 12. I attend to every detail in each project that I undertake.

_____ 13. In scheduling my personal work flow I take account of my own capabilities as well as the requirements of the task.

_____ 14. When returning to a project, I begin exactly where I left off regardless of the difficulty.

_____ 15. I take notes during meetings, presentations, and discussions, outlining important data.

Scoring: Give yourself 1 point for each true and 0 for each false response. Total your score. Scores of 0-5 indicate a severe time-management problem. Scores from 6-10 indicate you are developing some good time-management skills. Scores of 11-15 show superb time-management skills. Keep up the good work!

EXERCISE 2 ■ GOAL-SETTING PRACTICE

Choose a goal for a course you are now taking, a job, or your personal life. Write the goal statement so that it is clear and specific. Develop an implementation plan that includes establishing priorities, developing a work strategy, and scheduling activities to accomplish this goal. Share the results of your plan in a small group or with a partner. How realistic is your goal and plan of implementation?

EXERCISE 3 ■ LEARNING FROM EFFECTIVE MANAGERS

Interview a manager or supervisor you know who appears to be highly organized. Determine which of the behaviors we have presented in this module that person practices regularly. Does the person practice other behaviors that make him or her an effective organizer and planner? Share your interview results with a small group or the class as directed by your instructor.

EXERCISE 4 ■ MONITORING AND LEARNING TO MANAGE YOUR TIME

This exercise will take one week to complete. Create a time log similar to the one shown in Figure 7. Record how you spend each 60-minute block of time. Briefly describe the activity, whether it was required (controlled by someone or something else) or discretionary (under your control), and how productive the activity was using a scale of very productive (5) to very unproductive (1).

After one week, summarize your results and carefully examine how you are spending your discretionary time. Identify ways in which you can make your discretionary time more productive. Develop and begin to implement the use of effective time-management strategies. After four to five weeks of implementation, ask for feedback from a friend, roommate, or family member about your new behaviors, and critically evaluate your time-management skills. How successful have you been? What additional changes and strategies can you use to continue to improve your management of time?

Time	Activity	Required (R) Discretionary (D)	Unproductive/ Productive (1-5)
5:00			
6:00			
7:00			
8:00			
9:00			
10:00			
11:00			
12:00			
1:00			
2:00			
3:00			
4:00			
5:00			
6:00			
7:00			
8:00			
9:00			
10:00			
11:00			
12:00			

FIGURE 7
Daily Time Log

■ Use Exhibits 1–5 with In-Basket Exercise 1,
Exhibits 6–10 with In-Basket Exercise 2,
Exhibits 11–17 with In-Basket Exercise 3,
Exhibits 1, 18–19 with In-Basket Exercise 4,
Exhibits 1-20 with In-Basket Exercise 5.

EXHIBIT 1
Planning Calendars

JUNE

Sunday	Monday	Tuesday	Wednesday	Thursday	Friday	Saturday
			15	16	17	18
19	20	21	22	23	24	25
26	27	28	29	30		

JULY

Sunday	Monday	Tuesday	Wednesday	Thursday	Friday	Saturday
					1	2
3	4	5	6	7	8	9
10	11	12	13	14	15	16

EXHIBIT 2
Guerin-Fiedler Policy Manual

POLICY MANUAL

Guerin-Fiedler has a 23-year-old reputation of outstanding quality and service. We, as a company, are justly proud of this reputation and intend to keep quality and service as the hallmark of Guerin-Fiedler.

This manual has been prepared to provide our managers with guidelines developed by this company with respect to personnel and procedures. Strict adherence to these procedures is required to assure consistency in management.

Recruitment and Hiring:
Every applicant to this company will be considered on his or her ability to do a job. No position will be closed to anyone due to race, religion, gender, or ethnic origin.

Educational Requirements:
The following two departments have minimum educational requirements because of the technical nature of the work.

> *Research:*
> Senior level personnel will have an advanced degree in the physical sciences. Entry level personnel will have a bachelor's degree in the physical sciences and two years experience in a research lab or an advanced degree in the physical sciences.

> *Sales:*
> Senior level personnel will have a bachelor's degree in the physical sciences or minimum of five years experience with the company.

Training:
Entry level personnel will have a bachelor's degree from a recognized university or college, preferably in the physical sciences, and will have completed Training Course SRA.

Vacation:
1st-year employees receive 1 week paid vacation. 2nd year employees receive 2 weeks paid vacation. 8 years or more receive 3 weeks paid vacation.

Educational Leave:
Senior level employees may receive two weeks in addition to vacation time for job-related educational conferences, meetings, and symposia.

Sick Leave:
All employees have five days sick leave each year. This may accrue for up to 3 years and may be exchanged for pay or for vacation time.

Training Updates:
All sales managers will spend two weeks each year at the home office and research center to have their pharmaceutical and administration training updated. The company will reimburse employees for travel expenses incurred at company request.

EXHIBIT 3
Guerin-Fiedler
Brief Job Description
for Area Sales Manager

GUERIN-FIEDLER
BRIEF JOB DESCRIPTION FOR AREA SALES MANAGER

An area sales manager is responsible for all duties related to staffing and managing sales personnel, for seeing that all administrative tasks are carried out for Guerin-Fiedler in his or her assigned area, and for smooth and efficient functioning of the sales area. Specifically these duties include:

Personnel:
- Interview and make final hiring decisions on employees in his or her area.
- Conduct orientation training.
- Assign sales areas.
- Conduct training at bimonthly meetings.
- Conduct informal training as necessary.
- Set sales quotas.
- Monitor work.
- Terminate, if necessary.
- Recommend for training courses.
- In the case of a vacancy in the sales force, the sales manager is responsible for the accounts in that sales area until the vacancy is filled.

Administrative:
- Review weekly report forms of personnel and uses them for biweekly reports.
- Conduct bimonthly one- or two-day meetings for sales representatives.
- Oversee pay and reimbursements for area.

GUERIN-FIEDLER

MEMORANDUM

TO: All Area Sales Managers
FROM: Carter Youngbear, Director of Sales, Guerin-Fiedler
DATE: June 15
RE: New Product, THI

The pending FDA approval, expected before the end of the month, is our go-ahead for detailing THI. As you know, this is the first drug developed for specific treatment of the liver in diagnosed cases of hepatitis.

Time is crucial. Our only competition at the moment in this market is the less specific drug development for treatment of both hepatitis and cirrhosis. We estimate our lead time to be six to eight months.

All area sales managers will set up meetings for their sales reps before July 1 to ensure that they are fully informed on this drug and all its research. Drew Morse from research will be available to conduct these meetings.

We want every sales representative to be fully informed and completely prepared on THI when FDA approval comes.

EXHIBIT 4
Guerin-Fiedler Memorandum

EXHIBIT 5
Guerin-Fiedler Memorandum

GUERIN-FIEDLER

MEMORANDUM

TO: Chris Nelson, Sales Manager, Area S III
FROM: Jay Cavanaugh, Director of Development and Training
DATE: June 1
RE: Medical Student Assignments

As in years past, Guerin-Fiedler has selected 100 outstanding medical students to work as special sales representatives for two months during the summer. Area S III has been selected to receive six of these students. They will arrive in your area, ready for orientation and assignment, Tuesday, July 5.

These students are able to get past a nurse/receptionist and in to see a doctor who has previously been unavailable to our sales reps. This method has not been used to full advantage in the past. We are asking that no more than two students be assigned to a representative at a time and that students be assigned to one rep for July and another for August.

Keep in mind that these students are our future clients and have been selected for their potential leadership in medicine. Their positive attitude toward us will be an asset for this company.

Students assigned to Area S III are:

Allen, Jennifer	Cavera, John
Fuentes, Michael	Katz, Gail
Peterson, Jon	Sung, Harold

GUERIN-FIEDLER

MEMORANDUM

TO: Chris Nelson, Sales Manager, Area S III
FROM: Jake Rose, Director of Personnel
DATE: June 10
RE: George Brown, Training

George Brown, Sales Representative Area S III, has been scheduled for our June 20-24 area sales manager training session. George has passed all the preliminary steps in the process and is being considered along with two other sales representatives for an area manager's vacancy in Montana.

Scheduling for training sessions remains at the option of the area sales managers, but we felt you should know that the three candidates for the job are all slated for the same training-testing session. The hiring regional manager will make final selection based on performance in that session.

EXHIBIT 6
Guerin-Fiedler Memorandum

EXHIBIT 7
Guerin-Fiedler Memorandum

GUERIN-FIEDLER

MEMORANDUM

TO: Chris Nelson, Sales Manager, Area S III
FROM: Jay Cavanaugh, Director of Development and Training
DATE: June 30
RE: Schedule, Drew Morse

The following days are available for Drew Morse to come to your area for the training session on THI:

June 16, 18, 23, and 24.

Please indicate immediately which of these dates you want reserved for your area.

We need to be ready to introduce THI as soon as the FDA gives us the okay. We expect this approval any day.

All sales reps must be trained by July 1. Since Drew must cover all areas, we need to hear from you at once regarding your date selection.

GUERIN-FIEDLER

MEMORANDUM

TO: All Area Managers
FROM: Carter Youngbear, Director of Sales, Guerin-Fiedler
DATE: June 10
RE: HSP

A number of sales reps have been asked by doctors why they should prescribe HSP when the generic digoxin is 58 percent cheaper for their patients, and most patients who use this drug are elderly and on fixed incomes. We would like for them to assure the physicians that the extra money is more than worth the difference in quality in the two drugs.

We maintain the highest quality control standards in the industry, and a doctor can be sure that a patient is getting exactly what is prescribed when that patient takes HSP. Be sure that all your sales reps are aware of this fact, since most of them will be facing this question. I advise bringing it up for discussion at your next area meeting.

EXHIBIT 8
Guerin-Fiedler Memorandum

EXHIBIT 9
Guerin-Fiedler Letter

GUERIN-FIEDLER

Chris Nelson, Sales Manager, Area S III
Charleston, SC

Dear Chris,

I need an answer from you about our new drug HSP. It's come up twice now with Dr. Elkins. I need to call him Tuesday of next week and don't think I can evade him again. He wants to know why he should prescribe HSP for his patients over any generic digoxin since HSP is considerably more expensive.

Please give me some guidance on this. He's been a hard man to see in the past, and I'd hate to lose him now that he's agreed to take the time to see me.

Thanks,

Edwin Strend

Edwin Strend
Sales Representative

P.S. I couldn't get you by phone—they said there was trouble on the line. If you need to call me, I'll be working at home all Monday afternoon.

EXHIBIT 10
Paul Cooke letter

June 16

Chris Nelson,
Sales Manager, Area S III
Guerin-Fiedler
Charleston, S.C.

Dear Chris,

I appreciate your coming for an on-job training session with me next week when I make some calls. You had indicated the 23rd or 24th would be good days for you, so I set up some firm appointments with three of the physicians that I have had the most trouble getting to listen to me on the 23rd. I am really eager to find out what is wrong in my approach with them.

Thanks,

Paul Cooke

Paul Cooke

EXHIBIT 11
The Plymouth Hotel Letter

THE PLYMOUTH HOTEL
CHARLESTON

Chris Nelson, Sales Manager, Area S III
Guerin-Fiedler

Dear Chris,

The bimonthly meeting that you have regularly scheduled for the 4th
Monday and Tuesday of each month for our Yorktown Room will need to
be changed since the Yorktown Room will be used by a major corporation
that is holding a series of meetings in June. We have reserved the
Mayflower Room for you instead. It will hold a meeting of fifteen people
very comfortably. If you need a projector this month, please notify us three
days in advance of the meeting.

I am sure the accommodations in the Mayflower Room will please you. If I
do not hear from you I will assume that this arrangement is satisfactory.

Sincerely,

Gina Sadiq

Catering
The Plymouth Hotel
Charleston

P.S. If you need the larger room, it will be available anytime after July 1.

GUERIN-FIEDLER

MEMORANDUM

TO: Chris Nelson, Sales Manager, Area S III
FROM: Drew Morse
DATE: June 15
RE: THI Meeting Preparation

In preparation for the meeting I will be conducting, please have available slide projector, flip chart, or large chalkboard. Sales reps will all need to take notes even though I will be giving handouts. Please advise them to come prepared.

EXHIBIT 12
Guerin-Fiedler Memorandum

GUERIN-FIEDLER

MEMORANDUM

TO: Chris Nelson, Sales Manager, Area S III
FROM: Pat Ryan, Regional Manager
DATE: June 7
RE: Bimonthly Meeting

Now that everything seems to be aimed at THI's introduction to the market, I want to remind you of the importance of this month's area meetings. We have some information on drugs and some price change information that sales reps need to clearly understand. Also, the new weekly schedule forms require explanation.

Since July 1 is the date when all these changes go into effect, you cannot afford to wait until July. We have found that the two-day meeting normally held can be reduced to one day if everyone is prepared for one, very long day.

EXHIBIT 13
Guerin-Fiedler Memorandum

EXHIBIT 14
Guerin-Fiedler Memorandum

GUERIN-FIEDLER

MEMORANDUM

TO: Chris Nelson, Sales Manager, Area S III
FROM: Pat Ryan, Regional Manager
DATE: June
RE: Bimonthly Meeting

I think we have found the right person to fill the vacancy in your area. Sandy Markham is a microbiology major with three years experience in a hospital lab. She is eager to get into sales and is both knowledgeable and personable.

Sandy is returning next week to Richmond and will be available for a joint interview with the two of us any day next week. Let me know and I'll set it up.

In the future, if you foresee any vacancies, let me know. We need as much lead time as possible to find really high caliber people.

GUERIN-FIEDLER

MEMORANDUM

TO: Chris Nelson, Sales Manager, Area S III
FROM: Fred Mason, Sales Representative
DATE: June 3
RE: Student Assignments

I would like to formally state a complaint about medical student assignments. I spent this summer with four students, and I cannot see an advantage for any sales reps in such a situation. Making arrangements for their lodging most nights on the road was a headache. Since much of the area I travel through is mountainous and the few motels fill up rapidly in the summer, finding one with three rooms vacant can be a real chore. There are some physicians that I have a hard time seeing, but when I show up with four other people, it becomes impossible.

In the future, I would appreciate not being considered for the dubious honor of looking after students.

EXHIBIT 15
Guerin-Fiedler Memorandum

EXHIBIT 16
Letter from Donna Atkinson

June 14

Chris Nelson, Sales Manager, Area S III
Guerin-Fiedler
Charleston, S.C.

Dear Chris,

I'd like to have your permission to miss this month's district meeting June 27 and 28.

I managed to set up an appointment at the Walker Clinic in Toueville to talk to the monthly physicians meeting. There are 10 doctors in the group, and it's a real break, as you know, to get so many at once. At any rate, that's on the night of the 27th.

Since it's a four-hour drive to district for me, it's really difficult to make either day. By the way, I've tried calling, but your phone's been down. What an inconvenience that must be to you!

Sincerely,

Donna Atkinson
Sales Representative

GUERIN-FIEDLER

MEMORANDUM

TO: Chris Nelson, Sales Manager, Area S III
FROM: Pat Ryan, Regional Manager
DATE: June 3
RE: Medical Student Assignments

Your area is receiving some medical students this summer. Properly assigned, they are a great resource that is not charged to your area. They need orientation to your particular area and judicious assignments.

As you know, you do have the authority to refuse these students. If you feel they will disrupt your area, you must notify me immediately and Cavanaugh in Training by June 17.

EXHIBIT 17
Guerin-Fiedler Memorandum

GUERIN-FIEDLER

MEMORANDUM

TO: Chris Nelson, Sales Manager, Area S III
FROM: Drew Morse
DATE: June 15
RE: Schedule Change, THI Meeting

A small snag in the FDA review process on THI necessitates my being in Washington, D.C., on the date I had set to come to your area. Since FDA approval is delayed approximately two weeks, my meeting with your sales reps can take place early in July and still precede the release of the drug. At present, the dates that I could come to your area are:

     June 30
     July 5
     July 7
     July 11

Please contact my office as soon as possible regarding this date.

EXHIBIT 18
Guerin-Fiedler Memorandum

EXHIBIT 19
Sales Rep Information
Area S III

SALES REP INFORMATION, AREA S III

Sales reps assigned to Chris Nelson, Sales Manager, Area S III:

Atkinson, Donna	Brown, George
Caruthers, Alfonso	Cooke, Paul
Dietrich, Carl	Mason, Fred
Novis, Jane	Orwin, Richard
Peel, Martina	Robinson, Paula
Strend, Edwin	Ali, Catherine

Outstanding Performance January – March

Brown	Caruthers
Novis	Peel
Ali	

Sales reps needing further training:

Cooke	Mason
Robinson	

EXHIBIT 20
Guerin-Fiedler Memorandum

GUERIN-FIEDLER

MEMORANDUM

TO: All Area Managers
FROM: Fran Lee, Personnel Records
DATE: June 8
RE: Personnel Information Update

We are updating our files for the new employee insurance coverage. Please send us the following information on all your personnel: birth date, height, weight, number of miles driven per week, age of car, number of children, and educational degrees.

We must have this information as soon as possible. Please note that this will need to be repeated every six months.

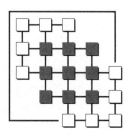

MODULE 7
DECISION-MAKING SKILLS: REACHING CONCLUSIONS

INTRODUCTION

Consider all the decisions necessary to carry out the goals of a major effort—from launching a space satellite to producing and marketing a new line of automobiles. Some decisions can have a major impact on people and work. Other decisions may be more routine yet still require that managers select an appropriate course of action.

Decision making is the process through which managers identify problems and attempt to resolve them. All managers are called upon to make decisions, although the kinds of decisions they must make vary with their level of authority and type of assignment. In fact, a manager's responsibility as a decision maker is very important. Poor decisions can be disastrous to a department or even an organization. Good decisions keep work flowing and enable the organization to achieve its goals.

Skill as a decision maker is a distinguishing characteristic of most successful managers. Managers may not *always* make the right decision, but they can use their knowledge of appropriate decision-making processes to increase their odds of success. And while managers are not necessarily born with good decision-making skills, there are ways they can learn to maximize decision-making capabilities.

Decision-making skills can be identified by observable and measurable behaviors. We are going to examine five categories of decision-making behaviors: (1) identifying problems; (2) generating alternatives; (3) evaluating alternatives; (4) reaching decisions; and (5) choosing implementation strategies.

The purpose of this module is to introduce concepts that can help you more fully understand the demands of managerial decision making. The module presents a variety of situations that are typical of many managers' experiences. In these situations you are asked to assume the role of manager and make decisions. By participating in these situations, you will have an opportunity to learn and practice decision-making skills.

319

The module is organized so that you will develop a before-practice assessment of your decision-making skills by completing the Decision-Making Process Questionnaire (DMPQ). This questionnaire assessment instrument will measure your skills at the present time. We then present an overview of decision making. Next, through in-basket exercises, you will have an opportunity to practice these skills. Feedback from your instructor will help you judge the quality of your own responses and provide guidance on improving specific behaviors.

After a review and summary, you will retake the DMPQ and compare your after-practice assessment results with your earlier results. You will also complete the Dozen Decisions Questionnaire (DDQ). This is another assessment instrument that examines how you actually behave in situations where decision-making skills are needed. It will give you more insight into your behaviors in situations requiring decision-making skills.

ASSESSING DECISION-MAKING SKILLS

Complete the DMPQ on the following pages before proceeding with the rest of the module. It is both a teaching tool and a means of evaluating your present decision-making skills level. Take time to complete the instrument carefully. Your answers should reflect your behaviors as they are now, not as you would like them to be. Be honest. This instrument is designed to help you discover where you are now so you can work to improve your decision-making skills.

The Decision-Making Process Questionnaire (DMPQ)

The Decision-Making Process Questionnaire (DMPQ) evaluates your current decision-making behaviors. It asks you to rate yourself according to the frequency of your behaviors in five categories that comprise decision-making skills. These behaviors are part of most managerial experiences, but you will find that the questions are applicable to your own experience even if you are not yet a manager. If you do not have experience in a management level position, consider a group you have worked with either in the classroom or in an organization such as a fraternity, sorority, club, church, or service group.

Use the following scale to rate the frequency with which you perform the behaviors described in each question. Place the corresponding number (1–7) in the blank preceding the statement.

Rarely	Irregularly	Occasionally	Usually	Frequently	Almost Always	Consistently
1	2	3	4	5	6	7

_____ **1.** I review data about the performance of my work and/or my group's work.

_____ **2.** I seek outside information, such as articles in business magazines and newspapers, to help me evaluate my performance.

_____ 3. When examining data, I allow sufficient time to identify problems.

_____ 4. Based on the data, I identify problem areas needing action.

_____ 5. To generate alternative solutions, I review problems from different perspectives.

_____ 6. I list many possible ways of reaching a solution for an identified problem.

_____ 7. I research methods that have been used to solve similar problems.

_____ 8. When generating alternative courses of action, I seek the opinions of others.

_____ 9. I explicitly state the criteria I will use for judging alternative courses of action.

_____ 10. I list both positive and negative aspects of alternative decisions.

_____ 11. I consider how possible decisions could affect others.

_____ 12. For each alternative, I estimate the probabilities of its possible outcomes.

_____ 13. I study information about problems that require my decisions.

_____ 14. I determine if I need additional data in light of my objectives and the urgency of the situation.

_____ 15. To reach a decision, I rely on my judgment and experience as well as on the available data.

_____ 16. I support my choices with facts.

_____ 17. Before finally accepting a decision, I evaluate possible ways to implement it.

_____ 18. I choose the simplest and least costly methods of putting my decisions into effect.

_____ 19. I select resources and state time frames as part of my implementation strategy.

_____ 20. I choose implementation strategies that help achieve my objectives.

DMPQ Scoring

The scoring sheet in Figure 1 summarizes your responses for the DMPQ. It will help you identify your existing strengths and pinpoint areas that need improvement. Right now, fill in the before-practice assessment column and add the five category scores to obtain a total score. Enter that total score in the space indicated. After completing the module, you will take the DMPQ again and fill in the after-practice assessment column.

DMPQ Evaluation

Figure 2 shows score lines for your total score and for each individual category measured on the DMPQ. Each line shows a continuum from the lowest score to the highest. Place a B (before-practice) where your personal score falls on each of

FIGURE 1
Decision-Making Process
Questionnaire (DMPQ) Scoring

Skill Area	Items	Assessment	
		Before Practice	After Practice
Identifying problems	1,2,3,4		
Generating alternatives	5,6,7,8		
Evaluating alternatives	9,10,11,12		
Reaching decisions	13,14,15,16		
Choosing implementation strategies	17,18,19,20		
TOTAL SCORE			

these lines. The score lines in Figure 2 show graphically where you stand with regard to five decision-making behaviors. If you have been honest with yourself, you now have a better idea of your relative strengths and weaknesses in the categories of behavior that make up decision making.

Learning to Use the DMPQ Skills

You have completed the initial evaluation of your decision-making skills. In the DMPQ, you rated the frequency with which you demonstrate behaviors in the five categories of decision making. This questionnaire provides a baseline against which you will assess improvements that have taken place after you have completed this module.

Before moving on, think about what you have learned in this questionnaire. What areas of your decision-making skills are weakest? These will require the most attention during the remainder of the module. What areas are your strongest? Use this module to fine-tune these areas so that you may take full advantage of them. In areas where you already perform well, learning some new things can lead to even greater performance.

The DMPQ will help you identify decision-making behaviors that are appropriate for both management and personal situations described in this module. After you have completed the module and have had an opportunity to put into practice what you have learned, retake the DMPQ. Then, compare your after-practice scores with your before-practice scores. This comparison will show you where you have progressed and where further work is needed.

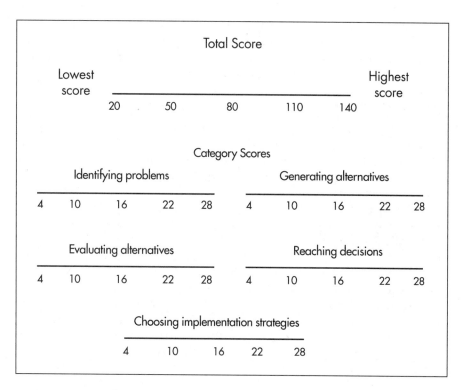

FIGURE 2
Decision-Making Process
Questionnaire (DMPQ) Evaluation

UNDERSTANDING DECISION MAKING

Decision making is a vital managerial skill that can be time-consuming and stressful. While the kinds of decisions required vary with the manager's level of authority and type of assignment, all managers must make some decisions. A manager's responsibility as a decision maker is very important. If he or she makes a wrong decision, or one that does not maximize opportunities, the results can be disastrous.

Most managers try to make decisions about problems as quickly as possible. The natural tendency is to select the first solution that comes to mind. However, in many cases the first solution is not the best one. Many managers implement solutions that marginally satisfy the problems at hand instead of choosing the best solution.

Take a moment now and think about decisions you have made, either at work or in your personal life, that you now consider ineffective. Without dwelling on them too long, ask yourself: What could I have done differently? Could I have paid closer attention to the factors involved, or the information I had? Did I look for all the information I needed, or did I just seek the minimum amount? Should I have sought other alternatives or consulted other sources?

For the manager, decision making involves the ability to demonstrate skills in five areas: (1) identifying problems; (2) generating alternatives; (3) evaluating alternatives; (4) reaching decisions; and (5) choosing implementation strategies. In the next section, we are going to examine these five categories of behavior.

Identifying Problems

The first category of decision-making skills is to identify problems. Managers should regularly review data about their department or area of responsibility, including outside information and reports and information from within the organization. Discrepancies between actual and desired conditions alert managers to potential problems.

Identifying problems is not an easy task when you consider the role human behavior plays in organizations. A problem may be deeply rooted in one individual's past experience, in the complexity of the organization, or in some combination of individual and organizational factors. Managers must be sure to identify problems as accurately as possible.

To identify problems accurately, managers need accurate and reliable information. Inaccurate or incomplete information can waste time and lead a manager to miss the underlying causes of a problem. Keep in mind that even if quality information is collected, managers may misinterpret it, or some factor beyond the manager's control may affect problem identification.

One technique that you may use to assist you in problem identification is to break down the problem into a series of smaller steps that lead to a resolution. These steps can be stated as a series of "yes" or "no" questions. Consider choices that, in your judgment, move you closer to your goal. Reject choices that you feel move you away from your goal.

The first question should focus on the goal. Once you have determined your goal, a series of questions may be generated. These questions will outline the various steps that you must take or the various conditions that you must meet to reach your goal. For example, later in the module, you will examine data on sales volume for Galaxie Vacuum Cleaners, Inc. The data presented indicates that sales volume will very likely decline in the future. Since your goal is increased volume this is identified as a problem. The primary question in this example involves how to treat the problem. To lead you to solve the problem, you could ask yourself: "Should dollar sales volume be increased?" This is a simple question answered by either "Yes" or "No." The answer will establish the target of the decision. You would then formulate a series of other questions that deal with the conditions needed to achieve your goal.

Generating Alternatives

Once a problem has been identified correctly, a manager should generate various ways to solve the problem. First, the manager must identify what goal he or she is trying to achieve. Then the manager can think of several alternatives for solving the problem that will achieve the goal.

In actual on-the-job situations, many resources are available to help the manager generate alternatives, for example, company data, pertinent publications, and personal experience. Managers may rely on their training, experience, education, and knowledge of the situation to generate alternatives. Another valuable means of generating alternatives is to draw on ideas solicited from other company employees such as superiors, colleagues, subordinates, and groups within the organization. They may offer valuable approaches and perspectives.

A common problem in managerial decision making is that alternatives are evaluated one at a time as they are proposed, so the first acceptable (although frequently not optimal) alternative is chosen. Consider the following attributes of good alternative generation:

- The evaluation of each proposed alternative is postponed.
- Alternatives are proposed by all individuals involved in the problem.
- Alternative solutions are consistent with organizational goals or policies.
- Alternatives take into consideration both the short-term and the long-term consequences.
- Alternatives build on one another.
- Alternatives solve the problem that has been defined.

Several alternative solutions should be generated before any of them are evaluated. Do not be too quick to focus in on the first solution that comes to mind.

Evaluating Alternatives

Once alternatives are generated, you must carefully assess each alternative. Which solution will be the best? Fundamental to this process is the ability to assess the relative advantages and disadvantages of each alternative under consideration. Predetermined criteria such as the anticipated costs, benefits, uncertainties, and risks of the alternative may be used in the evaluation process. The result of the evaluation should be a ranking of the alternatives.

Reaching Decisions

Considering and selecting an alternative would seem to be a straightforward proposition—simply look at all the alternatives and select the one that best solves the problem. In reality, the choice is rarely clear-cut. The best decisions are those that are based on a careful examination of the facts. This means that judgment is needed in interpreting the information at hand and in determining whether sufficient information is available to reach a decision.

Choosing Implementation Strategies

The bridge between reaching a decision and evaluating the results is the implementation phase of decision making. When decisions involve taking action or making changes, choosing ways to put these actions or changes into effect becomes an essential managerial task.

The keys to effective implementation are sensitivity to those who will be affected by the decision and proper planning. Those who implement the decision must understand the choice and why it was made. They also must be motivated and committed to its successful implementation. This can be done by involving employees in the early stages of the process.

The strategies that are used to implement decisions can seriously affect the decisions themselves, altering their costs, their acceptance by others in the organization, their time requirements, and their success in accomplishing their objectives.

Decision-Making Skills and Their Relationships to Other Managerial Skills

All managerial skills are interwoven to some degree. Decision making is most closely connected to the skills of perception, organizing and planning, and decisiveness.

Decision making involves perceiving a set of facts or data and analyzing their meaning, as well as reaching a conclusion, which is really the essence of decision making. The skill of perception is used in the other phases of decision making as well. It is fair to say that decision making is grounded in the ability to critically analyze facts. Thus, the more skilled the manager is in perception, the more skilled he or she is likely to be in decision making.

Decision making is also related to decisiveness or the ability to take action. The manager who has followed the steps of the decision-making process, even to the point of developing implementation strategies, may not always be skilled at putting into effect decisions he or she has made. Decisiveness must accompany decision-making skills if the manager is to act on the decisions he or she has made. All of these skills combine with decision making for effective management.

PRACTICING DECISION MAKING

Decision-making skills consist of the following component behaviors:

- *Identifying problems*—The specific area requiring action must be identified based on examination of information and data.
- *Generating alternatives*—A decision always involves a choice among possible courses of action. Skill in the decision-making process requires developing alternative ways of dealing with issues.
- *Evaluating alternatives*—A skilled decision maker weighs possible courses of action according to explicitly stated criteria.
- *Reaching decisions*—The skilled manager chooses one course of action based on carefully evaluated data and his or her authority. Careful judgment is required here.
- *Choosing implementation strategies*—This is the final step in decision making. Managerial skill is demonstrated by selecting strategies that best accomplish the objectives of the decision.

The next section of in-basket exercises focuses on each component of decision making. Each exercise is followed by questions that direct your attention to the appropriate behaviors.

Before you begin the exercises, take time to review your scores on the five parts of the DMPQ that you completed earlier. Then, as you work to complete the exercises, keep in mind the behaviors noted in this questionnaire. The questions in the DMPQ deepen your understanding of basic decision-making considerations.

In-Basket Exercise 1: Identifying Problems

The manager skilled in decision making regularly reviews information relating to his or her area of responsibility, including outside data and reports as well as information from within the company. This kind of review will help the manager identify problems and the decisions that are required to resolve them.

Situation:

You are Jesse Walters, the new marketing manager for Galaxie Vacuum Cleaners, Inc. Your principal duty is developing marketing strategies for Galaxie products. Your task at the moment is to examine sales data to help you evaluate previous marketing strategies. In your review of the information, you should identify possible problems.

On your desk are the materials shown in Exhibits 1 through 4 that relate to the sales of Galaxie products. Read these, and then answer the questions that follow.

Your decision-making skills focus:

- Compare data on company performance with that of other firms in the industry that may help you pinpoint areas requiring decisions.
- Examine the data to spot changes over time that may reveal problems requiring action.
- Gather accurate and reliable information.
- Carefully interpret the information.

Questions for In-Basket Exercise 1:

1. Examine each item in Exhibits 1 through 4. For each exhibit, summarize what information is important for marketing.

2. What can you infer about existing marketing strategies based on an examination of the data?

3. What problems for Galaxie are indicated in the data?

4. What decisions will have to be made about the problems indicated in the data?

In-Basket Exercise 2: Generating Alternatives

Generating various ways to solve problems to achieve objectives is part of decision making. In this step, the manager must rely heavily on his or her experience and expertise. However, researching ways in which similar problems have been handled and seeking other people's advice will help the manager generate alternatives. The manager should bear in mind the limits of his or her decision-making authority.

The situation below provides you with an opportunity to generate alternative solutions to a problem.

Situation:

You are Tony Mark, production manager for Competitive Computers, Inc., a manufacturing firm that specializes in the production of parts for electronic instruments. You are now working on a project for Platheon, Inc., a major supplier of high-tech products. It is December. You are about halfway to completion dates for the Platheon contract. A major problem has arisen in supervisor–employee relations. As a result, production is down and employee turnover is up.

Exhibits 5 through 9 provide information about the problem. Examine the materials carefully. These will help you generate possible ways to solve the problem.

Your decision-making skills focus:

- State the goals and objectives to be achieved.
- View the problem from varying perspectives.
- Seek others' opinions and inputs.
- Generate several varied alternatives.
- Consult with those directly involved in the problem.

Questions for In-Basket Exercise 2:

1. What specific goals should you, Tony Mark, production manager at Competitive Computers, Inc., consider in generating alternative solutions to the problems with employees and supervisors on the Platheon contract?

2. List three possible approaches to the problems with employees working on the Platheon contract.

3. What could you do to help produce additional alternatives?

4. When generating alternatives, how would you handle limits on your authority as production manager?

5. Review your answers to all of the preceding questions. Then list five specific steps that could be taken to alleviate the Platheon problems.

In-Basket Exercise 3: Evaluating Alternatives

The manager who is skilled in decision making evaluates possible courses of action methodically, noting all probable consequences of each alternative. The manager must consider financial burdens and the impact of alternatives on others.

When evaluating alternatives, it is helpful to list the advantages and disadvantages of each one, keeping in mind your goals and objectives. As a manager, you will derive these goals from the goals of your company and your division. The questions that follow lead you through this process.

Situation:

You are Dahabo Halsey, sales manager for Marathon Hosiery Manufacturers, Inc. Marathon produces medium-priced pantyhose that are marketed in drugstores, convenience stores, and supermarkets.

Recently, Marathon purchased a plant that manufactures women's cosmetics. Plans are to distribute these to the outlets that carry Marathon Hosiery. You must choose between using the same sales force for both cosmetics and hosiery, or acquiring a new and separate sales force for the cosmetics line. Salespersons write orders, deliver merchandise, stock shelves, and arrange displays.

A file on your desk contains the information shown in Exhibits 10 through 14 that may influence your choice in this matter. This information will guide you in evaluating the alternatives you face. After you examine this material, respond to the questions that follow.

Your decision-making skills focus:

- State criteria you will use in your evaluation.
- Determine the value of each alternative.
- Assess the advantages and disadvantages of each alternative.
- Consider specific drawbacks of each possible action.
- Note the impact of each alternative on company goals as well as on goals of your own division.

Questions for In-Basket Exercise 3:

1. In a memo to you, the president of Marathon specified some goals for your sales division. What are they?

2. Considering these goals, what are some general criteria by which you may judge possible decisions with respect to sales?

3. Now, bearing these criteria in mind, what are the advantages of using the existing sales force to sell both hosiery and cosmetics? What are the disadvantages?

4. What are the advantages of selecting a new and separate sales force for the cosmetic line?

5. What are the disadvantages of selecting a new and separate sales force for the cosmetic line?

6. The president of Marathon has informed you that it is the company's goal to recover the cost of investment in the Mountaindale plant in three years. Will this affect your evaluation of the alternatives? Explain.

IN-BASKET EXERCISE 4: REACHING DECISIONS

The best decisions are those that are based on a careful examination of the facts. Of course, judgment is needed in interpreting the information at hand and in determining whether there is sufficient data for reaching decisions.

Situation:

You are Leslie Goff, site location manager for Better Bookstores, Inc. Better Bookstores is a rapidly expanding retail chain. Today is March 15. You are trying to find suitable locations for new stores. Use the information shown in Exhibits 15 through 19 to help you reach decisions about site locations. Examine the data carefully. Then, respond to the questions that follow. These questions will help you reach decisions through analysis of relevant information.

Your decision-making skills focus:

- Base your judgments on the facts.
- Carefully examine all the information.
- Determine whether sufficient information is available.
- Select the best choice.

Questions for In-Basket Exercise 4:

1. What specific objectives should you, Leslie Goff, keep in mind as you look for data that will help you reach a decision about site recommendations?

2. You have been directed to locate sites for new stores. You are looking for areas that meet the guidelines noted by Janetta Russell (Exhibit 15). What information about these guidelines is contained in the data you have just reviewed?

3. Using the data available to you, reach a decision about bookstore locations.

4. What information (not in your file) could influence your decision about site locations?

5. Considering that today is March 15 and your report is due by the end of March, should you delay your final decision until you get information on real estate, rental, and shipping costs? Explain.

In-Basket Exercise 5: Choosing Implementation Strategies

When decisions involve taking action or making changes, choosing ways to put these actions or changes into effect is an essential part of the decision-making process. The strategies that are used to implement decisions can seriously affect the decisions themselves, affecting their costs, their acceptance by others in the organization, their time requirements, and their success in accomplishing objectives.

Situation:

You are to assume the role of Mickey Larsen, sales manager for Manatee Typewriters, Inc. Some time ago, Manatee secured the rights to a new type of computer/printer. After careful consideration, a decision was made to manufacture and market this under the name of COMPUPRINTER.

The task of product promotion has been assigned to the marketing department, which has planned an extensive campaign that will begin shortly. Sales are your department's responsibility. A decision has been made to push sales aggressively during the first six months of the year in order to maximize market penetration during this introductory period. It is your job to implement this directive. You are considering several possible implementation strategies.

Today is December 15. On your desk is a file of information (shown in Exhibits 20 through 23). Study the file, and then answer the questions that follow. These questions will give you guided experience in choosing implementation strategies.

Your decision-making skills focus:

- Clearly identify the decision you are to implement.
- Establish guidelines.
- Be aware of how your implementation strategies will affect other parts of your organization and vice versa.
- Choose the strategy that appears to have the highest probability of successfully implementing the target decision.
- Assign responsibility.
- Plan properly.

Questions for In-Basket Exercise 5:

1. While many decisions have been made in connection with the COMPUPRINTER, one is specifically your concern, and you must find ways to implement it. Which decision is that?

2. You are considering possible ways to make your sales campaign successful. You have listed these in your memo of December 1. Two methods provide special inducements to the customer, and one grants incentives to the sales force. What are some guidelines that would help you choose your strategy?

3. What information about the marketing and service departments should you take into account in developing your strategy?

4. Choose a sales strategy. Support your choice.

ASSESSING CHANGE

The purpose of this module has been to help you develop your decision-making skills through in-basket exercises. Your attention has been focused on the different behaviors that make up decision-making skills. You have seen that decision-making skills involve:

- *Identifying problems*—As Jesse Walters, your task was to examine sales data to help you evaluate previous marketing strategies. In your review of the data, you were asked to identify possible problem areas in which you had to take some action.
- *Generating alternatives*—As Tony Mark, production manager for Competitive Computers, Inc., you were working on a project for Platheon, Inc. and a major problem arose in supervisor–employee relations. You were asked to examine the materials carefully and develop alternative ways of dealing with the problem.
- *Evaluating alternatives*—In the role of Dahabo Halsey, sales manager for Marathon Hosiery Manufacturers, Inc., you examined the materials on your desk and systematically evaluated the alternative solutions to a problem.
- *Reaching decisions*—As Leslie Goff, site location manager for Better Bookstores, Inc., you were facing a decision involving finding suitable locations for the expanding retail chain. You made your decision based on careful examination of the information provided about site locations.
- *Choosing implementation strategies*—In the role of Mickey Larsen, sales manager for Manatee Typewriters, Inc., you were asked to choose from among several strategies to implement a decision.

At the beginning of this module, you completed the DMPQ to provide a baseline against which you could measure improvements in your decision-making skills. Now it is time to assess some of these improvements.

First, retake the DMPQ. When you have completed it, compare your answers with those you gave earlier to see how much you have strengthened your decision-making skills.

The Decision-Making Process Questionnaire (DMPQ)

Use the following scale to rate the frequency with which you perform the behaviors described in each question. Place the corresponding number (1–7) in the blank preceding the statement.

Rarely	Irregularly	Occasionally	Usually	Frequently	Almost Always	Consistently
1	2	3	4	5	6	7

_____ **1.** I review data about the performance of my work and/or my group's work.

_____ 2. I seek outside information, such as articles in business magazines and newspapers, to help me evaluate my performance.

_____ 3. When examining data, I allow sufficient time to identify problems.

_____ 4. Based on the data, I identify problems areas needing action.

_____ 5. To generate alternative solutions, I review problems from different perspectives.

_____ 6. I list many possible ways of reaching a solution for an identified problem.

_____ 7. I research methods that have been used to solve similar problems.

_____ 8. When generating alternative courses of action, I seek the opinions of others.

_____ 9. I explicitly state the criteria I will use for judging alternative courses of action.

_____ 10. I list both positive and negative aspects of alternative decisions.

_____ 11. I consider how possible decisions could affect others.

_____ 12. For each alternative, I estimate the probabilities of its possible outcomes.

_____ 13. I study information about problems that require my decisions.

_____ 14. I determine if I need additional data in light of my objectives and the urgency of the situation.

_____ 15. To reach a decision, I rely on my judgment and experience as well as on the available data.

_____ 16. I support my choices with facts.

_____ 17. Before finally accepting a decision, I evaluate possible ways to implement it.

_____ 18. I choose the simplest and least costly methods of putting my decisions into effect.

_____ 19. I select resources and state time frames as part of my implementation strategy.

_____ 20. I choose implementation strategies that help achieve my objectives.

DMPQ Scoring and Evaluation

Follow the scoring directions found on page 321 and in Figure 1. Complete the after-practice assessment column for the DMPQ and compare your before- and after-practice assessment totals. Plot your after-practice scores in Figure 2. In which categories did your scores improve? Think about what has made your progress possible. Perhaps you can apply your insights to categories where your performance has lagged.

The Dozen Decisions Questionnaire (DDQ)

A second method to assess change in your decision-making skills is through the Dozen Decisions Questionnaire (DDQ). In the DDQ, you review twelve decisions made by other managers. In the space provided, you indicate whether you agree or disagree with each decision. Your answers will give you more insight into your behaviors in situations requiring decision-making skills. Your instructor will review your answers with those of your classmates and compare these with the responses and explanations given by a panel of management consultants.

1. Morrie Janow manages the service department of the Westport Air Conditioning Company. Westport services both home and commercial establishments on an annual contract basis. A major selling point for Westport has been the guarantee of seven-day, round-the-clock service for its contract customers. Although a premium is charged for nighttime and weekend service, the company barely breaks even on these calls. Recently, Westport was asked to join a pool of area air-conditioning companies that would rotate responsibility for off-hours service. The decision is left to Janow. He decides not to join. Do you agree or disagree with Janow's decision?

   Agree _____   Disagree _____

2. The Pet Plant and Flower Shop is a small retail flower shop managed by Sim Carrington. Most of its business is conducted via telephone with nearby residents, who are predominantly young artists, musicians, and writers. Currently the shop features flowers and plants. Carrington is considering adding a line of books on horticulture and plant psychology that market surveys indicate appeal to impulse buyers. He decides to add the book line. Do you agree or disagree with Carrington?

   Agree _____   Disagree _____

3. Bonheure Stores, Inc., operates twenty small convenience-type stores that limit their inventory to a select line of high-priced gourmet foods and wines. Purchases are made through a central purchasing office. A market survey has indicated that sales at the Seasquare store, located near Greerly University, would increase by 10 percent if a lower-priced food line were added to the stock. Lisle Ianello, manager of the Seasquare Store, has been asked to make a recommendation. She recommends that the Seasquare store stay with the current luxury line. Do you agree or disagree with Ianello's recommendation?

   Agree _____   Disagree _____

4. Cole Northern is sales manager for Condor Office Supplies, Inc., located in downtown Danford. Recently, many new business and professional offices have located in suburban Danford. Northern is considering the following ways to solicit business from these new firms: a) a mail-out followed by a personal sales visit, b) an ad in the *Danford Leader*, a local

weekly newspaper, and c) an ad in the business section of the *Daily Tribune*, a newspaper with statewide circulation. Northern decides to advertise in the *Tribune*. Do you agree or disagree with his decision?

Agree _____   Disagree _____

5. Due to competing products, Saber Safety Pin Company finds that its sales volume has declined over a period of years. Currently sales appear to have stabilized, with Saber appealing to a corps of conservative customers who prefer the old-fashioned safety pin to other types of fasteners. George Peck is the new manager of the Sales and Merchandising Division of Saber. Recently, he conducted a brainstorming session with the staff in his division. Its purpose was to generate suggestions for new uses for the safety pin with the goal of expanding sales. The following nontraditional uses were suggested: a) as a device for fastening papers together (like a paper clip); b) as a decorative pin with punk appeal; and c) as a speedy hem repairer and button replacer. After reviewing these ideas, Peck decided to reject them. Do you agree or disagree with his decision?

Agree _____   Disagree _____

6. Kim Tucker has been submitting vouchers for reimbursement of travel expenses without supporting receipts. Upon review, Ron Barrington, sales manager for Caltrol Suppliers, finds that compared to vouchers submitted by other members of the sales staff, some of Kim's vouchers appear to be overstated and others appear to be understated. On balance, however, the amounts claimed by Kim are in line. Barrington is not quite sure how to handle the situation and is considering the following alternatives: a) Warn Tucker that future vouchers will have to be accompanied by verifying receipts if they are to be paid, or b) ignore the matter since, on balance, her claims are in line with those of other salespersons. Barrington chooses to ignore the matter. Do you agree or disagree?

Agree _____   Disagree _____

7. Terenson's sells fine paintings, prints, and sculpture to a predominantly corporate clientele. Several of Terenson's customers have expressed interest in renting, rather than buying, some of the art used in their offices. Norell DuSoir, sales manager at Terenson's, agrees to rent. Do you agree or disagree with her decision?

Agree _____   Disagree _____

8. Mercado Electronics has received a subcontract to produce microreceptors. A firm delivery date has been set for six months from the date of contract. Mercado has a small but efficient staff adept at the semi-skilled light assembly work required for the microreceptors. Chris Loffer, production manager at Mercado, is aware that in order to meet the delivery date staff-hours will have to be increased. She is considering

scheduling the existing staff for three hours of daily overtime for the next six months or hiring four new employees. Loffer decides to hire the new employees. Do you agree or disagree with her decision?

Agree _____ Disagree _____

9. Residents of Winchly have organized a food co-op that buys fresh produce from nearby farms. A number of nonprofit nursing homes have been invited to join. Fees consist of an annual charge based upon the total number of persons served by the institution. It is estimated that the cost of food sold at the co-op is about 30 percent less than food purchased from suppliers. Co-op members must pledge to purchase a minimum amount; in the case of nursing homes, this amount is based on the number of patients served by the home. The patients in the nursing homes have special food needs that vary widely from patient to patient. Lon Tinsley, food service manager for the Amerada Nursing Home, has considered joining the co-op, but he decides not to join. Do you agree or disagree with Tinsley's decision?

Agree _____ Disagree _____

10. New Freeport Bank services the year-round residents of this small beach resort community. Almost all customers have maintained accounts at the bank for many years and enjoy its friendly personal atmosphere. The number of depositors has shown little growth. The population swells to four times its normal size during the summer, but most summer residents seem to demand speedier service than that offered at New Freeport Bank. At its last meeting, the board of directors of New Freeport Bank talked about purchasing an automated teller machine that would operate twenty-four hours a day. The board asked Britt Levinson, manager of the bank, to examine the issues involved and make a recommendation. Levinson recommends purchase of an ATM. Do you agree or disagree with her decision?

Agree _____ Disagree _____

11. J.O. Morely is manager of the Repair and Maintenance Department of the Nexus Power Company. Currently, Nexus is installing power lines in a new subdivision in the town of Maxwell. Work on the new installations has coincided with frequent power outages, with the result that there has been a sharp increase in complaints and demands for service by residents of Maxwell. Morely has been considering the following ways of handling the situation: increase the existing maintenance staff so that service calls can be expedited, or inform Maxwell residents that the situation is a temporary one that will be corrected when the new lines are in place. She decides to ask for an increase in staff. Do you agree or disagree with her decision?

Agree _____ Disagree _____

12. The school board of Coahula County has voted to add a computerized math program to the learning lab for students with special needs. The program is to be operational in time for the new school year, which is three months away. Jess Centavo, director of Special Programs for the Coahula Department of Education, is considering the following ways of meeting the board's directive: develop the program locally with the aim of tailoring it to the special needs of the local students, or purchase a ready-made generic program that is geared to students who have problems learning math. The cost of the generic program is 10 percent higher than the annual salary of a computer programmer. Centavo decides to develop the program locally. Do you agree or disagree with his decision?

Agree _____   Disagree _____

DDQ Scoring and Evaluation

Complete the DDQ scoring form in Figure 3. Compare your responses with the feedback your instructor will provide about the most appropriate responses for the twelve decisions.

FIGURE 3

Dozen Decision Questionnaire (DDQ) Scoring

Question	a	b	c	d	e	Response
1						
2						
3						
4						
5						
6						
7						
8						
9						
10						
11						
12						

SUMMARY

If you are committed to excellence as a manager, you will be aware of the importance of good decision-making skills. Managers who are recognized as great decision makers spend much time examining and analyzing information, considering alternatives, and exercising sound judgment. These managers know that good decisions produce great outcomes.

In this module you found that decision-making skills require a manager to demonstrate skills in five categories of behavior: (1) identifying problems; (2) generating alternatives; (3) evaluating alternatives; (4) reaching decisions; and (5) choosing implementation strategies. Decision-making skills are not tied to specific places or events. Once learned, they are applicable wherever and whenever you need to make decisions. They can be used in all types of situations, managerial or personal. You will certainly be able to apply what you learn here to your own workplace or personal life.

You may not be the chief executive officer, but your decisions as a manager will always affect your organization. Decision making is a challenging skill. No one can be right all the time. No one can achieve his or her goals all the time. But as your decision-making skills improve, so will your decisions. Consequently, you will accomplish more of your goals. Your organization will benefit and so will you.

It's up to you to exercise good decision making skills so that your impact will be positive. To remember key steps in practicing decision making and to identify situations in which the skills are needed, use the action guide shown in Figure 4. Frequent review of the information will help you become a more effective manager.

FIGURE 4
Decision-Making Skills Action Guide

You Show Decision-Making Skills When You:

- Identify problems
- Generate alternatives
- Evaluate alternatives
- Reach decisions
- Choose implementation strategies

You Should Show Decision-Making Skills When:

- Data or information to identify problems are examined
- Alternative action choices must be determined
- Alternatives need to be judged or evaluated
- Decisions or action choices must be made
- Decisions need to be put into effect

SKILL-BUILDING EXERCISES

EXERCISE 1 ■ EXAMINING DECISION MAKING: AN ORGANIZATIONAL VIEW

Identify a significant decision recently made by a major company in your city, or look in recent issues of *Business Week, Wall Street Journal,* or *Fortune* for a company that has made an important decision. In the decision you identified, did the manager or managers appear to use good decision-making skills? Can you describe the categories of behavior (identifying the problem, generating alternatives, evaluating alternatives, reaching a decision, and choosing implementation strategies) that they used?

EXERCISE 2 ■ DECISIONS ON CAMPUS ISSUES

Imagine that you are appointed to a task force charged with selecting a site to locate a new $40 million student union on your campus. Your task force is made up of ten members from all areas of campus. You should: identify the problem, generate and evaluate alternatives, and reach a decision. What information do you need to make this decision? Where will the members of the task force go to obtain the information? How difficult or easy was this decision? After the task force is finished, report to the class on your progress.

■ Use Exhibits 1–4 with In-Basket Exercise 1,
Exhibits 5–9 with In-Basket Exercise 2,
Exhibits 10–14 with In-Basket Exercise 3,
Exhibits 15–19 with In-Basket Exercise 4,
Exhibits 20-23 with In-Basket Exercise 5.

EXHIBIT 1
Index of Annual Purchases of Vacuum
Cleaners for Home Use

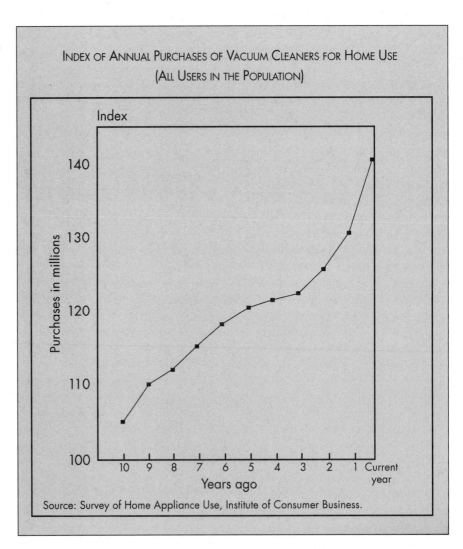

INDEX OF ANNUAL PURCHASES OF VACUUM CLEANERS FOR HOME USE
(ALL USERS IN THE POPULATION)

Source: Survey of Home Appliance Use, Institute of Consumer Business.

ANNUAL DOLLAR SALES OF GALAXIE VACUUM CLEANERS, INC.
(in millions of dollars)

Yearly Totals	Sales to Households	Sales to Office and Industrial Users	Total Sales
10 years ago	$19	$10	$29
9 years ago	19	11	30
8 years ago	18	12	30
7 years ago	17	14	31
6 years ago	15	14	31
5 years ago	13	26	39
4 years ago	12	32	44
3 years ago	10	40	50
2 years ago	8	44	52
1 year ago	8	45	53
Current year	8	45	53

Source: Data Analysis Department, Galaxie Vacuum Cleaners, Inc.

EXHIBIT 2
Annual Dollar Sales of Galaxie Vacuum Cleaners, Inc.

EXHIBIT 3
Galaxie Vacuum Cleaners, Inc.
Annual Dollar Sales over Past Decade

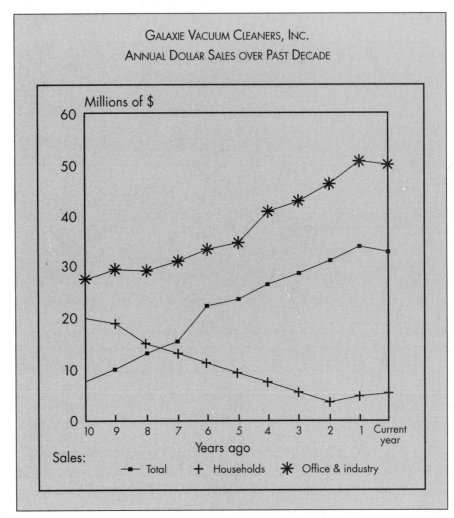

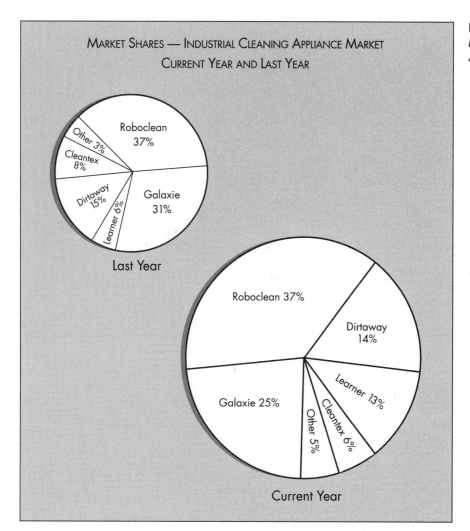

MARKET SHARES — INDUSTRIAL CLEANING APPLIANCE MARKET
CURRENT YEAR AND LAST YEAR

Last Year

Roboclean 37%
Galaxie 31%
Dirtaway 15%
Cleantex 8%
Other 3%
Learner 6%

Current Year

Roboclean 37%
Dirtaway 14%
Learner 13%
Cleantex 6%
Other 5%
Galaxie 25%

EXHIBIT 4
Market Shares — Industrial Cleaning
Appliance Market

EXHIBIT 5
Competitive Computers, Inc.
Memorandum

COMPETITIVE COMPUTERS, INC.
MICA VALLEY DRIVE

MEMORANDUM

TO: Tony Mark, Production Manager
FROM: Maria Castilho, Plant Manager
DATE: June 1
RE: Platheon Contract

Although the new Platheon contract calls for great care and very exacting skills (allowable tolerances are minimal), I hesitate to ask you to transfer any of our current supervisors to this new job because completion dates for other contracts are very tight.

Do you have any suggestions?

EXHIBIT 6
Competitive Computers, Inc.
Memorandum

COMPETITIVE COMPUTERS, INC.
MICA VALLEY DRIVE

MEMORANDUM

TO: Tony Mark, Production Manager
FROM: Jay Worth, Personnel Manager
DATE: December 1
RE: Employee Relations

As you know, Kelly Madden, line supervisor, was hired six months ago. Kelly had previously worked for the Argonaut Corporation, but was forced to move to a milder climate for health reasons. References and recommendations from past employers were excellent and indicated outstanding performance in both supervisory and technical areas.

We are, therefore, very surprised at the number of complaints we have been receiving from employees supervised by Madden. These complaints, for the most part, refer to work assignments and output expectations.

We have not received complaints in this number about other supervisors. Do you know what the problem is?

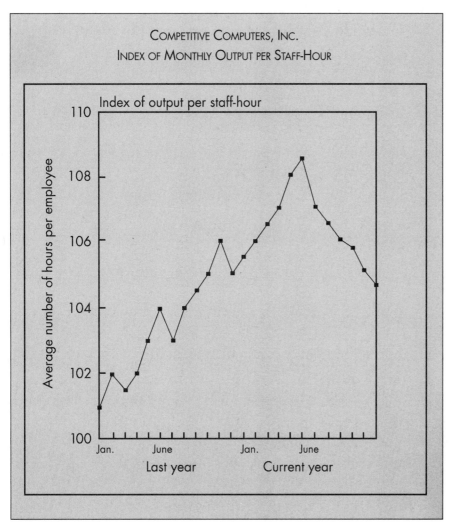

EXHIBIT 7
Competitive Computers, Inc.
Index of Monthly Output per
Staff-Hour

EXHIBIT 8
Competitive Computers, Inc.
Employee Turnover Index by Month

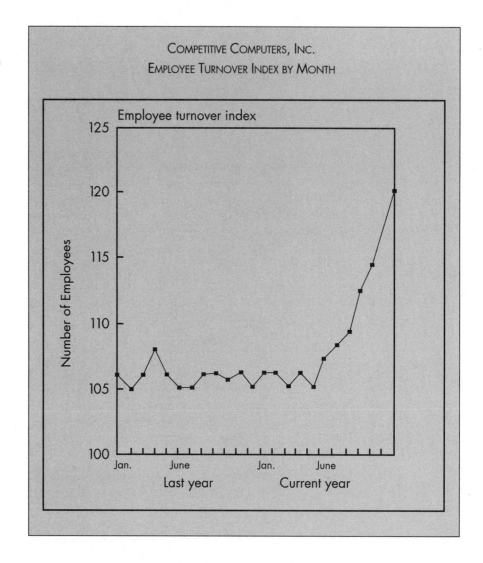

COMPETITIVE COMPUTERS, INC.
MICA VALLEY DRIVE

MEMORANDUM

TO: Maria Castilho, Plant Manager
FROM: Tony Mark, Production Manager
DATE: December 3
RE: Platheon Contract

I would like your help on a difficult matter. Your secretary tells me that you will be out of town until Thursday, so I've asked her to leave this memo on your desk where you will be sure to see it as soon as you return. When you look at the reports on the Platheon contract, everything seems great. Quality control is very high, and we have fully met Phase Two of the contract on the target date.

However, we are having a problem with the employees. They are quitting in record numbers. Although, so far, we have been able to replace them, the effect on output per staff-hour is severe. If this continues it is doubtful that we will make Phase 3 on time.

Maria, you and I know how difficult that Platheon job is. In fact, we hired a special person, Kelly Madden, to supervise it because it required special expertise. Kelly says that because the work is difficult and the specifications exacting, the employees must be closely supervised in their work. From the turnover data, I would say that the employees are not responding too well to Kelly's methods. Perhaps we can talk about all of this when you return.

EXHIBIT 9
Competitive Computers, Inc.
Memorandum

EXHIBIT 10
Marathon Hosiery Manufacturers, Inc.
Internal Memorandum

MARATHON HOSIERY MANUFACTURERS, INC.

INTERNAL MEMORANDUM

TO: All Sales Personnel and Route Salespersons
FROM: Dahabo Halsey, Sales Manager
DATE: January, current year
RE: Commission

Beginning January 1, this year, commissions will be paid to all route salespersons as follows:

Dollar Sales	Commission Rate
Criterion level	Base rate only

Percentage over criterion:

1 – 10	1% of that segment
11 – 20	2% of that segment
21 – 30	3% of that segment
31 – 40	5% of that segment
41 or more	7% of that segment

Thus, the higher your dollar sales, the higher will be your overall average rate of commission.

MARATHON HOSIERY MANUFACTURERS, INC.

INTERNAL MEMORANDUM

TO: Dahabo Halsey, Sales Manager
FROM: Kerr Watts, President
DATE: January, current year
RE: Acquisition of Cosmetics Plant

With the acquisition of the cosmetics plant in Mountaindale, we plan to sell a full line of cosmetics which we will market under the name of ISIS GLAMOURIZERS.

This new line should boost our revenues considerably, since profit margins on cosmetics are substantially above those on hosiery, i.e., in drugstores, convenience stores, and supermarkets.

We have not decided between the following alternatives: 1) using the current hosiery sales force to sell, make deliveries, and service displays for the new cosmetics line, or 2) hiring a new sales force for the cosmetics line. Since you are the sales manager, we feel the decision should be yours.

In making your decision, bear in mind that we should be able to recover our investment in the Mountaindale plant in three years. As for sales, we expect you to more than double your net in two years and to triple it in three years.

Attached are some data that bear on the matter. Please let me know your decision ASAP.

EXHIBIT 11
Marathon Hosiery Manufacturers, Inc.
Internal Memorandum

EXHIBIT 12
Where Consumers Purchase Facial
Cosmetics

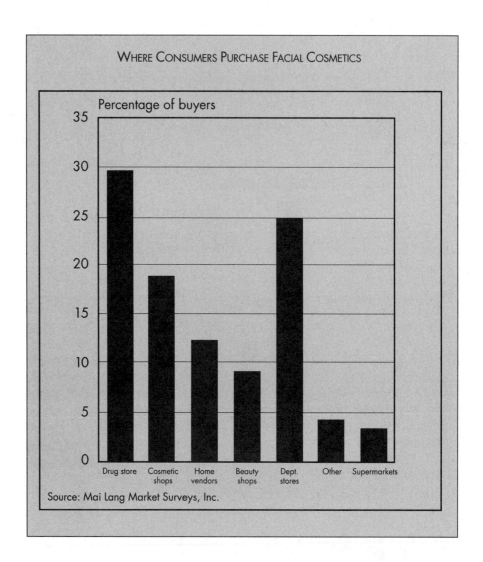

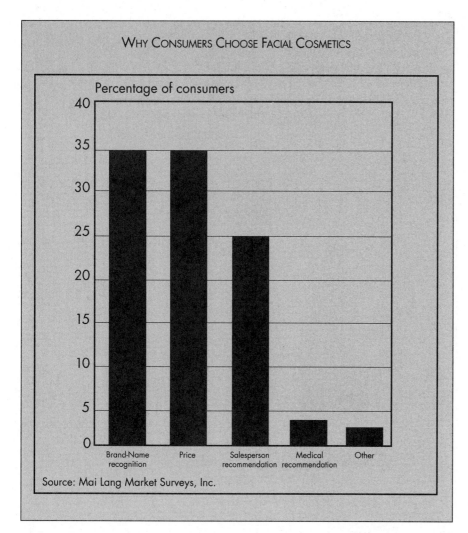

EXHIBIT 13
Why Consumers Choose Facial
Cosmetics

EXHIBIT 14
Marathon Hosiery Manufacturers, Inc.
Percent of Sales to Various Retail
Outlets Last Year

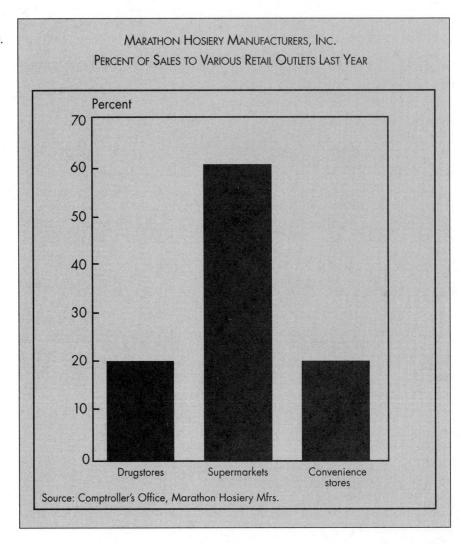

BETTER BOOKSTORES, INC.

MEMORANDUM

TO: Leslie Goff, Site Location Manager
FROM: Janetta Russell, President
DATE: February 18
RE: Locations for new bookstore

Our stores have been very successful, thus far, and we plan to continue to open new units.

I am depending on you to locate at least two areas where the market is not already saturated, where there is strong potential demand, and where shipping and real estate or rental costs are reasonable.

We need your recommendations in time for the meeting of the executive committee on March 30th.

EXHIBIT 15
Better Bookstores, Inc.
Memorandum

NASUS MARKET RESEARCH GROUP, INC.
SITE SEARCH REPORT

We have identified ten urban areas with populations between 50,000 and 75,000 and with fewer than three full-service bookstores in the area. These are listed by code number as shown below, together with the number of full-service bookstores currently in operation in the area.

Area	Number of Full-Service Bookstores Currently in Operation
0101	1
0102	0
0103	0
0104	1
0105	0
0106	1
0107	0
0108	2
0109	0
0110	0

EXHIBIT 16
Nasus Market Research Group, Inc.
Site Search Report

EXHIBIT 17
Percent Distribution of Books Sold in
Bookstores

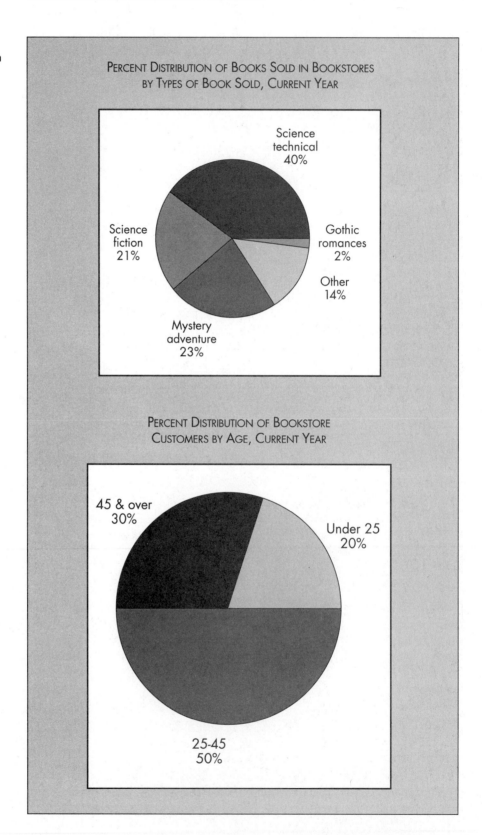

PERCENT DISTRIBUTION OF BOOKS SOLD IN BOOKSTORES
BY TYPES OF BOOK SOLD, CURRENT YEAR

Science
technical
40%

Science
fiction
21%

Gothic
romances
2%

Other
14%

Mystery
adventure
23%

PERCENT DISTRIBUTION OF BOOKSTORE
CUSTOMERS BY AGE, CURRENT YEAR

45 & over
30%

Under 25
20%

25-45
50%

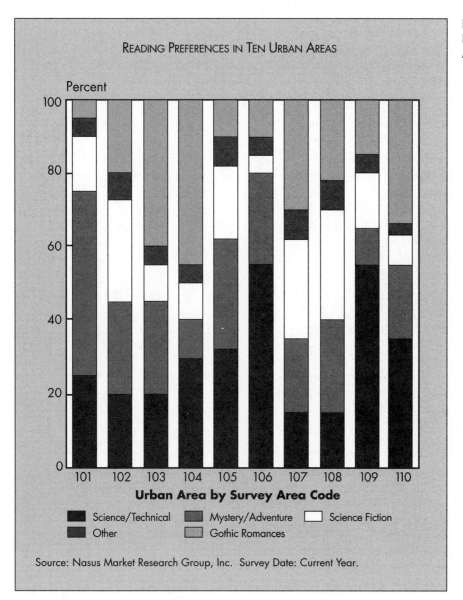

EXHIBIT 18
Reading Preferences in Ten Urban Areas

EXHIBIT 19
Age Distribution of Population
in Ten Urban Areas, Current Year

Area by Population Bureau Code	Under 25	25 – 45	45 & over	Total
0101	44.2	33.0	22.8	100.0
0102	42.6	15.0	42.4	100.0
0103	22.4	32.6	45.0	100.0
0104	46.0	30.0	24.0	100.0
0105	38.0	38.0	24.0	100.0
0106	24.8	45.2	30.0	100.0
0107	45.0	36.0	19.0	100.0
0108	32.0	35.0	33.0	100.0
0109	39.0	46.0	15.0	100.0
0110	26.0	22.0	52.0	100.0

AGE DISTRIBUTION OF POPULATION IN TEN URBAN AREAS, CURRENT YEAR (PERCENT)

Source: Population Analysis Bureau.

MANATEE TYPEWRITERS, INC.

MEMORANDUM

TO: Weil Friedman, Marketing Manager
FROM: Mickey Larsen, Sales Manager
DATE: December 1
RE: Plans for sales of COMPUPRINTER

As you know, we have been advised to aggressively sell the COMPUPRINTER during its first six months on the market. For your information, the sales division will choose one or more of the following strategies to push sales of this computer.

- Grant sales personnel a 5% additional commission (above regular commission rates) for each COMPUPRINTER sold during the first six months of next year. This will bring overall commission rates on this computer to 25% for sales made in January through June.
- Discount the established price by 15% on ALL orders placed during the initial six months period.
- Allow discounts to educational institutions only during this period.

We will let you know as soon as we finalize our plans.

EXHIBIT 20
Manatee Typewriters, Inc.
Memorandum

EXHIBIT 21
Manatee Typewriters, Inc.
Memorandum

MANATEE TYPEWRITERS, INC.

MEMORANDUM

TO: Mickey Larsen, Sales Manager
FROM: Weil Friedman, Marketing Manager
DATE: December 13
RE: Promotional campaign for COMPUPRINTER

As you know, our new COMPUPRINTER is a compact word processor and computer with built-in printer. The unit is no larger than a regular typewriter and has the memory and programming capacity of our V1-40s. Because of its compact construction and computer and print-out capability, we expect that it will have special appeal for both home and education markets.

To introduce the COMPUPRINTER, we have planned a media campaign using educational and general news publications as well as prime time on TV. Our campaign will be directed to both the educational establishment and to home users. The tie-in will be a "Sharing the Future" and "Help Your Child—Help Yourself" approach combined with a factual hard sell for the education market. The ads, TV spots, and news releases will first appear in January.

What are the final plans for the sales department in connection with the COMPUPRINTER? It's important that we coordinate our activities. Promotions are only as effective as the sales staff that backs them up.

EXCERPT FROM THE *DAILY EDUCATOR*, DECEMBER
MIDWAY MAP CORPORATION OFFERS SCHOOL DISCOUNTS

Midway Map, Inc., which recently introduced a line of holistic map projections for classroom use, has offered substantial discounts to local and state departments of education placing orders within the next three months. Midway has used this technique previously to introduce new products targeted to specific markets.

Pam Meers, Midway vice president in charge of new product promotions, says that discounts are particularly effective in the education market because funds in that market are tight and bargains go a long way toward overcoming any reluctance to be the first to try a new thing.

Anyone considering sales of products to education establishments should push sales now, because preparation of budgets for the coming year is already underway. Typically, products purchased in December through June are scheduled for delivery during the following September when a new school year begins. This gives manufacturers a lot of time to get their wares to the purchaser.

Promoting products in the education market that will later be sold to the public at large pays dividends, according to Meers. Parents, friends, and neighbors become aware of the products used by students and teachers in the classroom. If these products are good, they will promote interest in a very large group of potential consumers. And they build future markets as well, since students soon become independent consumers.

EXHIBIT 22
Excerpt from the *Daily Educator*

EXHIBIT 23
Manatee Typewriters, Inc.
Memorandum

MANATEE TYPEWRITERS, INC.

MEMORANDUM

TO: Mickey Larsen, Sales Manager
FROM: Kim Lu, Service Department
DATE: December 14
RE: COMPUPRINTER

Servicing **COMPUPRINTERS** is a whole new ball game for the service personnel. We need special training for this. Because of other demands for service, we have not been able to take time out for the required training.

I estimate that it will take 90 hours of training time for an experienced service representative to learn the **COMPUPRINTER**. In addition, we'll probably need to expand our service staff. So far, we have not received the go-ahead for either of these steps.

I am calling this to your attention because, as you know, if we sell **COMPUPRINTERS** without providing a service backup we are asking for trouble.

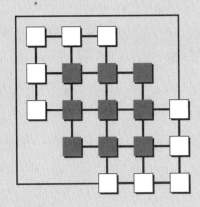

PART 4
ENABLING SKILLS: RECOGNIZING THE NEED FOR AND ADAPTING TO CHANGE

MODULE 8
Decisiveness Skills: Taking Action

MODULE 9
Flexibility Skills: Adapting to Change

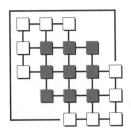

MODULE 8
DECISIVENESS SKILLS: TAKING ACTION

INTRODUCTION

Being a manager means being an activist, focusing on results, and making things happen. It does not mean being a passive keeper of administrative rules and procedures. Some of your responsibilities as a manager are to take action and give direction to subordinates. You must resolve hang-ups, delays, and disputes, take risks, and deal with other difficulties that are likely to occur in your department at one time or another. To do this, you must be decisive.

To be decisive is to display a range of assertive behaviors. In this module we are going to examine five components of decisive behaviors that managers must use: (1) taking the initiative, (2) giving opinions, (3) making rapid decisions, (4) defending decisions when challenged, and (5) taking risks to achieve results. Decisiveness is closely linked to decision making and leadership. It differs from these skills, however, in that it focuses on *taking action*. By contrast, decision making is concerned with the basis for the action, and leadership focuses on the ability to manage the behavior of others.

This module will help you develop and strengthen the skills involved in decisive behavior. You will assume the role of a manager in a variety of situations that require you to be decisive. In each situation, you will be provided with information—samples of material that typically find their way to the manager's desk. In the role of manager, you must use decisiveness skills to solve a potential problem. By actually participating in these exercises, you can learn and practice decisiveness.

The module is organized so that you will develop a before-practice assessment of your decisiveness skills by completing the Decisiveness Process Questionnaire (DPQ). This questionnaire is an assessment instrument that measures your skills at the present time. We then present a brief discussion of the components of decisiveness. Next, through in-basket exercises, you will have an opportunity to practice decisiveness behaviors. The exercises focus on one category of decisiveness at a time. Feedback from your instructor will help you judge the quality of your own responses and provide guidance on improving specific behaviors.

After a review and summary, you will have an opportunity to retake the DPQ and compare your after-practice assessment results with your earlier results. You will also complete the Decisiveness Action Demonstration Scale (DADS). This assessment instrument examines how you interpret actual behavior in situations where decisiveness skills are needed. It will give you more insight into your behaviors in situations requiring decisiveness.

Once you have completed this module, you may find that your training and practice will be reflected in immediate improvement, or you may find that your improvement may be more noticeable after you have had opportunities to perform on the job or in a nonwork-related situation.

ASSESSING DECISIVENESS SKILLS

Before proceeding with the rest of this module, complete the following questionnaire. It is both a teaching tool and a means for measuring your present level of decisiveness skills. Take time to complete the questionnaire carefully. Your answers should reflect your behaviors as they are now, not as you would like them to be. Be honest. The instrument is designed to help you discover where you are now in terms of decisiveness. Whatever your before-practice scores are, you can improve these skills by working through the exercises presented in the module.

The Decisiveness Process Questionnaire (DPQ)

The Decisiveness Process Questionnaire (DPQ) examines your current decisiveness skills in five areas. These skills are essential to managerial effectiveness. In responding to the questions, consider your work experience or relate the questions to your experience with a group in the classroom, a fraternity, a sorority, a club, or a service organization. You will find that the questions are applicable to your own experience even if you are not yet a manager.

After you have completed this module and have had an opportunity to put into practice the decisiveness skills you have learned, you will retake the questionnaire. Comparing your scores will help you evaluate the effectiveness of your practice.

Use the following scale to rate the frequency with which you perform the behaviors described in each question. Place the corresponding number (1–7) in the blank preceding the statement.

Rarely	Irregularly	Occasionally	Usually	Frequently	Almost Always	Consistently
1	2	3	4	5	6	7

_____ **1.** I take immediate action to resolve problems as they emerge.

_____ **2.** I improvise when it is necessary to keep things moving.

_____ 3. I change work priorities or procedures as needed without waiting for direction from others.

_____ 4. When required actions are not within my limits of authority, I inform the proper person that action is needed.

_____ 5. I volunteer my views without waiting to be asked.

_____ 6. I take a stand on controversial issues.

_____ 7. I support my views with facts and figures.

_____ 8. I link my conclusions to the goals and objectives of my group or organization.

_____ 9. I make decisions when they are needed, whether or not all the facts are in.

_____ 10 I have little difficulty making up my mind.

_____ 11. I present my decisions concisely without lengthy explanations or justifications.

_____ 12. I prefer to face the facts of a situation and deal with them now, rather than wait to see what happens.

_____ 13. When challenged, I support my choices firmly.

_____ 14. I hold to my point of view despite pressure to yield.

_____ 15. I go with what I think is right, even in the face of strong opposition.

_____ 16. When my choices are challenged by others, I stick to the issues and support my point of view.

_____ 17. I use structured techniques in appraising risks.

_____ 18. I count on my knowledge and experience to offset risks.

_____ 19. I match possible outcomes with probabilities that they will be achieved.

_____ 20. I balance risks against possible outcomes.

DPQ Scoring

The scoring sheet in Figure 1 summarizes your responses for the DPQ. It will help you identify your existing strengths and pinpoint areas that need improvement. Right now, fill in the before-practice score column. Add the five category scores to obtain a total score. Enter that score in the space indicated. After completing the module, you will take the DPQ again and fill in the after-practice score column.

DPQ Evaluation

Figure 2 shows score lines for your total score and for each category measured on the DPQ. Each line shows a continuum from the lowest score to the highest. Place the letter B (before-practice) where your personal score falls on each of these lines.

FIGURE 1

Decisiveness Behavior Questionnaire (DBQ) Scoring

Skill Area	Items	Assessment	
		Before Practice	After Practice
Taking the initiative	1,2,3,4		
Giving opinions	5,6,7,8		
Making rapid decisions	9,10,11,12		
Defending decisions when challenged	13,14,15,16		
Taking risks to achieve results	17,18,19,20		
TOTAL SCORE			

The score lines in Figure 2 show graphically where you stand with regard to five decisiveness behaviors. If you have been honest with yourself, you now have a better idea of your relative strengths and weaknesses in the categories of behavior that make up the skills of decisiveness.

Learning to Use the DPQ Skills

You have completed the initial evaluation of your decisiveness skills. In the DPQ, you rated the frequency with which you demonstrate behaviors in the five categories of decisiveness. This questionnaire provides a baseline against which you will assess improvements that have taken place after you have completed this module.

Before moving on, think about what you have learned about yourself in this evaluation. In what area of decisiveness skills are you weak? These will require the most attention during the remainder of the module. What areas are your strongest? Use this module to fine-tune these areas so you may take full advantage of them. For these stronger areas, learning only one or two new things may be all you need for significant improvement in your decisiveness skills.

Keep your own special needs in mind as you proceed. Review the DPQ frequently. Refer to it as you work through the material presented in the remaining sections of the module. The DPQ will help you identify decisiveness behaviors that are appropriate for the management situations described in this module. After you have completed the module and have had an opportunity to put into practice what you have learned, retake the DPQ. Then compare your after-practice scores with your before-practice scores. This comparison will show you where you have progressed and where further work is needed.

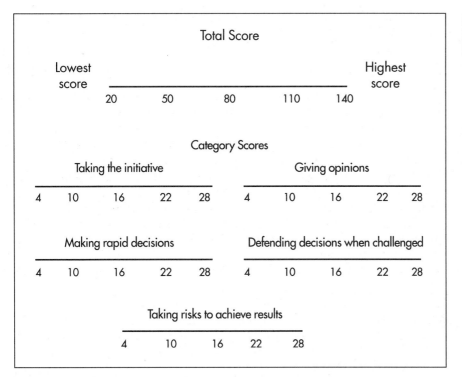

FIGURE 2
Decisiveness Behavior Questionnaire
(DBQ) Evaluation

UNDERSTANDING DECISIVENESS

To be decisive, a manager must make choices and take action—this ability to act is critical. Some decisions are so routine as to be unnoticeable; others are important and have serious consequences. Either way, managers who do not make choices and act on them are indecisive. They surrender authority and cannot effectively manage.

At times, weighing all the factors and evaluating the potential impact of a decision in order to decide what action to take may be a lengthy, complex process, and one that you cannot afford. As a manager you must be able to make up your mind based on minimal information, if necessary, and you must be willing to act on your decision. It is part of your responsibility to take these risks. Remember that your decisions will not always be right. If you aim for perfection, you are not likely to succeed, and you are more likely to become indecisive.

Decisiveness Skills Required of Managers

Decisiveness includes not only the ability to make decisions, but the ability to assert a point of view, to determine a course of action when time is of the essence, and to withstand opposition. Decisiveness skills can be divided into five categories of behavior: (1) taking the initiative, (2) giving opinions, (3) making rapid decisions, (4) defending decisions when challenged, and (5) taking risks to achieve results. In the next section, we will examine these five categories.

Taking the Initiative

Managers often must act quickly with limited time and information. Sometimes the urge to wait just a little longer is difficult for a manager to resist, but effective managers learn to determine the credibility of information, ascertain the importance of a threat or opportunity, and act accordingly. Managers must identify urgent issues, choose courses of action, improvise when necessary, state decisions firmly, and respond quickly to matters that require resolution.

Several steps will help a manager learn to take initiative. First, keep a positive mental attitude—make a habit of approaching tasks energetically and positively. Second, focus on the most important tasks. Learn to separate trivia from important jobs that must be done first. Finally, be persistent yet temper that persistence with patience.

Giving Opinions

For the decisive manager, giving opinions means asserting a point of view, even when it is in conflict with the views of others. It includes the willingness and ability to challenge decisions, comments, and actions with which you disagree as well as to firmly support those with which you concur. Successful managers know how to make requests and state points of view in a confident, straightforward manner, without becoming pushy, annoyed, or angry. They express their own perspectives as well as opinions on the perspectives of others.

Making Rapid Decisions

Managers must make decisions when they are needed, often before all the facts are gathered. Good managers make analysis the means instead of the end. In the real world, we almost never have enough information; we must take action based on our experiences and a sense of what is right. To make rapid decisions includes reaching conclusions quickly, making a choice without undue delay and vacillation, and taking action with minimal hesitancy.

Defending Decisions when Challenged

Managers are often called upon to defend their decisions. They may have to face confrontation and be subjected to pressure from others. Good managers know how to take a stand, carefully evaluate other possibilities, examine information, support their decisions with facts, and answer opposing arguments. Most importantly, they know how to be assertive. Being assertive involves making clear statements without being abusive or obnoxious, standing up to challenges by others, and confidently and firmly defending opinions. Nonassertive people suppress their feelings and actions, whereas assertive people express them.

Taking Risks to Achieve Results

Taking risks means trying new things and challenging old ways, often going against the odds to accomplish objectives. Risk involves uncertainty. Managers must always consider the possibility that their actions could lead to losses rather than gains. In fact, since almost every action contains some element of risk, the potential for failure is always present. Even if managers have all the information available, their decisions carry risks because they cannot predict or control environmental factors. In spite of these risks, however, successful managers maintain confidence in their decisions.

Not all decisions you make will turn out the way you expect—no one is right all of the time. Information is often incomplete and accidents and unexpected events may occur to change the expected results of some decisions. Still, risk will not stop an effective manager from taking action.

Decisiveness Skills and Their Relationships to Other Managerial Skills

Decisiveness is closely intertwined with other managerial skills such as flexibility, which is covered in another module. Decisive managers must use problem-solving skills such as perception, organizing and planning, and decision making. They must also have strong interpersonal and leadership skills. In essence, managers should develop all of their skills in order to exercise decisiveness effectively.

PRACTICING DECISIVENESS

Decisiveness skills cover the following component behaviors:

- *Taking the initiative*—Taking action when action is needed, improvising, and acting on new events and information without waiting for orders from others shows decisiveness.
- *Giving opinions*—Volunteering your views, taking stands on controversial issues, and defending your opinions are components of decisive behavior.
- *Making rapid decisions*—Making decisions when they are needed, without delay, without seeking consensus, and without fear of adverse reaction shows decisiveness.
- *Defending decisions when challenged*—A decisive manager defends his or her decisions in the face of challenge and will not yield to pressure.
- *Taking risks to achieve results*—Evaluating the risks and taking those risks in order to get what you want are major factors in decisive behavior.

This next section of in-basket exercises focuses separately on each component of decisiveness. In each exercise you will find questions that will help you practice a particular aspect of decisiveness.

Before you begin the exercises, review your scores on the five parts of the DPQ that you completed earlier. As you work to complete the exercises, keep in mind the behaviors noted in this measure of decisiveness. The questions in the DPQ deepen your understanding of decisiveness skills.

Situation:

As Collie Tiner, newly appointed plant manager of the Overland plant of the Harper Wells Company, you are in charge of all plant operations. The Overland plant produces, warehouses, and delivers video recorders and parts.

Your predecessor, Dan Everidge, was transferred to a new position as of January 15. You had to wind things up and train your replacement at your former job before reporting for duty at Overland. You are scheduled to begin work at your new job tomorrow, January 18.

This morning, Sunday, January 17, you learned that you must leave town immediately because of a personal emergency. You will be away for at least four days and will not be able to begin your job on the scheduled date. You have come to your new office today to see if you can take care of some pending matters before your departure.

You find the matters needing your attention in the in-basket on your desk. Many of these items are addressed to Dan Everidge, the former plant manager, but have not yet been attended to. A little while ago you phoned your secretary, Chris Wentworth, at her home but she is out of town.

You glance at your watch. It is 1:00 P.M. You must leave the office at 2:30 P.M. to catch your plane. You have only one and a half hours to take care of the matters in your in-basket, and your actions must be based on that material alone since Chris is not available to open the office files. You must make whatever decisions are required in the 90 minutes that are available to you.

IN-BASKET EXERCISE 1: TAKING THE INITIATIVE

Taking the initiative is an important aspect of decisiveness. Regrouping, improvising, and innovating when quick action is needed are all part of being decisive. In the following situation, you must initiate action to resolve problems needing your immediate attention.

Review the information shown in Exhibits 1 through 5. Refer to this information as you answer the questions that follow. Remember, your time is limited.

Your decisiveness skills focus:

- Identify urgent issues.
- Determine courses of action.
- Improvise when necessary.
- State your decisions firmly.
- Respond quickly to matters that require resolution.

Questions for In-Basket Exercise 1:

1. Each of the items in Exhibits 1 through 5 involves an issue that needs resolution. What are these issues?

2. Explain why these issues call for taking initiative.

3. Considering that you will be away from the office for the next several days, what decisions can you make now that will initiate prompt action on these matters? Write each decision as if it were a memo to the person involved.

IN-BASKET EXERCISE 2: GIVING OPINIONS

In the context of decisiveness, giving opinions means coming forward and asserting your point of view, even when it is in conflict with the views of others. It includes the willingness and ability to challenge decisions, comments, and actions with which you disagree as well as to firmly support those with which you concur. As a manager, when you give an opinion, you convey conviction in statements that do not provoke antagonistic reactions.

Refer to the information in Exhibits 6 through 10 and any previous information to answer the questions that follow.

Your decisiveness skills focus:

- Act on limited information.
- Make up your mind quickly.
- Adopt a clear point of view.
- Express yourself firmly.

Questions for In-Basket Exercise 2:

1. State your opinion on pay for unused sick leave (Exhibit 6).

2. Write a note to the employees' committee expressing your views on the dress code (Exhibit 6).

3. Express your views on the thermostat setting (Exhibit 7).

4. Express your views on Manny Foster's proposal (Exhibit 8).

5. Express your opinion on quality circles (Exhibit 9).

6. Express your opinion on recognition for secretaries (Exhibit 10).

In-Basket Exercise 3: Making Rapid Decisions

The essence of decisiveness is the ability to make up your mind quickly—to reach conclusions, make choices, and take action with minimal hesitancy. As a manager, you must make choices firmly and confidently. Refer to material in the previous exercises as well as to Exhibits 11 through 15 to answer the questions that follow.

Your decisiveness skills focus:

- Act on limited information.
- Take action without consulting others.
- Reach conclusions quickly.
- Present your decisions concisely.
- Make required decisions immediately.

Questions for In-Basket Exercise 3:

1. What is your decision with respect to the Sandwell proposal (Exhibit 11)?

2. Make a decision regarding Clem MacDonald's request (Exhibit 12).

3. Make a decision and reply to Tully Brent (Exhibit 13) .

4. Indicate your decision with respect to the Gratin letter (Exhibit 14).

5. Reply to Lee Marowitz with your decision (Exhibit 15).

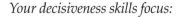

IN-BASKET EXERCISE 4: DEFENDING DECISIONS WHEN CHALLENGED

Decisiveness includes the ability to stand up to challenges by others and to be firm in the face of demands. It includes confidently and firmly defending your opinions, actions, and decisions against opposing views and pressures.

As Collie Tiner, plant manager at Harper Wells Company, your original positions on five controversial issues are challenged. Shown in Exhibits 16 through 20 are the issues, your original position, and the opposing arguments. You may need to refer to information in previous exhibits.

Your decisiveness skills focus:

- State your position firmly.
- Hold to your point of view in the face of opposition.
- Speak to the issues.
- Answer opposing arguments.

Questions for In-Basket Exercise 4:

1. State your defending argument for your original position on Issue 1: Special recognition for secretaries (Exhibit 16).

2. State your defending argument for your original position on Issue 2: Pay for unused sick leave (Exhibit 17).

3. State your defending argument for your original position on Issue 3: Quality Circles (Exhibit 18).

4. State your defending argument for your original position on Issue 4: Conflict between sales and production (Exhibit 19).

5. State your defending argument for your original position on Issue 5: Polling employees (Exhibit 20).

IN-BASKET EXERCISE 5: TAKING RISKS TO ACHIEVE RESULTS

A decisive manager takes risks to achieve results and maintains confidence despite uncertainty. Risk is inherent in any decision. As a manager, risk must not stop you from taking action. Taking risks means trying new things, challenging old ways, and often going against the odds to accomplish your objectives. The possibility exists that your decisions may turn out badly and even create new problems. Refer to Exhibits 21 through 25 to respond to the questions that follow.

Your decisiveness skills focus:

- Determine when a decision is needed.
- State the goal(s) of your decision.
- Consider all your options.
- Evaluate your options according to their degree of risk.
- Consider the possible benefits of your options.
- Determine what option is most likely to achieve your goals.
- Choose an option by balancing possible results against risks.

Questions for In-Basket Exercise 5:

1. Refer to the letter from Industrial Information Specialists (IIS) shown in Exhibit 21 and the information contained in Exhibit 22. Why do you need to make a decision about this matter? Explicitly state the goal(s) of such a decision. List some options for acting on the report from IIS. Now, rank the options in order of degree of risk to the company. Begin with 1 for the most risky option, 2 for the next riskiest, etc. Explain your rankings. What is your decision regarding this issue? Explain the risks involved and why you are willing to accept these risks.

2. What risk is involved in co-signing the mortgage for Lysle Wilbur as described in the Overland Commercial Bank proposal shown in Exhibit 23? Explain what factors offset the risks of loss. Would you take the risks involved? Why? How would the company benefit from your decision to take these risks?

3. With regard to the memo from Lee Jason (Exhibit 24) about the purchase of spools at a special price, what are the advantages and disadvantages of buying the spools now? What are the risks involved in making the purchase? What is your decision with regard to the purchase of the spools? Explain the risks your decision involves.

4. Refer to the letter from Marbury Associates shown in Exhibit 25 and rate the options listed in the Marbury letter in terms of risk to Harper Wells Company. Use 1 for the riskiest option, 2 for the next riskiest, etc. Which option offers the greatest possibility of benefit to Harper Wells? What option contains the greatest risk of loss for Harper Wells? Which option offers the least benefit to Harper Wells? Make a decision. Explain why you are willing to assume the risks involved.

ASSESSING CHANGE

The purpose of this module has been to help you develop your decisiveness skills through simulated managerial situations. Your attention has been focused on the five components of decisiveness skills:

- *Taking the initiative*—Your task as Collie Tiner was to take the initiative on matters needing your immediate attention. You were asked to rethink, improvise, and innovate in response to unforeseen variables that disturbed previous plans.
- *Giving opinions*—As Collie Tiner, you were asked to form opinions on a variety of matters and assert your point of view in controversial situations.
- *Making rapid decisions*—Your task was to make decisions quickly on matters ranging from hiring an outside maintenance organization to renewing your food services contract.
- *Defending decisions when challenged*—As plant manager, you were asked to defend decisions challenged by others.
- *Taking risks to achieve results*—In the role of Collie Tiner, you were asked to take some risks in order to resolve a difficult situation or reach a particular goal. This included a willingness to challenge others and to initiate a novel course of action.

At the beginning of this module, you completed the DPQ to provide a baseline against which you could measure changes in your decisiveness behaviors. Now it is time to assess some of these changes.

First, retake the DPQ. When you have finished, compare your answers with those you gave earlier to see how much you have strengthened your decisiveness skills.

The Decisiveness Process Questionnaire (DPQ)

Use the following scale to rate the frequency with which you perform the behaviors described in each question. Place the corresponding number (1–7) in the blank preceding the statement.

Rarely	Irregularly	Occasionally	Usually	Frequently	Almost Always	Consistently
1	2	3	4	5	6	7

_____ **1.** I take immediate action to resolve problems as they emerge.

_____ **2.** I improvise when it is necessary to keep things moving.

_____ **3.** I change work priorities or procedures as needed without waiting for direction from others.

_____ **4.** When required actions are not within my limits of authority, I inform the proper person that action is needed.

_____ **5.** I volunteer my views without waiting to be asked.

_____ **6.** I take a stand on controversial issues.

_____ 7.   I support my views with facts and figures.

_____ 8.   I link my conclusions to the goals and objectives of my group or organization.

_____ 9.   I make decisions when they are needed, whether or not all the facts are in.

_____ 10   I have little difficulty making up my mind.

_____ 11.   I present my decisions concisely without lengthy explanations or justifications.

_____ 12.   I prefer to face the facts of a situation and deal with them now, rather than wait to see what happens.

_____ 13.   When challenged, I support my choices firmly.

_____ 14.   I hold to my point of view despite pressure to yield.

_____ 15.   I go with what I think is right, even in the face of strong opposition.

_____ 16.   When my choices are challenged by others, I stick to the issues and support my point of view.

_____ 17.   I use structured techniques in appraising risks.

_____ 18.   I count on my knowledge and experience to offset risks.

_____ 19.   I match possible outcomes with probabilities that they will be achieved.

_____ 20.   I balance risks against possible outcomes.

DPQ Scoring and Evaluation

Follow the scoring directions found on page 379 and in Figure 1. Complete the after-practice assessment column for the DPQ and compare your before- and after-practice scores. Plot your after-practice scores in Figure 2. In which categories did your scores improve? Think about what has made your progress possible. Perhaps you can apply your insights to categories where your performance has lagged.

The Decisiveness Action Demonstration Scale (DADS)

Now you are asked to complete another questionnaire, the Decisiveness Action Demonstration Scale (DADS), as a second method to assess change. In the DADS, you review the actions of other managers in situations where decisive behaviors are required. Then you decide whether the actions they took really were decisive enough. This questionnaire will give you more insight into ways you would use the skill of decisiveness in specific situations.

The DADS describes ten different situations in which a manager took action. Indicate whether you agree or disagree that the action taken was the most decisive of the options considered. Check the appropriate space. As you proceed, keep in mind the behaviors noted in the DPQ.

     1.   Frank Sayantani manages the warehouse at Crumer's, a wholesale distributor of auto parts. Crumer's has just received an emergency order

from Harlow and Sons, a valuable new customer. The order is for a group of assorted-size hoses. A delivery truck is about to leave the warehouse. If the order is placed on this truck, it will reach the customer the next day.

Frank checks the warehouse inventory and finds that, although he can fill most of the order, there will be some shortages. The inventory will be replenished in a few days. At that time, the order could be filled completely.

Frank has a decision to make. Should he send out part of the order now and part later? This will involve an additional shipping charge to the customer. Should he wait a few days and fill the order completely? The total charge for shipping would be smaller then. Should he notify sales and ask the sales manager to make the decision? Should he contact the customer and ask the customer to decide?

Frank decides to ship part of the order immediately with a notice to the customer that the rest will be arriving in a few days. Do you agree or disagree that this was the most decisive of Frank's possible actions?

Agree _____   Disagree _____

2. Betty Daller is the store manager at Sadler's, a popular candle store in the Melody Mall in Evetsville. Right now she is speaking to Mr. and Mrs. Feenberg, who have been vacationing in Evetsville. The Feenbergs wish to return a candelabra they purchased on sale a few days ago. They say that the candelabra is chipped, and that it had been glued together in a way that was unnoticeable except on very close examination. When they bought the candelabra, they were told that it was in perfect condition, or so they claim.

The salesperson who sold the candelabra is out on vacation. Betty points to a sign that is prominently displayed in the store. The sign reads, "Sale items are not returnable." The Feenbergs insist that since the merchandise they purchased was misrepresented, this rule does not apply in their case. They continue to argue and are attracting the attention of other customers in the store.

Betty knows that she must resolve the situation. She wonders whether she should allow the Feenbergs to return the candelabra and get their refund. Perhaps she should allow them to exchange the item for another of like value. Or should she hold fast to established store policy and tell the Feenbergs that she will not accept the item and that is final? Perhaps she should try to reach the vacationing salesperson and check the Feenberg's story.

Betty decides to accept the return and give the Feenbergs a refund. Do you agree or disagree that this was the most decisive action she could take?

Agree _____   Disagree _____

3. Terry Hesley is the store manager for the Westbridge unit of Gimbley's. Gimbley's is a small, family-owned chain of retail food stores. Most management positions are held by members of the family. Terry is one of

the few exceptions. She has been allowed free rein in the store and has put many changes and new ideas into effect.

The success of the Westbridge store has been outstanding. Its sales and net profits have outrun all other units of Gimbley's. Terry thinks she is ready for a higher management position. She considers asking her boss, Mike Gimbley, for a promotion. Perhaps she should summarize both her educational qualifications and practical accomplishments in written form and send a letter to Mike. Should she send a copy to Kirk Gimbley, the president of the firm? Or should she wait for performance review time next month and see if she gets the promotion she wants? Should she send her resume to other firms to see if she could get a better position?

Terry decides to send out her resume. Do you agree or disagree that this was the most decisive action she could take?

Agree _____   Disagree _____

4. Jon Gardner was hired recently as director of the Creative School for Children. With the sweep of a new broom, Jon quickly set about making changes. The staff has not reacted well. Recently, teachers have refused to obey an order to remain in their classrooms with their students during rest periods. Instead, they leave the classroom doors open while they socialize with each other in the hall outside the classrooms.

Jon has called one of the teachers, Anna Piper, into his office to discuss the matter. Piper tells Jon that it has been customary for the teachers to take a break while the children are resting. The teachers do not understand why this practice cannot continue. They resent the change and feel that a previously held privilege has been removed needlessly.

Jon feels he must take some action to maintain his authority as director. He is considering one or more of the following: (1) firing Anna Piper as an example to the rest of the staff; (2) rescinding the rest period ruling; (3) meeting with the staff in a rap session and discussing the rest period ruling as well as other changes he has made; and (4) meeting with the staff and warning that anyone violating the rest period or other rules will be fired.

Jon calls a staff meeting and announces that rules must be followed. Anyone who refuses to follow the established rules will be dismissed. Do you agree or disagree that Jon took the most decisive action?

Agree _____   Disagree _____

5. Rick Tourage is the site manager for D & D Construction Company. A number of sites are scheduled to be poured today, among them Site X in the Nostrand Hills office park. This site is a difficult one and requires special attention.

Because of preconstruction leases, it is important to get the Nostrand Hills building completed on time. Rick has selected five of his most experienced men to work on the site.

Due to some unexplained mixup in scheduling, the concrete truck has arrived two hours early. If the truck waits for the assigned crew to arrive as scheduled, the concrete most likely will thicken and spoil. If the truck leaves, it will not be able to return the same day, and both the truck and the crew will have to be rescheduled for another day. Moreover, the crew will have to be paid downtime for today.

Rick ponders ways to resolve the situation. He can try to get crew members to Nostrand Hills quickly. This would mean withdrawing them from various other sites to which they had been assigned. He can phone the concrete company and insist that it send another truck at the time that had been scheduled, noting that otherwise it must assume the additional costs involved, including the penalties for construction delay. He can ask the truck to wait and take a chance that the concrete will be OK.

Rick phones the crew members and tells them to report to Nostrand Hills immediately. Do you agree or disagree that this was the most decisive action Rick could take?

Agree _____   Disagree _____

6. Joan Ingram, manager of Howell Creek Publishing Company, recently hired Mel Williams as a proofreader. Mel has had much experience in proofing copy and also in technical writing.

Mel cannot resist making changes in sentence construction, wording, and punctuation while he proofreads. The writers at Howell Creek are complaining, saying that Mel changes the meaning of what they had written. Joan has been asked to meet with her manager to discuss the matter.

At the meeting, Joan feels that she has been put on the carpet for her decision to hire Mel. Her manager tells her that Mel is clearly overqualified for the job of proofreader and this is causing a lot of trouble with the writing staff.

Joan reviews her options. She can admit she was wrong in hiring Mel and fire him; she can promise to speak to Mel and instruct him to limit himself to proofreading, the job for which he has been hired; she can try to get Mel transferred to a writing job, for which he is clearly qualified. Joan decides to speak to Mel. Do you agree or disagree that this is the most decisive action Joan could have taken?

Agree _____   Disagree _____

7. Al Gelvinsky is the plant manager at Dundee's Lumber Company. Last week, an employee at Dundee's was seriously injured because he did not wear his safety goggles, as required. Since the accident, tension in the plant has been high. To ease the situation, Al calls supervisors and employees together with the purpose of exploring ways to assure compliance with the safety regulations. At the meeting, Al asks the participants for suggestions. The room is silent. Finally, after several uncomfortable seconds, a supervisor says that employees ask for accidents because they simply refuse to wear safety gear, even when warned repeatedly about the dangers of going without it.

There is an immediate buzz of angry voices. An employee declares that the accident occurred because safety goggles slow them down, and the supervisors have been speeding up the work without regard for the safety of the employees. Both supervisors and employees begin to shout accusations at each other.

The meeting appears to have disintegrated into chaos. It is obvious that not only must the matter of safety regulations be reviewed, but also the whole question of employee/supervisor relationships must be addressed.

Al considers ways he can best handle the situation. He can try to call the meeting to order, by pounding with the gavel he holds in his hand; he can dismiss the meeting and call another, after people have had a chance to cool off; he can dismiss the meeting and appoint committees to research the situation.

Al pounds the gavel on the desk in front of him until there is silence. Then he proceeds with the meeting, setting forth some ground rules so that all will have a chance to be heard. Do you agree or disagree that Al chose the most decisive action?

Agree _____   Disagree _____

8. Jo Blass manages special feature production for a television station. At the regular Friday planning meeting, Bill Jones and Kim Lu, two members of the local news staff, present an outline for a new series on local businesses operated by women. Jo thinks the series is a good idea.

Bill and Kim submit a list of firms they will cover in their series. Included in the list is the Green Granny Catering House, a catering firm in which Bill's wife is a partner.

Jo knows that Green Granny is a very successful and highly unusual firm, and that its activities would be of interest to the TV audience. However, she fears that including this firm in the series may seem self-serving of Bill and may open the feature staff to charges of conflict of interest.

Jo thinks about what she should do. She considers the following possibilities. She can instruct Bill and Kim to delete Green Granny from their list; she can remove Bill from the series; or she can allow Bill and Kim to go ahead as planned, including Green Granny in the series.

Jo tells Bill and Kim to go ahead with their plans. Do you agree or disagree that this was the most decisive action Jo could take?

Agree _____   Disagree _____

9. Lonnie Hogan is the comptroller for the Davis and Smith Agency. Every three months, Lonnie makes a detailed financial report to the board of directors meeting. Bo Davis, president of the firm, has insisted on this quarterly report ever since the company made a costly investment error a few years ago due to incomplete information about their financial status.

Lonnie was out on vacation all of last week. However, before she left, she completed her report and instructed her secretary to make five copies, one for each member of the board of directors.

This morning, when Lonnie returns from her vacation, she finds that no duplicates have been made. The meeting is scheduled for 10 A.M. It is now 8 A.M. The report is lengthy, and it will take about an hour to make the five copies.

Lonnie instructs her secretary, Gary, to copy the report immediately. Gary responds that this is impossible because the only office copy machine is in use. Another report, also on the agenda for today's directors' meeting, is being copied. The machine will be free in about an hour.

Lonnie ponders her options. She can forget the copies and outline the report verbally, submitting only one copy to the firm's president for review. She can wait for the copy machine to be free and ask her secretary to bring the copies to the meeting, even if they are late. She can send her secretary down the street to Copy-quick and have the report copied there. Or she can insist on immediate access to the copier, since her task is a direct assignment of the president of the firm.

Lonnie decides to skip duplicating the report. Do you agree or disagree that this was the most decisive action Lonnie could take?

Agree _____   Disagree _____

10. Ronnie Herman is the head of sales at Apex Real Estate Agency. Apex arranged with a local travel agency to award a Caribbean cruise to the salesperson who achieved the highest dollar sales for the quarter. The travel agency agreed to donate the cruise as a promotional device.

The quarter has ended, and Val Lormer is clearly the winner. Ronnie phones Apex to find out when Val can pick up the tickets, only to learn that the phone has been disconnected. The travel agency has closed its doors. It is out of business!

Ronnie has not counted on paying for the cruise with Apex funds, nor has he permission to do so. Ronnie reviews his options. He can apologize to Val and explain the situation. Val shouldn't be too disappointed because she has received some hefty commissions on her sales. He can try to contact the cruise line directly and explain the situation in the hope that the cruise line will give Apex the tickets. Or he can have Apex pay for the tickets.

Ronnie decides to contact the cruise line. Do you agree or disagree that this is the most decisive behavior on Ronnie's part?

Agree _____   Disagree _____

DADS Scoring and Evaluation

Complete the DADS scoring form in Figure 3. Compare and be prepared to discuss your responses with the feedback your instructor provides about the most appropriate responses for the ten decisiveness situations.

FIGURE 3
Decisiveness Action Demonstration
Scale (DADS) Scoring

Question	Agree	Disagree	Response
1			
2			
3			
4			
5			
6			
7			
8			
9			
10			

SUMMARY

The more you practice the skills of decisiveness, the more effective you become as a manager. In this module you found that decisiveness required a manager to demonstrate skills in five categories. These were (1) taking the initiative, (2) giving opinions, (3) making rapid decisions, (4) defending decisions when challenged, and (5) taking risks to achieve results.

Working through the five in-basket exercises, you were asked to exercise decisiveness skills in the role of Collie Tiner, plant manager of the Harper Wells Company. In this role you focused on taking the initiative and being innovative in response to unforeseen variables, asserting your opinions in controversial situations, making rapid decisions and defending these decisions, and being aware of and taking risks.

You are now ready to apply the experience gained in this module to a work situation or other activity in which you are involved. As you practice these skills, you will experience the pleasure of positive feedback from others. Feedback from persons with whom you work will help you gauge whether you are using your decisiveness skills appropriately. Successful and competent managers continually work to improve their decisiveness skills.

FIGURE 4
Decisiveness Skills Action Guide

You Show Decisiveness When You:

- Take the initiative
- Give your opinions
- Make rapid decisions
- Defend your decisions when challenged
- Take risks to achieve results

You Should Show Decisiveness Skills When:

- Situations require action
- Opinions are requested
- Quick decisions are needed
- Your position is challenged
- You must go for what you want, even though results are not guaranteed

FIGURE 4
Decisiveness Skills Action Guide

To remember key steps in practicing decisiveness skills and to identify situations in which the skills are needed, use the action guide shown in Figure 4. Frequent review of the information will help you become a better manager.

SKILL-BUILDING EXERCISES

EXERCISE 1 ■ BEING ASSERTIVE

You are a project manager for a Fortune 500 company. In your mail today, you find the following memo: "Congratulations, you have been appointed as regional chair to collect money for the United Way Campaign. We are sure you will find it both an honor and a privilege to serve in this capacity for such a worthy cause." The memo is from an unknown volunteer. The task clearly does not fit with your long-term goals. Further, you have never indicated your interest in this position. Respond to this request in an assertive manner and defend your decision.

EXERCISE 2 ■ EXAMINING DECISIVE BEHAVIOR IN OTHERS

Select the most decisive person you know and conduct an interview with that individual. Include in your interview protocol questions around the components of decisiveness discussed in this module. Ask for specific examples. Report your findings to a small group or to the class as directed by your instructor.

■ Use Exhibits 1–5 with In-Basket Exercise 1,
Exhibits 6–10 with In-Basket Exercise 2,
Exhibits 11–15 with In-Basket Exercise 3,
Exhibits 16–20 with In-Basket Exercise 4,
Exhibits 21–25 with In-Basket Exercise 5.

EXHIBIT 1
Harper Wells Company
Memorandum

HARPER WELLS COMPANY

MEMORANDUM

TO: Dan Everidge, Plant Manager
FROM: José Picone, Warehouse Supervisor
DATE: January 10
RE: Year-end Inventory

Our year-end inventory check shows a 10% unexplained inventory shrinkage. We usually have only a 2-3% discrepancy at year end. 10% is definitely out of the ordinary.

I think we need quick action on this. What should we do?

HARPER WELLS COMPANY

MEMORANDUM

TO: Dan Everidge, Plant Manager
FROM: Chris Wentworth
DATE: January 15
RE: Merchandise Order

Jim Turner of Video Ventures called regarding a cassette order. He says that he phoned an order to the warehouse two weeks ago for eight cartons of cassettes that were featured for sale in today's newspaper ads.

The order was due Thursday, January 14, but has not been delivered. The warehouse people say they never heard of it, and that the trucks will not be able to get to Video until Thursday, January 21.

What do we do?

EXHIBIT 2
Harper Wells Company
Memorandum

HARPER WELLS COMPANY

MEMORANDUM

TO: Dan Everidge, Plant Manager
FROM: Norm Wilson, Shipping Supervisor
DATE: January 12
RE: Town Video Rentals, Inc.

Town Video has returned five recorders that were delivered last December, just before Christmas. All of the recorders have been used. My guess is that the Town people needed them temporarily to take care of increased business over the holidays. Now that things have slowed down, they'd like to get rid of them.

Of course, Lon Colbert at Town Video says that there is something wrong with the recorders. We can't find anything.

How should we handle this?

EXHIBIT 3
Harper Wells Company
Memorandum

EXHIBIT 4
Overland Chamber of Commerce
Letter

> OVERLAND CHAMBER OF COMMERCE
> 13 MAYO WAY
>
> Kim Matsuo, President   Dominick Cole, Director
>
> January 10
>
> Dear Mr. Everidge:
>
> Our membership is very interested in learning about the use of video recorders in business operations, and we are looking forward to hearing you next Tuesday, January 19, as scheduled.
>
> Dinner will be served at 6 P.M. in the Marshes room of the Newcomb Hotel; your talk will follow immediately.
>
> You will be our guest for dinner, of course.
>
> Sincerely yours,
>
> *Dominick Cole*
>
> Dominick Cole, Director

HARPER WELLS COMPANY

MEMORANDUM

TO: Dan Everidge, Plant Manager
FROM: Nolle Johnson, Risk Management Supervisor
DATE: January 12
RE: On-premises accident

Margo Fuller, one of our assemblers, caught her heel in the carpeting outside of your office. She twisted her ankle and will be unable to stand on her foot for about ten days. In all likelihood, she will apply for workers' compensation since she has only four days sick leave. This will not look good on our insurance record.

The accident could have been avoided if Maintenance had fixed the carpeting earlier. Ozzie Arnold, Maintenance Superintendent, was notified about the carpeting at least one month ago. I spoke to him this morning, and he says that new carpeting has been ordered, but it won't be here for another month.

We're likely to have another accident if something isn't done before then.

EXHIBIT 5
Harper Wells Company
Memorandum

EXHIBIT 6
Harper Wells Company
Memorandum

HARPER WELLS COMPANY

MEMORANDUM

TO: Collie Tiner, Plant Manager
FROM: Dan Everidge, Former Plant Manager
DATE: January 12
RE: a) Sick Leave, b) Dress Code

I'll be in Hawaii, listening to the rustle of the palm trees, by the time you read this memo. You are going to enjoy the plant. I know that you can take over with very little direction from me, and I feel quite comfortable about leaving before you arrive.

I'd like to call your attention to a couple of matters that I feel need your input. A proposal has come up to pay employees for unused sick leave. This practice has been used successfully elsewhere to cut down on absenteeism. Our managers and supervisors are divided on the issue. Some feel that the proposed practice assumes that employees are dishonest in their sick leave utilization; others say it penalizes sick employees. You need to send a letter to Tully Brent expressing your point of view.

Another unsettled issue is the dress code. The employees committee has taken strong exception to a recent requirement that all office employees dress in formal business clothing. The committee argues that since this is a manufacturing plant, and line workers wear casual work clothes, making office staff dress differently is unreasonable. This may seem like a minor issue, but it is creating quite a stir around here. Perhaps you should take a stand and end the dispute once and for all. Good luck.

HARPER WELLS COMPANY

M E M O R A N D U M

TO: Dan Everidge, Plant Manager
FROM: Clem MacDonald, Production Supervisor
DATE: January 11
RE: Thermostat Setting on Climate Control System

We lowered the thermostat as per your instructions. The purpose of this was to encourage faster movement in assembly operations. (It was conjectured that too much heat relaxed the assemblers and resulted in assembly slowdowns.)

For the past two weeks, we have kept the thermostat at 62 degrees. Instead of speeding up the operation, the opposite has occurred. Everyone says their fingers are too cold to work properly.

The cool temperatures seem to be counterproductive. What should we do?

EXHIBIT 7
Harper Wells Company
Memorandum

EXHIBIT 8
Ericson Security Systems, Inc.
Letter

ERICSON SECURITY SYSTEMS, INC.
32 MARSHALL STREET
OVERLAND

January 15

Collie Tiner, Plant Manager
Harper Wells Company

Dear Collie:

I heard the good news about your transfer to Overland. Whoever thought that when we attended Brookwood College, and majored in history, we'd both end up in the video business.

Yes, I deal with video too. My company designs individualized plant security systems. We use closed circuit T.V.'s and/or video recorders, depending on the needs of the customer. Perhaps we can do business with each other since your firm manufactures recorders and cassettes.

I'd like you to consider the possibility of an arrangement whereby you would supply and bill the customer directly for the recorders that would be needed in our system. We would expect a percentage of sales for this, of course. What do you think? In any event, let's meet for lunch and talk.

Sincerely,

Manny Foster

Manny Foster, President
Ericson Security Systems

MANAGEMENT OPINION QUARTERLY
HARLEM, ILLINOIS

January 14

Collie Tiner, Plant Manager
Harper Wells Company

Dear Collie:

We are collecting opinions on Quality Circles (small groups of employees from line to management who meet together regularly to exchange ideas on plant operations). We want to know whether, in your opinion, Quality Circles would help or hinder the operations of your firm, and why.

Because this is such an important current issue, we are asking only the most knowledgeable and experienced plant managers to respond to our survey. We need your reply quickly, so we can include it, along with others, in our next issue of Management Opinion.

Specifically address the questions of whether employee participation in decisions affecting their work is good for production, good for morale, or both. Will it have a measurable effect on productive efficiency, or simply a morale or attitudinal effect? We'd like you to think specifically in terms of your own plant when you reply. We have always valued your opinion and have depended on you in the past for some of our most valuable insights. We know we can count on you again. Many thanks.

Sincerely yours,

Landrum Chester, Editor

EXHIBIT 9
Management Opinion Quarterly Letter

EXHIBIT 10
Harper Wells Company
Memorandum

HARPER WELLS COMPANY

MEMORANDUM

TO: All Managerial Personnel
FROM: Tully Brent, President
DATE: January 4
RE: National Secretaries Week

According to the newspapers, many women's organizations are objecting to the candy and flowers approach to secretaries week. Also, at least 10% of company secretaries are males who would probably prefer beer and skittles.

Kidding aside, our secretaries form an important part of our support staff, and I believe special recognition is warranted for this group of employees. Do you agree? If so, how do you think we should proceed—use tried and true methods like luncheons, candy and flowers, or do something else?

We need your reply by the end of this month.

MAXWELL MACHINERY MAINTENANCE, INC.
LASWELL HEIGHTS, OVERLAND

Tony Sendwell   1-611-323-9829
President   January 10

Dear Plant Manager:

Have you considered using an outside maintenance organization for
machine and equipment repairs? Let us show you how a contract with us
can save you money, and get the job done faster and better.

Please phone my office, and we'll set up an appointment. We are offering
a special introductory rate to firms that act quickly.

Sincerely,

Tony Sandwell

Tony Sandwell

HARPER WELLS COMPANY

MEMORANDUM

TO: Collie Tiner, Plant Manager
FROM: Clem MacDonald, Production Supervisor
DATE: January 15
RE: Contract completion dates

___

Our sales staff is promising delivery without regard to production requirements. It is not possible to complete all orders by the dates promised.

Is there some way we can coordinate their promises with our possibilities?

EXHIBIT 13
Harper Wells Company
Memorandum

HARPER WELLS COMPANY

M E M O R A N D U M

TO: Collie Tiner, Plant Manager
FROM: Tully Brent, President   CONFIDENTIAL
DATE: January 15
RE: Computer Contract

We have received a contract for production of a new type of video recorder that can be operated by remote control.

Employees working on this contract must be highly skilled and must also receive security clearance.

Can you handle it? We need an immediate reply.

EXHIBIT 14
Essen Nutrition Systems
Letter

ESSEN NUTRITION SYSTEMS
"FOR THE HEALTH OF IT"

January 2

Dear Plant Manager:

Our contract to run your food services expires on January 5th. At this time there will be a 15% increase in charges for service. Prices for food will vary, as usual, according to current market prices.

According to the terms of our existing contract, if we do not hear from you to the contrary within 15 days, the existing contract is renewed for one year as amended above.

Sincerely yours,

Geri Gratin

Geri Gratin
Contract Officer

HARPER WELLS COMPANY

MEMORANDUM

TO: Collie Tiner, Plant Manager
FROM: Lee Marowitz, Personnel Director
DATE: January 15
RE: Health Maintenance Organizations (HMO)

We will have an opportunity shortly to enter an HMO. This would replace our present employee health insurance policy.

HMO coverage is more restricted than that currently in effect, but the costs are considerably lower and preventive health checkups are paid for.

Because of the seriousness of the changes involved, perhaps we ought to give our employees a chance to vote their preferences. The alternative is to make a decision without consulting the employees.

Although we have no obligation to confer with the employees on any changes in medical/health coverage, if changes are disliked, we may face a morale problem.

We need to take some action before January 21.

EXHIBIT 15
Harper Wells Company
Memorandum

EXHIBIT 16
Issue 1
Special Recognition for Secretaries

Issue 1: Special recognition for secretaries.

Your original position: Opposed. Secretaries perform a job as do other personnel employed by the firm. There is no reason to single out this classification for special recognition.

Opposing argument: This job is unique because a secretary is often called upon to anticipate and act upon needs related to the boss's job as well as to his or her own job. Additionally, a secretarial job requires a special combination of diverse skills, e.g., the ability to take orders and follow directions without input or questions, and the ability to take the initiative and make decisions on behalf of the employer under some circumstances. The assignment requires a high degree of flexibility and personal loyalty. A secretary deserves special recognition from the person to whom he or she is assigned.

EXHIBIT 17
Issue 2
Pay for Unused Sick Leave

Issue 2: Pay for unused sick leave.

Your original position: Opposed. Sick leave is a facet of medical insurance. Its purpose is to protect employees against loss due to illness. It is not part of the vacation or wage and salary system.

Opposing argument: Employees who put in more time on the job ought to be rewarded accordingly. You must agree that employees with a good health record put in more hours than those who are out sick a lot. Why not compensate them for that? The way to do this is to compensate for unused sick leave. This also discourages malingering.

Issue 3: Quality Circles (vertical groups of employees from line to management who meet to discuss work and suggest methods for improving production).

Your original position: Support Quality Circles. People with hands-on job experience know where the bugs are and can offer suggestions for improving operations. Meeting with management allows interchange of ideas, produces useful information, and encourages interest in job.

Opposing argument: Quality Circles are window dressing only. All the real decisions are made by management. Employees know this and will not take these meetings seriously.

EXHIBIT 18
Issue 3
Quality Circles

Issue 4: Conflict between sales and production. Sales staff promises delivery dates without regard to production schedules.

Your original position: Production should inform sales of output schedules so sales staff can set more realistic delivery dates.

Opposing argument: If we don't deliver the product when customers need it, they will take their business elsewhere. It's up to production to adjust schedules to meet the customers' needs, not vice versa.

EXHIBIT 19
Issue 4
Conflict between Sales and Production

Issue 5: Polling employees on a possible change from the current health insurance policy to a health maintenance organization.

Your original position: Oppose. This is a management decision. In making this decision, management will take many factors into consideration, including possible effects on employee morale.

Opposing argument: Health benefits are part of the wage and salary structure of the employees. In the interest of good employee relations, these benefits should not be changed arbitrarily.

EXHIBIT 20
Issue 5
Changing Health Benefits

EXHIBIT 21
Industrial Information Specialists

INDUSTRIAL INFORMATION SPECIALISTS
253-333-4444

January 11

Dan Everidge, Plant Manager
Harper Wells Company

Dear Mr. Everidge:

This is in regard to our testing of Kit Weston on January 8. According to our contract with you, all warehouse employees who receive, sort, and/or pack orders are tested annually for physiological response to a series of critical questions relating to the handling of inventory (the so-called "lie detector test"). The tests are usually given at year end or shortly thereafter.

This is the third annual test administered to Kit Weston. In the preceding two tests, results were within normal range. In this last test, however, Weston showed unusually marked responses to several critical questions. Our opinion is that Weston has failed to reach acceptable norms on the test.

Results of "lie-detector" tests have been studied for effectiveness in detecting false statements. These studies indicate that tests are effective in 35% to 60% of the situations studied. The probability that these percentages would occur due to chance alone is less than 5%.

Sincerely yours,

Hsiu-Lien Charles, President

HARPER WELLS COMPANY
OVERLAND PLANT
PERFORMANCE EVALUATION

Name: Kit Weston

Evaluator: José Picone,
Warehouse Supervisor

Position: Material Handler

December 30 Last Year

Performance Rating Scale

1	2	3	4	5
Needs Improvement	Fair	Good	Superior	Excellent

Performance Category	Rating
Attendance	5
Accuracy in Order Filling	5
Accuracy in Order Sorting	5
Quantity of Packages Handled	4
Interactions with Other Employees	5
Response to Supervision	4
Willingness to Work Overtime	5
Flexibility	4
Overall Rating	**4.6**

EXHIBIT 22
Harper Wells Company
Performance Evaluation

EXHIBIT 23
Overland Commercial Bank
Letter

OVERLAND COMMERCIAL BANK
WATERWAY LANE

January 15

Dan Everidge, Plant Manager
Harper Wells Company

Dear Dan:

Lysle Wilbur, the newly appointed comptroller for your Overland plant, has asked us to issue a mortgage on a home she wishes to purchase. The price of the home is $144,000, and the appraised value, according to an appraisal issued by a CLA (Certified and Licensed Appraiser) is $180,000.

Our usual practice is to issue mortgages at 80% of purchase price, or of appraised value, whichever is lower. This requires the buyer to make a down payment of at least 20%. However, Ms. Wilbur has asked us to base the mortgage on the higher appraised value rather than on the purchase price. The results would be that the entire purchase price of the home would be covered by the mortgage, with no down payment required. We are willing to do this if your company guarantees the mortgage.

It is not unusual for companies to underwrite mortgages on the homes of key employees. Would you be willing to co-sign in the company's name with Wilbur, especially since the value is there? Ms. Wilbur knows that we have written this letter to you.

Sincerely yours,

Kirk Wallace, Loan Officer

HARPER WELLS COMPANY

MEMORANDUM

TO: Collie Tiner, Plant Manager
FROM: Lee Jason, Purchasing Agent
DATE: January 15
RE: Materials Purchase

The Crewitt Corporation is offering a special price on No. 2 fine wire spools, provided that we place a minimum order of 100 gross. While this will give us far more spools than we need to fill current and immediately prospective orders, the price savings are so great that it would pay to store the surplus.

There is a very small chance that the spools will warp if subjected to sharp temperature change, such as might occur if cartons of spools were removed from the air conditioned warehouse and placed in the noonday sun. But this is not likely to happen.

Orders must be placed by Tuesday, January 19, to take advantage of the sale price. Do I have your approval?

EXHIBIT 24
Harper Wells Company
Memorandum

EXHIBIT 25
Marbury Associates
Letter

MARBURY ASSOCIATES
COUNSELORS AND ATTORNEYS AT LAW
BRANHAM BUILDING

January 12

Tully Brent, President
Harper Wells Company

Dear Tully:

Continental Video Systems has offered to withdraw their suit for Patent infringement, if your firm agrees to stop manufacturing the V-29 type recorder. (I understand from Dan Everidge that you have discontinued manufacturing this type of recorder anyway.) While this can avoid court action, and the consequent litigation costs, I don't think Continental has a case. Of course, you can never guarantee what a jury will do even when the facts are clear!

The risk of settling on the basis proposed is that Continental refuses to guarantee that they will not bring suit later. However, since the statute of limitations has only six months to run, by the end of June, you'll be in the clear anyway, *provided that you forego your right to manufacture the V-29s.*

In summary, your options are as follows:

1.　Accept Continental Video's offer to withdraw without guarantee that no further action will be taken. Since the statute of limitations has only six months to run, the risks of a new action from Continental are small. This will save you the costs of litigation.

2.　Make a counter offer. We suggest that you ask for Video's agreement to cease and desist from further legal action with respect to the V-29, and a clause emphasizing that the agreement does not constitute an admission of infringement on your part.

3.　Agree to nothing and take the case to court. I think we'll win. In that event, you will retain the right to manufacture the V-29. If you want to go this route, we can also file countersuit for recovery of costs involved in litigation.

Which option do you want to go with?

Sincerely,

Winnie Marbury

Winnie Marbury
Attorney-at-Law

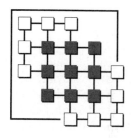

MODULE 9
FLEXIBILITY SKILLS: ADAPTING TO CHANGE

INTRODUCTION

Imagine yourself as the navigator of a small skiff. Changes in the wind, current, or weather all require adjustments in speed or direction for the boat to make it to port. As navigator, you must not only recognize when these adjustments are needed but also determine the adjustments to be made and make them. If you fail, the boat will remain at sea.

Similarly, as a manager you must deal with shifting situations and unforeseen occurrences. Like the navigator of the skiff, you must adjust plans, assignments, procedures, and behaviors in order to stay on course and reach goals. As a manager, your ability to be flexible may make the difference between a successful outcome and an unsuccessful one.

Successful managers recognize that to build viable organizations, they must view adapting to change as an integral part of their responsibility. This means changing old methods of control and command that emphasized bureaucracy, rigidity, and impersonal human relationships to new methods of participation, involvement, entrepreneurship, and flexibility. This is the fundamental challenge faced by organizations as they strive for managerial excellence and learn to deal with changing cultures, strategies, and practices.

This module explores the skills needed to understand and manage change. It is based upon the viewpoint that the best way to manage change is to develop and practice the skills of flexibility.

Flexibility allows the manager to make adjustments needed to remain on course. It is the ability to maintain constructive behavior in stressful situations, to remain calm when pressured by time, people, or situations, and to change courses of action in order to deal appropriately with new situations, people, personalities, and assignments. Flexibility is demonstrated by the following behaviors: (1) working with new, changing, and ambiguous situations, (2) working under pressure, (3) dealing with different personal styles, (4) handling feedback, and (5) resolving conflicts.

This module will help you develop and strengthen these flexibility skills. You will assume the role of manager in a variety of exercises. In each exercise, you will be provided with information—samples of material that typically find their way to the manager's desk. In the role of manager, you must use flexibility skills to solve a potential problem. By actually participating in exercises, you can learn and practice flexibility.

The module is organized so that you will develop a before-practice assessment of your flexibility skills by completing the Flexible Behaviors Questionnaire (FBQ). This questionnaire measures your flexibility skills at the present time. We then present a brief discussion of the components of flexibility. Next, through exercises, you will have an opportunity to practice flexible behaviors. The exercises focus on one category at a time. Feedback from your instructor will help you judge the quality of your own responses and provide guidance on improving specific behaviors.

After you have completed the exercises, you will have an opportunity to retake the FBQ and compare your after-practice assessment results with your earlier results. You will also complete the Flexibility Display Scale (FDS). This assessment instrument examines how you interpret actual behavior in situations where flexibility skills are needed. It will give you more insight into your own behaviors in situations requiring flexibility.

Once you have completed this module, you may find that your practice will result in immediate improvement, or you may find that your improvement is noticeable after you have had opportunities to perform on the job or in a nonwork-related situation.

ASSESSING FLEXIBILITY SKILLS

Before proceeding with the rest of this module, complete the questionnaire on the following pages. It is both a teaching tool and a means of measuring your present level of flexibility skills. Take time to complete the questionnaire carefully. Your answers should reflect your behaviors as they are now, not as you would like them to be. Be honest. This instrument is designed to help you discover where you are now so you can work to improve your flexibility skills.

The Flexible Behaviors Questionnaire (FBQ)

The Flexible Behaviors Questionnaire (FBQ) examines your current flexible behaviors in five areas. These behaviors are essential to managerial effectiveness. As you respond to the questions, consider your work experience or groups you have worked with in a classroom, fraternity, sorority, club, or service organization. You will find that the questions are applicable to your own experience even if you are not yet a manager.

After you have completed this module and have had an opportunity to put into practice the flexibility skills you have learned, you will retake the questionnaire. Comparing your before- and after-practice scores will help you evaluate the effectiveness of your practice.

Use the following scale to rate the frequency with which you perform the behaviors described in each question. Place the corresponding number (1–7) in the blank preceding the statement.

Rarely	Irregularly	Occasionally	Usually	Frequently	Almost Always	Consistently
1	2	3	4	5	6	7

_____ 1. I manage a variety of assignments with varying demands and complexities.

_____ 2. I adjust work plans to account for new circumstances.

_____ 3. I modify rules and procedures in order to meet operational needs and goals.

_____ 4. I work with ambiguous assignments when necessary and use these when possible to further my goals and objectives.

_____ 5. I rearrange work or personal schedules to meet deadlines.

_____ 6. In emergencies, I respond to the most pressing needs first.

_____ 7. I change my priorities to accommodate unexpected events.

_____ 8. I manage my personal work overload by seeking assistance or by delegating responsibility to others.

_____ 9. I vary the way I deal with others according to their needs and personalities.

_____ 10. I help others improve their job performance or I assign tasks that will further their development.

_____ 11. I accept the authority of my manager but continue to demonstrate my initiative and assertiveness.

_____ 12. I work well with all types of personalities.

_____ 13. I measure my performance on the job against the feedback I receive.

_____ 14. I correct performance deficits that have been brought to my attention.

_____ 15. When I disagree with my manager's appraisal of my work, I discuss our differences.

_____ 16. I seek training and assignments that can help me improve my job-related skills.

_____ 17. In disagreements concerning work-related issues, I look at matters impersonally and concentrate on the facts.

_____ 18. I make compromises to get problems moving toward resolution.

_____ 19. I look for new and better ways to accomplish my duties and responsibilities.

_____ 20. I offer to negotiate all areas of disagreement.

FIGURE 1

Flexible Behaviors Questionnaire (FBQ) Scoring

Skill Area	Items	Assessment	
		Before Practice	After Practice
Working with new, changing, and ambiguous situations	1,2,3,4		
Working under pressure	5,6,7,8		
Dealing with different personal styles	9,10,11,12		
Handling feedback	13,14,15,16		
Resolving conflicts	17,18,19,20		
TOTAL SCORE			

FBQ Scoring

The scoring sheet in Figure 1 summarizes your responses for the FBQ. It will help you identify your existing strengths and pinpoint areas that need improvement. Right now, fill in the before-practice assessment column and add the five category scores to obtain a total score. Enter that score in the space indicated. After completing the module, you will take the FBQ again and fill in the after-practice assessment column.

FBQ Evaluation

Figure 2 shows score lines for your total score and for each category measured on the FBQ. Each line shows a continuum from the lowest score to the highest. Place the letter B (before-practice) where your personal score falls on each of these lines.

The score lines in Figure 2 show graphically where you stand with regard to the five flexible behaviors. If you have been honest with yourself, you now have a better idea of your relative strengths and weaknesses in the categories that make up the skills of flexibility.

Learning to Use the FBQ Skills

You have completed the initial evaluation of your flexibility skills. In the FBQ, you rated the frequency with which you demonstrate behaviors in the five categories of flexibility. This questionnaire provides a baseline against which you will assess changes that have taken place after you have completed this module.

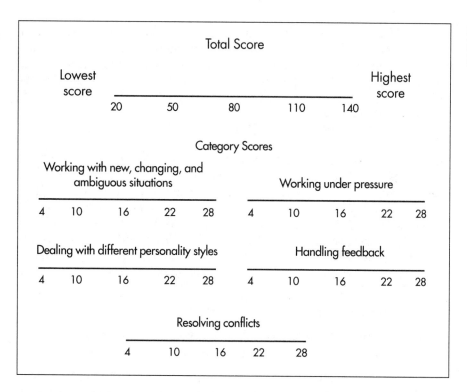

FIGURE 2
Flexible Behaviors Questionnaire (FBQ) Evaluation

Before moving on, think about what you have learned about yourself in this evaluation. In what areas of flexibility skills are you weak? These will require the most attention during the remainder of the module. What areas are your strongest? Use this module to fine-tune these areas so you may take full advantage of them. For these stronger areas, learning only one or two new things may be all you need for significant improvement in your flexibility skills.

Keep your own special needs in mind as you proceed. Review the FBQ frequently. Refer to it as you work through the material presented in the remaining sections of the module. The FBQ will help you identify flexible behaviors that are appropriate for the management situations described in the exercises. After you have had an opportunity to put into practice what you have learned, retake the FBQ. Then, compare your after-practice scores with your before-practice scores. This comparison will show you where you have progressed and where further work is needed.

UNDERSTANDING FLEXIBILITY

Managers need flexibility to deal with conflict, change, and pressure. They must deal with circumstances they do not anticipate and with problems that, at first glance, may appear hopeless. When such problems occur frequently or are quite pressing, they may have heavy personal impact on the manager. Managerial stress then becomes personal distress. It is not the intent of this module to teach you how to deal with personal stress. However, you probably are aware that the ability to cope with external pressures goes a long way toward relieving the personal stress that such pressures generate. Flexibility increases your ability to cope with external pressures.

Looked at in another way, flexibility is the skill that allows you to keep control over events that threaten to go out of control. The flexible manager implements changes that keep situations from deteriorating. These changes respond to current needs and, at the same time, promote progress toward goals. As a manager you must work well under pressure and learn to resolve conflicts productively. Effective managers must also deal with all personality types and must be able to give and receive criticism constructively.

Rigid managers can't perform these tasks well. They find it very difficult to change, to deal positively with all personalities, or to resolve conflicts—in short, they are seldom flexible. This usually means failure as a manager.

The Flexibility Process

Flexibility is a process that leads to adaptive actions. The process consists of the following steps:

1. *Generating new perspectives:* Looking at the situation from different viewpoints may lead to different interpretations. This phase of flexibility opens doors to new possibilities for action.
2. *Developing new options:* If you pay attention to alternative ways of dealing with new or changing situations and pressures, you will become more flexible.
3. *Reordering priorities:* When you rearrange priorities, new possibilities for change may surface. You can then solve problems more easily.
4. *Revising goals:* At times it is helpful to set new goals that more realistically take into account the "here and now" of a situation. New goals can remove obstacles that interfere with the achievement of more basic organization objectives. A flexible manager revises goals as necessary.
5. *Taking adaptive actions:* The previous four steps will lead you to new and constructive ways of meeting difficult situations.

Flexibility Skills Required of Managers

Flexibility covers a range of behaviors. It requires that a manager demonstrate skills in five categories: (1) working with different and ambiguous situations, (2) working under pressure, (3) dealing with different personal styles, (4) handling feedback, and (5) resolving conflicts. Flexibility is the ability to offer constructive suggestions, to remain calm, and to modify your behavior when appropriate. In the next section, we will briefly describe these behaviors.

Working with New, Changing, and Ambiguous Situations

The manager must cope with a variety of sometimes confusing situations. Frequently, the course of action isn't suggested, or the lines of authority may be interpreted in many ways. Responsibility for problem solving sometimes isn't clear. Flexible managers, however, adapt and take clear action to solve problems.

Working under Pressure

Work overload, conflicting demands, and emergencies are some of the pressures that call for flexibility on the part of the manager. For example, some situations cause a conflict between customer needs and other job requirements. A flexible stance can help managers effectively cope with these situations.

Dealing with Different Personal Styles

As a manager, you must work with many people and accommodate the varying personal styles of others, including superiors, subordinates, colleagues, and customers. You will find that frequently, all these people have separate agendas and conflicting personality styles.

A person's style is his or her habitual way of interacting with others. Some people, for example, are assertive, while others are compliant. Extroverts are outgoing while introverts are reserved when interacting with others. People with compatible behavioral styles tend to like each other and naturally get along better than do people with incompatible styles. An essential managerial skill is knowing how to adapt to different personal styles.

Personal style is especially important when an employee and a manager with incompatible styles come in contact with each other. When that occurs, tension often results. This tension usually pushes the employee away from the manager and makes that person seem to be a "difficult" employee. In order to avoid this tension, a manager should practice flexibility.

Accepting and understanding that employees are different and need to be managed differently is basic to successful management. If managers are able to identify personality traits in their employees, they can manage the way the employees would like to be managed. The bottom-line benefit will be greater productivity and more personal satisfaction in all relationships.

Handling Feedback

Feedback, either formal or informal, is frequently a call for change in some aspects of job performance. Feedback can be given verbally or nonverbally; its purpose is to verify facts or feelings. Feedback that gives information on the consequences of certain actions is central to any human relationship in which learning is desired or necessary.

Feedback is often taken for granted. It may, however, be the most important aspect of interpersonal communication. The effective use of feedback skills—both giving feedback and receiving feedback—helps reduce the probability of misunderstanding and misinterpretation.

Effective feedback is never easy, but a manager has the primary responsibility of making it work. The following guidelines are designed to facilitate the feedback process.

- Describe rather than evaluate. Describe objectively what the person did and any feelings it aroused in you, but do not label or evaluate the behavior. The person receiving the feedback is less likely to feel threatened or defensive.
- Offer feedback but do not impose it. Offer feedback as one person's perceptions, not as "the truth." Give information as something the person can consider and explore, not as a command that he or she change.
- Deal in specifics, not generalities. Describe concrete events and exact incidents. Avoid extremes and absolutes.
- Give feedback promptly. Feedback given soon after the behavior, except when the individual is upset or otherwise not ready to listen, is better than that given when details are no longer clear in anyone's mind.
- Examine your motives. Be sure your intentions are to be helpful, not to show how perceptive and superior you are or to hurt the other person.
- Focus on the behavior or problem, not the person. Focus on the problem and its solution rather than on personality or personal traits.

When feedback is not handled effectively, both defensiveness and disconfirmation can occur. If an individual feels threatened or punished by the feedback, both the message and the interpersonal relationship are blocked. Self-protection becomes paramount, and now the focus is more on self-defense than on listening. Criticism of one's behavior is often perceived as a threat or attack. Common reactions are anger, aggression, competitiveness, and avoidance.

When a manager is receiving feedback, he or she should view it impersonally and objectively. Feedback can help the manager move ahead. A nondefensive posture will promote a flexible and productive response to feedback.

Resolving Conflicts

Conflict is a disagreement between two or more people in which their concerns appear to be incompatible. The main sources of conflict in organizations are disputes over shared resources, differences in goals, interdependence of work activities, and differences in values or perceptions.

Individuals respond to conflict in two ways: trying to satisfy their own concerns or cooperating with others to maintain a satisfactory relationship. A closer look at these two basic dimensions reveals five methods of dealing with conflicts. As seen in Figure 3, these methods are (1) competing, (2) accommodating, (3) avoiding, (4) collaborating, and (5) compromising.

Competing is assertive and uncooperative behavior in which individuals pursue their own concerns at another person's expense. Competing is most helpful in situations where quick, decisive action is vital, such as in emergencies. It is also useful where unpopular courses of action, such as discipline or cost cutting, must be implemented.

Accommodating is the opposite of competing and consists of unassertive and cooperative behavior. Accommodating is a useful strategy for the manager when the issue at stake is much more important to the other person than it is to the

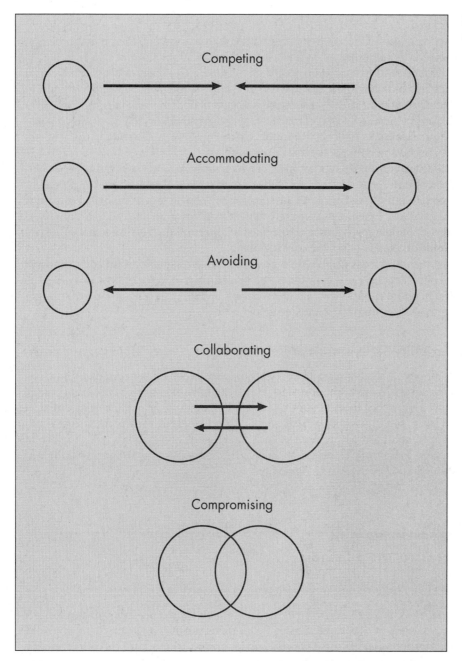

FIGURE 3
Approaches to Interpersonal Conflict

manager. Satisfying another's needs as a goodwill gesture will help maintain a cooperative relationship and build up credits for later issues.

Avoiding is unassertive and uncooperative behavior in which individuals do not pursue either their own concerns or those of others. In avoiding the conflict, a person might diplomatically sidestep an issue, postpone it, or withdraw from the situation. Avoiding is useful when the issue under disagreement has passing importance or is relatively trivial to the manager. If the manager has little power or encounters a situation that is very difficult to change, avoiding may be the best use of his or her time.

Collaborating is the opposite of avoiding; it consists of assertive and cooperative behavior. It involves an attempt to work with the other person to find a solution that fully satisfies the concerns of both parties. This joint problem-solving involves a lot of communication and creativity on the part of each party to find a mutually beneficial solution. Collaborating is a necessity in cases where the concerns of both parties are important.

Compromising falls somewhere between assertive and cooperative behaviors. The objective is to find a mutually acceptable middle ground that is expedient and partially satisfies both parties. Most conflicts are resolved through compromise. Since compromise always involves give and take, flexibility is needed. Redefining issues and priorities while reviewing new information draws people of opposing views closer together.

A compromise is useful when goals are moderately important and not worth the effort of collaboration or the possible disruption of competition. It is often the best hope for situations where both parties are of equal power and are strongly committed to mutually exclusive goals.

Flexibility Skills and Their Relationships to Other Managerial Skills

Flexibility is always used in conjunction with other managerial skills, such as interpersonal skills and leadership. Flexibility is the skill most likely to encourage fresh approaches to the issues involved. For example, flexibility is essential in problem solving where a manager is called upon to formulate and execute creative solutions to problems. Since the essence of flexibility is the ability to modify behaviors to adapt to new situations, other managerial skills are strengthened by practicing flexibility.

PRACTICING FLEXIBILITY

Flexibility skills consist of the following component behaviors:

- *Working with new, changing, and ambiguous situations*—You must manage a variety of situations, modify work plans when changes occur, change old procedures to meet goals, and continue to manage despite vaguely defined authority limits.
- *Working under pressure*—When deadlines are short or assignments extremely demanding, you have to change your own or others' work assignments, schedules, and priorities.
- *Dealing with different personal styles*—Personal styles as well as management styles differ. The ability to deal with these differences is part of being flexible.

- *Handling feedback*—You need to be flexible when you are given feedback on your own performance. Look at the facts, discuss disagreements, and improve by modifying your unproductive behaviors.
- *Resolving conflicts*—You show flexibility when you are able to negotiate and compromise in order to resolve conflicts.

The following five in-basket exercises are set in one of two interlocking companies. In each exercise, you are asked to assume a different role—to be a different person within these companies—as well as to deal with a different situation. The roles and circumstances change, although the companies' objectives stay the same. These exercises will help you practice flexible behaviors.

The exercises focus separately on each component of flexibility. In the first exercise, you must work with a changing and ambiguous situation. The next exercise will require you to work under pressure. In the third exercise you will be asked to deal with different personal styles. The fourth exercise focuses on handling feedback. Finally, in the fifth exercise you will be asked to resolve a conflict.

Before you begin the exercises, review your scores on the FBQ. As you complete the exercises, keep in mind the behaviors noted in this measure of flexibility. The questions in the FBQ deepen your understanding of flexibility skills. After reading about the background of the two organizations, practice your flexibility skills in the exercises.

Background Information on Plusultra and Clayplay

The following exercises are set in two interlocking companies, Plusultra, Inc., and Clayplay, Inc. One company produces ultralon; the other packages and markets ultralon for sale to retail and other establishments. Organizational charts for the companies are shown in Exhibits 1 and 2.

Ultralon is a compound that has been developed and patented by Ozzie Kliner, a research chemist. It has certain unique qualities. At room temperature, ultralon is a pliable solid. When heated to 200 degrees Celsius, ultralon liquefies and can be poured into preformed molds and allowed to cool and harden. If treated cryogenically (frozen), ultralon loses its plasticity and becomes fixed in shape, and indestructible.

Kliner developed ultralon in the basement laboratory of his family home in Palma Miros, Florida. At the time, Kliner was employed by the Conidium Corporation, producers of agricultural pesticides. Kliner left Conidium five years ago and formed Plusultra. Although Kliner has retained personal ownership of ultralon patents, rights to manufacture ultralon have been granted exclusively to Plusultra.

In addition to ultralon, Plusultra produces chemical compounds such as fertilizers and pesticides, usually under subcontract to other firms. Ownership of Plusultra is held closely. It is distributed as follows: Ozzie Kliner, 60 percent; attorney Lee Winslin, 10 percent; Aubrey Marx, vice president of sales and marketing, 28 percent. Two percent of stock is held in reserve by the corporation.

To date, there has been little demand for ultralon from industrial firms. Some time ago, Kliner decided to offer ultralon to the consumer market. With two colleagues, Jo Fendat and Ardie Morton, Kliner organized Clayplay, Inc.

Clayplay packages and markets ultralon for direct use by consumers. Its customers are art and hobby outlets and schools. The product is used like clay. Plusultra owns 25 percent of Clayplay. The remaining 75 percent is divided equally among Kliner, Fendat, and Morton. Both Plusultra and Clayplay are small firms with fewer than 100 employees between them.

IN-BASKET EXERCISE 1: WORKING WITH NEW, CHANGING, AND AMBIGUOUS SITUATIONS

As a manager, you are often asked to oversee situations in which events shift rapidly, requirements are not clearly stated, and lines of authority are vague or ambiguous. To deal with these circumstances, you need to change previously established plans, rules, or procedures. In other words, you must be flexible.

In the following in-basket, you assume the role of a manager whose authority limits are not explicitly defined. At the same time, you must deal with new demands made on the department you manage.

Situation:

You are Allie Blauhut, production manager for Plusultra, Inc. Your job is to direct the processing of products so delivery schedules are met, costs are contained, quality is maintained, and customers are satisfied. You make decisions to enable the firm to meet these goals.

Until very recently, authority lines have been very clear to you. They have been set forth on the organizational chart of your firm (shown in Exhibit 1). Your line supervisors report to you, and you in turn report to Kilmer Gordon, plant manager. Within the limits of your authority, you either initiate necessary action or act on the changes suggested by the line supervisors or instituted by the plant manager.

Recently, the executive committee of Plusultra voted to launch a team approach to company operations. Teams have been organized to deal with problems and other matters. Each manager has been assigned a team. Today, you will be meeting with your team.

The memorandum announcing team formation and other pertinent information is in a file on your desk (Exhibits 1 through 8). The program has been given the acronym TEN. It stands for Try Excellence Now. You will also find references to other matters of concern. Refer to the file of information as you answer the questions that follow.

Your flexibility skills focus:

- Revise your perspectives.
- Realign your priorities.
- Use new resources.
- Try novel approaches.

Questions for In-Basket Exercise 1:

1. Having already scheduled processing of K-287 for the Southwestern Insecticide Company and processing of ultralon for Clayplay you are presented with the following changes:

   ■ A new order has been received for K-287 from another company. Since no delivery date has been set, there appears to be little pressure for early delivery. However, it would be cost-effective to process this new order immediately.

   ■ Jo Fendat, president of Clayplay, has complained about the way the deliveries of ultralon to Clayplay are handled by Plusultra.

   ■ Processing the new order for K-287 means delaying the processing of a prior order for ultralon for which no delivery date had been established.

   ■ Your newly established TEN circle will be meeting today. Ozzie Kliner has suggested that you ask the circle to consider problems faced by your department.

   How would you deal with these matters in a way that demonstrates flexibility?

2. A decision must be reached on these matters today. The memo from Kliner is unclear about the authority of your TEN circle. Suppose you refer the scheduling issues to your TEN circle and then disagree with its recommendation. How would a flexible stance help resolve the situation?

3. Suppose your circle members agree that more time is needed for an in-depth study of order scheduling and order filling? Demonstrate flexibility by dealing with this in a way that accommodates the need for an immediate decision without ignoring the advice of the circle.

4. Read Exhibit 8. This letter from Jo Fendat introduces some new considerations, and the situation changes. The letter specifies a firm delivery date and emphasizes the importance of meeting that delivery date. Reevaluate your previous responses as you respond to these new events. An initial flexible response would be to review your options. What are your options? Should you discuss the matter with your TEN circle?

IN-BASKET EXERCISE 2: WORKING UNDER PRESSURE

As a manager you will sometimes be faced with work overload, tight deadlines, emergencies, and other events that place you under heavy pressure and personal strain. Responding flexibly to these events can ease the tensions and pressure.

In the situation that follows, you must deal with increasing pressures. Your task is to remain flexible. In the process, you will find relief from the personal strains induced by the situation.

Situation:

Assume the role of Petey Perrin, packaging manager for Clayplay. You will recall that Clayplay's entire operation consists of selling, packaging, and shipping ultralon to customers who use it for recreational and artistic purposes. You are under heavy pressure to meet delivery schedules. According to the information shown in Exhibits 9 through 13, you find yourself caught between opposing pressures—one to reduce costs and the other to get a large order out on time. You will see that flexibility skills will help you solve this dilemma. Study the information shown in Exhibits 9 through 13 and answer the questions that follow.

Your flexibility skills focus:

- Redefine your task.
- Revise your priorities.
- Choose between conflicting goals.
- Change and compromise in order to reach your target goal.
- Temporarily suspend rules to meet urgent needs.

Questions for In-Basket Exercise 2:

1. As of October 15, you have been informed that work on the Zuyder order is two days behind schedule because of machine breakdowns. The order is scheduled for shipping on October 17. This is an important order, and the customer has made some commitments that depend on the delivery date you have promised. Overtime is strongly discouraged. Display flexibility in handling this situation. Explain.

2. Read Exhibit 13. You must face the increased pressure that is generated by this memorandum from Fendat to Morton. In addition to delays on the Zuyder order due to downtime, you also must contend with a direct order from the president of Clayplay to bulk-package ultralon immediately. Deal with this by using your flexibility skills.

IN-BASKET EXERCISE 3: DEALING WITH DIFFERENT PERSONAL STYLES

As a manager, you must work with many people. You will find that frequently they have separate personal agendas and conflicting personality styles. Adapting to these differences by displaying flexibility will help you become a better manager.

In the following in-basket exercise, you are required to meet with three company executives. You must use flexibility in dealing with their different personalities and diverse personal agendas.

Situation:

In this situation, you, Glynne Bonney, sales manager for Clayplay, will be meeting with the executives of Clayplay. The purpose of the meeting is to discuss sales. Present will be Jo Fendat, president of the firm, Ardie Morton, vice president of operations, and Ozzie Kliner, executive committee chair.

Profiles of each of these persons along with data on sales performance and other information are shown in Exhibits 14 through 18. Read the profiles and examine the charts and memos. Then explain the facts and make your suggestions in a way that is most likely to be acceptable to each conferee, given their individual agendas and personalities.

Your flexibility skills focus:

- Change perspectives.
- Rethink relationships.
- Vary your own approaches.
- Restructure issues in terms of common agendas.

Questions for In-Basket Exercise 3:

1. You are meeting with the top executives of your company, and you are in the hot seat. You need to explain, defend, and recommend action on the sales performance of your staff. You must deal with three very different persons, each with a somewhat different agenda, a different degree of authority and power, and a different personal style. Explore a flexible approach to this situation.

2. How do you deal with the different personality styles of each of the company executives while meeting with all three of them at once? Be specific on your approach at the meeting.

3. Need your behavior change significantly if you meet with each executive separately? Explain.

4. You are meeting with all three executives together. Display flexibility by making a statement that addresses the common agenda, avoids arousing conflicts due to differences in individual agendas, and adapts to the varied styles of the participants.

IN-BASKET EXERCISE 4: HANDLING FEEDBACK

A major part of the manager's responsibility is to give feedback to others. But managers also receive feedback, usually from their own managers. Feedback may be offered informally—over lunch, for example—or in a formal, regularly scheduled performance appraisal. In any event, the purpose of the feedback is to encourage the manager to make adjustments as needed to improve performance.

In the exercise that follows, you will be dealing with a formal performance appraisal, an evaluation of your own performance by the president of your organization.

Situation:

As Kilmer Gordon, plant manager for Plusultra, you are responsible for overall plant management. You supervise other managers. In turn, you report to Ozzie Kliner, president of the firm. You are expected to have a general knowledge of all plant operations, to be able to delegate responsibilities effectively, and to coordinate all production and shipping operations. You also represent the plant in the community.

On your desk is the performance evaluation you have received from Ozzie Kliner, shown in Exhibit 19. The performance appraisal requires you to respond to feedback about your own performance. Read this and then answer the questions that follow. Your flexibility skills will assist you in this task.

Your flexibility skills focus:

- Accept the need for change.
- Find new ways of doing things.
- Change perspectives.

Questions for In-Basket Exercise 4:

1. Kliner has placed responsibility for order conflicts and machine break-downs on you, the plant manager. It would be easy to respond to these statements defensively, since orders are not really under your control and machine breakdowns are usually unforeseen and accidental. However, what would be a more flexible (and hence a more adaptive) way of dealing with this criticism?

2. Kliner's suggestion that you join NAPM could be seen as adding yet another responsibility to your job. However, from another perspective, it would be seen differently. What are some ways you can view this suggestion?

IN-BASKET EXERCISE 5: RESOLVING CONFLICTS

Conflict resolution is an area where flexibility is essential. You can reduce conflict by identifying areas of agreement and using a flexible approach to differences. The following in-basket exercise provides experience in resolving conflicts.

Situation:

In this exercise, you assume the role of Tully Justin, marketing manager for Clayplay. You have been advertising ultralon play and art kits in recreational industry magazines and newspapers.

Glynne Bonney, sales manager, has asked you to encourage retailers to place their own ultralon ads in local newspapers. Bonney suggests that an appropriate way to do this is to offer the retailer advertising allowances. Bonney believes that these allowances are a marketing expense and should be charged to your budget. You disagree. If Bonney wants to offer advertising allowances to retailers, you feel they should be charged to sales. The issue needs to be resolved.

You have reviewed some information about conflicting views of the sales and marketing departments with respect to promotional allowances to retailers. Read the memos in the file shown in Exhibits 20 through 23, and then answer the questions that follow.

Your flexibility skills focus:

- Consider new information.
- Redefine issues.
- Compromise on lesser issues in the interest of furthering broader goals.

Questions for In-Basket Exercise 5:

1. Your (Tully Justin's) memo of October 11 notes that you already have made plans for the remainder of the year. You indicate that you are not willing to change these plans, and you refuse to accept budget responsibility for promotional allowances to retailers. It looks as if you and the sales department are pretty far apart. Generally, what would be a more flexible approach?

2. As marketing manager, you do not oppose promotional allowances. You simply state that you do not consider these to be your responsibility. Your objection appears to be based on the fact that such charges would interfere with your budget. You now have received information that you did not have when you developed this budget—that customers are requesting promotional allowances. Given this information, what would be a flexible way to handle Bonney's request?

ASSESSING CHANGE

The purpose of this module has been to help you develop your flexibility skills through simulated managerial situations. Your attention has been focused on the components that make up flexibility skills. You have seen that flexibility skills involve:

- *Working with new, changing, and ambiguous situations*—In the role of Allie Blauhut, you had to deal with new demands made on your department, change old procedures to meet goals, and continue to manage despite vaguely defined authority limits.
- *Working under pressure*—As Petey Perrin, you were faced with increasing pressures when deadlines were short and assignments extremely demanding. As pressures increased, you had to change your own or others' work assignments, schedules, and priorities.
- *Dealing with different personal styles*—Your task as Glynne Bonney was to meet with three company executives. You had to use flexibility in dealing with their different personalities and diverse personal agendas.
- *Handling feedback*—As Kilmer Gordon, plant manager, you were dealing with a formal performance appraisal, an evaluation of your own performance by the president of your organization.
- *Resolving conflicts*—You assumed the role of Tully Justin and were required to demonstrate flexibility by negotiating and compromising in order to resolve conflicts.

At the beginning of this module, you completed the FBQ assessment instrument to provide a baseline against which you could measure later changes in your flexibility behaviors. Now it is time to assess some of these changes.

First, retake the FBQ. A comparison of your before- and after-practice responses will demonstrate the extent to which you have increased the frequency of your flexibility behaviors. When you have retaken this questionnaire, compare your answers with those you gave earlier to see how much you have strengthened your flexibility skills. Next, you will take the Flexibility Display Scale (FDS) that follows the FBQ.

The Flexible Behaviors Questionnaire (FBQ)

Use the following scale to rate the frequency with which you perform the behaviors described in each question. Place the corresponding number (1–7) in the blank preceding the statement.

Rarely	Irregularly	Occasionally	Usually	Frequently	Almost Always	Consistently
1	2	3	4	5	6	7

_____ **1.** I manage a variety of assignments with varying demands and complexities.

_____ **2.** I adjust work plans to account for new circumstances.

_____ 3. I modify rules and procedures in order to meet operational needs and goals.

_____ 4. I work with ambiguous assignments when necessary and use these when possible to further my goals and objectives.

_____ 5. I rearrange work or personal schedules to meet deadlines.

_____ 6. In emergencies, I respond to the most pressing needs first.

_____ 7. I change my priorities to accommodate unexpected events.

_____ 8. I manage my personal work overload by seeking assistance or by delegating responsibility to others.

_____ 9. I vary the way I deal with others according to their needs and personalities.

_____ 10. I help others improve their job performance or I assign tasks that will further their development.

_____ 11. I accept the authority of my manager but continue to demonstrate my initiative and assertiveness.

_____ 12. I work well with all types of personalities.

_____ 13. I measure my performance on the job against the feedback I receive.

_____ 14. I correct performance deficits that have been brought to my attention.

_____ 15. When I disagree with my manager's appraisal of my work, I discuss our differences.

_____ 16. I seek training and assignments that can help me improve my job-related skills.

_____ 17. In disagreements concerning work-related issues, I look at matters impersonally and concentrate on the facts.

_____ 18. I make compromises to get problems moving toward resolution.

_____ 19. I look for new and better ways to accomplish my duties and responsibilities.

_____ 20. I offer to negotiate all areas of disagreement.

FBQ Scoring and Evaluation

Follow the scoring directions found on page 432 and in Figure 1. Complete the after-practice assessment column for the FBQ and compare your before- and after-practice scores. Plot your after-practice scores in Figure 2. In which categories did your scores improve? Think about what has made your progress possible. Perhaps you can apply your insights to categories where your performance has lagged.

The Flexibility Display Scale (FDS)

Now you are asked to complete another questionnaire, the Flexibility Display Scale (FDS), as a second method to assess change. In the FDS, you assume the role of manager in ten situations. You must select from among several responses the one that in your opinion shows the greatest flexibility given the facts at hand. This questionnaire gives you more insight into your behaviors in situations requiring flexibility skills. Select only one response.

1. You are the manager of the billing department for the Better Foundation Company. You have come to the office on this first day of the company-wide vacation period in order to catch up on some work. You are about to open the office door when you realize that you have left the key to the alarm system locked in your desk. If you open the door without immediately turning off the alarm, it will be set off, and the police will come to the office. Under the circumstances, the most appropriate thing to do is to:

_____ a) Forget the whole idea and go home.

_____ b) Phone your boss and ask him or her to come down to the office with an alarm key.

_____ c) Open the door anyway and explain to the police when they arrive why the alarm went off.

_____ d) Phone the police before entering and explain that the alarm will go off.

_____ e) Wait around in the hope that someone else may show up at the office with an alarm key.

2. You are an attorney. You have just checked your listing in the Yellow Pages. To your dismay, you note that the listed phone number is incorrect. Which is the most appropriate action you could take?

_____ a) Ask for a refund of the charge paid for the listing.

_____ b) Change your phone number to the one shown in the Yellow Pages.

_____ c) Ignore the matter.

_____ d) Contact the phone company and demand that the number shown in the Yellow Pages be answered by a recording that informs the caller of the correct number.

_____ e) Refuse to place any further listings in the Yellow Pages.

3. Jolene Arkin, head teller at the Dexter State Bank, has just asked you, the branch manager, to allow her to go home because she is feeling ill. It is 1 P.M. on Friday, and the traffic in the bank lobby is already backing up. The customers are becoming impatient with the delays. Under the circumstances, which of the following would be the most suitable way for you to handle the matter?

_____ a) Ask Jolene to wait until the crowd thins.

_____ b) Give Jolene permission to leave and close her teller window.

_____ c) Give Jolene permission to leave, and stay at Jolene's window yourself until the crowd thins.

_____ d) Ask a neighboring teller to alternate between his or her own window and Jolene's window.

_____ e) Ask your secretary to take over for Jolene.

4. Eudomics, Inc., is a dating service that prides itself on the careful investigation and selection of registrants. Its purpose is to match people with similar interests and compatible history for a sizable fee. You are the manager of the firm. You have just interviewed an applicant who does not meet the requirements Eudomics sets for its clientele. The applicant is anxious to register. Under the circumstances, the most appropriate thing you can do is to:

_____ a)   Refer the applicant to another service, explaining that this service will better meet his needs.

_____ b)   Tell the applicant that registration is full at the present time and that Eudomics will contact him when registration opens.

_____ c)   Allow the applicant to register, but ignore the registration.

_____ d)   Inform the applicant that he does not meet the Eudomics profile and suggest he try elsewhere.

_____ e)   Suggest that the client make changes that will help him meet your requirements.

5. You are the city manager of Flaxfield. Over the holiday weekend, a severe windstorm damaged the roof of the Flaxfield Public Library. The entire city, including the library, is operating within a tight budget. There is little room for unplanned expenditures. Usually, repairs to city property are taken care of by the four-person city maintenance crew. However, half of the crew has phoned in sick on this first day after the holiday weekend. Further, the city has had little occasion to repair roofs and does not have roofing materials on hand. Under the circumstances, the most appropriate action that you, the city manager, could take is to:

_____ a)   Hire an outside roofer to repair the roof.

_____ b)   Order roofing materials and work with the crew on hand.

_____ c)   Ask the council to approve an emergency appropriation for repair of the library roof at its next meeting, scheduled in two weeks.

_____ d)   Accept the situation and wait until next year to request funds for repairs in the regular budget.

_____ e)   Ask volunteers to repair the roof.

6. The Colfacts Tool Company manufactures tempered steel parts for biomedical instruments. You are the plant manager. Kao Vang, sales manager of Colfacts, has just given you a brochure issued by Nagana, Inc. Nagana produces similar parts overseas. However, its prices are approximately 20 percent below those of Colfacts'. An appropriate way for you to respond is to:

_____ a)   Immediately request an increase in automation at the Colfacts plant.

_____ b)   Ask Vang for more facts on Nagana's products so that a careful comparison can be made between these and Colfacts' products.

_____ c)   Ignore the brochure since price setting is not part of the plant manager's responsibility.

_____ d) Refer the brochure to the comptroller's office and request a cost analysis of Colfacts' plant operations.

_____ e) Ask the executive board to reduce prices.

7. You are the manager of AZY Home Appliances, Inc., in Tremont. AZY sells washing machines, dryers, refrigerators, and other appliances to home builders and to retail customers. Wholesale prices for builders are about one-third below those for individual consumers. There has been little new construction in Tremont. Sales to builders have been sparse. Inventory is aging. According to weekly reports, building permits are up in other cities. Under the circumstances, an appropriate action to take is to:

_____ a) Start a training program for your sales staff.

_____ b) Advertise in out-of-town newspapers.

_____ c) Reduce prices to consumers.

_____ d) Update your inventory in the expectation that building activity will increase in Tremont.

_____ e) Offer additional discounts to builders.

8. You are the principal of the Apple County Public School. Most of the school's students are the children of migrant workers who typically attend for one semester and then move on to another school district, usually out of state. On a recent statewide test, scores for the Apple County School were considerably below statewide norms. There has been much criticism in the press regarding these scores, and District Superintendent Simmie Woods has asked you to respond to the situation. An appropriate response would be to:

_____ a) Send a memo to the teachers and ask for their suggestions.

_____ b) Send letters to the news media noting that migrant children cannot be judged by the same standards as children of a stationary population.

_____ c) Ask Woods for assistance in devising a new curriculum specifically targeted to meet the special needs of migrant children.

_____ d) Ask for a transfer to a new school.

_____ e) Accept the situation and continue with the usual program.

9. You are the plant manager for the Crispy Chip Company, which processes corn and potato chips. In the warehouse storage bins are corn and potatoes. Neither product is in full supply. Unless an additional shipment of corn or potatoes is received, the mash machines will be able to operate for only a few hours for each food item. In addition, the machines and cooking tanks will have to be thoroughly cleaned between each product. These procedures will waste electric power and labor. The processing cannot be postponed without risking spoilage of the potatoes and corn in the warehouse. A way for you to deal with the situation suitably would be to:

_____ a) Accept the overuse of electricity and labor since spoilage of the potatoes and corn will be at least as costly.

_____ b) Create a new product called POCO, a blend of potato and corn mash, and process both corn and potato mash together.

_____ c) Try to find additional shipments of corn and potatoes so that full batches of these can be cooked.

_____ d) Sell the corn and potatoes to a produce wholesaler.

_____ e) Contact your immediate superior and ask for direction.

10. You are a bank examiner for the government regulatory agency. You have inspected the books and records of the Meridian State Bank, and you now need to confer with Hi Faider, vice president in charge of loans. Faider has been out of the office since shortly after you began your examination, and your efforts to reach Faider have been unsuccessful. An appropriate way for you to handle this situation is to:

_____ a) Meet with the president of the bank instead of with Faider.

_____ b) Meet with your own supervisor and report the situation.

_____ c) Write Faider a registered letter and set a date for a meeting.

_____ d) Continue to call Faider until you reach him.

_____ e) Set a meeting date and ask the president of the bank to instruct Faider to be present.

FDS Scoring and Evaluation

Complete the FDS scoring form in Figure 4. Compare and be prepared to discuss your responses with the feedback your instructor provides about the most appropriate responses for the ten flexibility situations.

SUMMARY

This module has explored skills associated with flexibility. It is based upon the viewpoint that the best way to adapt to change is to develop and practice the skills of flexibility.

The purpose of this module has been to provide an opportunity for you to develop flexibility skills through practice. You have assumed many different managerial roles, and you have been placed in varying situations in order to develop flexibility. As noted earlier, flexibility skills are made up of the following behaviors: (1) working with new, changing, and ambiguous situations, (2) working under pressure, (3) dealing with different personal styles, (4) handling feedback, and (5) resolving conflicts.

We presented flexibility as a process in which a series of steps leads to change and adaptive actions. The steps in the flexibility process were (1) generating new

Question	a	b	c	d	e	Response
1						
2						
3						
4						
5						
6						
7						
8						
9						
10						

FIGURE 4
Flexibility Display Scale (FDS) Scoring

perspectives, (2) developing new options, (3) reordering priorities, (4) revising goals, and (5) taking adaptive actions. Adaptive actions will help you deal with the pressures, shifts, conflicts, and differences that you will inevitably face on your job.

In working through this module, you have practiced flexibility in several exercises. Perhaps you have started applying the experience gained in this module to your work situation. If so, you already may have had the pleasure of positive feedback from others. Feedback from persons with whom you work will help you gauge whether or not you are using your flexibility skills in an appropriate manner. Your manager or instructor can help you immeasurably by observing your behavior and providing opportunities for you to use what you have learned. Therefore, by all means, enlist the cooperation of your manager or instructor so that he or she may guide you in the full development of flexibility.

Popular literature warns that organizations' futures depend on their managers' ability to be flexible. Keep in mind that excellent managers continually strive to be flexible and adapt to change.

To remember key steps in practicing flexibility skills and to identify situations in which the skills are needed, use the action guide shown in Figure 5. Frequent review of the information will help you become a more effective manager.

FIGURE 5
Flexibility Skills Action Guide

You Show Flexibility When You:
- Generate new perspectives
- Develop new options
- Reorder priorities
- Revise goals
- Take adaptive actions

You Should Show Flexibility Skills When:
- New, changing, and ambiguous situations must be addressed
- Working under pressure is required
- Various personal styles are presented
- Feedback must be handled
- Conflicts must be resolved

SKILL-BUILDING EXERCISES

EXERCISE 1 ▪ PLANNING FOR CHANGE

As a manager, one of the problems you face involves mistakes made by employees who perform a particular task. The same mistakes seem to occur in more than one department. You believe a training program for the people concerned will help reduce errors.

You are aware, however, that your supervisors may defend existing procedures simply because the introduction of training may imply criticism of the way they have been operating. You realize too, that the supervisors may fear making changes because some employees may be concerned with not doing well in the training program.

Develop a plan, along with a recommendation for your subordinates and supervisors, on how training will be implemented to reduce errors.

EXERCISE 2 ▪ EXAMINING FLEXIBLE BEHAVIOR IN OTHERS

Choose an organization in which you are a member (a place where you are employed, a church, sorority, campus club, or professional group). Describe a situation where a manager showed flexible behavior as described in the module. Be sure to describe specifically how flexibility was demonstrated.

- With reference to the situation, indicate whether you agree or disagree that the action taken by the manager: (1) improved the situation, (2) averted possible problems, (3) was in accord with basic organizational goals, and (4) adapted to situational changes.

- With what you now know about flexibility, would you recommend a different response than the manager chose? If so, describe the flexible action that you would recommend. How could this have affected the outcome?

■ Use Exhibits 1–8 with In-Basket Exercise 1,
Exhibits 3, 9–13 with In-Basket Exercise 2,
Exhibits 14–18 with In-Basket Exercise 3,
Exhibit 19 with In-Basket Exercise 4,
Exhibits 20–23 with In-Basket Exercise 5.

EXHIBIT 1
Plusultra, Inc.
Organizational Chart

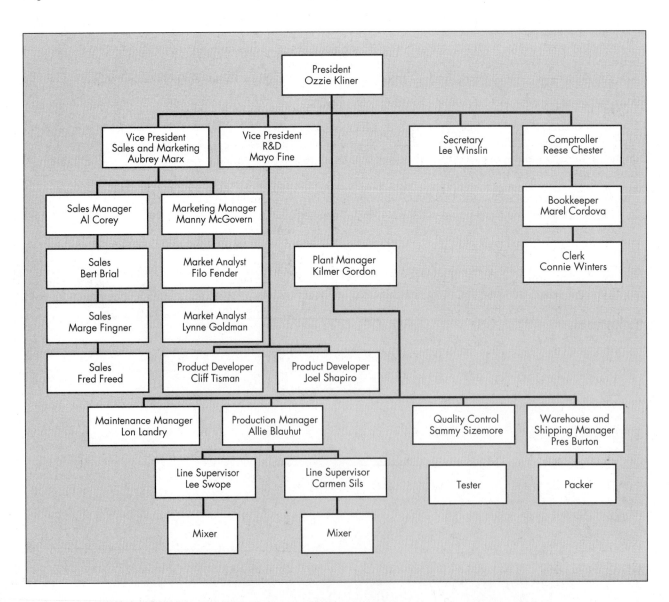

EXHIBIT 2
Clayplay, Inc.
Organizational Chart

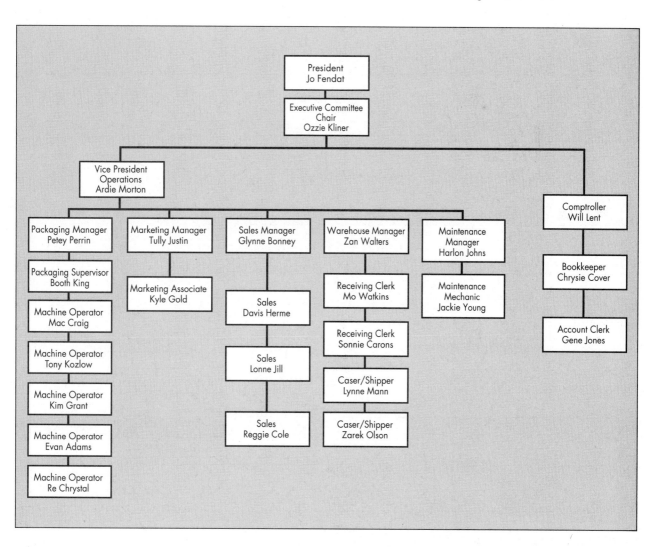

EXHIBIT 3
Calendars – August, September, and
October

AUGUST						
Sunday	Monday	Tuesday	Wednesday	Thursday	Friday	Saturday
			1	2	3	4
5	6	7	8	9	10	11
12	13	14	15	16	17	18
19	20	21	22	23	24	25
26	27	28	29	30	31	

SEPTEMBER						
Sunday	Monday	Tuesday	Wednesday	Thursday	Friday	Saturday
						1
2	3	4	5	6	7	8
9	10	11	12	13	14	15
16	17	18	19	20	21	22
23	24	25	26	27	28	29
30						

OCTOBER						
Sunday	Monday	Tuesday	Wednesday	Thursday	Friday	Saturday
	1	2	3	4	5	6
7	8	9	10	11	12	13
14	15	16	17	18	19	20
21	22	23	24	25	26	27
28	29	30	31			

EXHIBIT 4
Plusultra, Inc.
Memorandum

PLUSULTRA, INC.

MEMORANDUM

TO: Allie Blauhut, Production Manager
FROM: Ozzie Kliner, President
DATE: August 22
RE: TRY EXCELLENCE NOW! (TEN)

As a firm, we have always been good. But in today's business climate, good is not enough. The time has come for us to go for EXCELLENCE!

Toward this end, we are organizing our company into TEN circles. These circles will work with people, problems, and ideas to make us the best we can be.

Everyone in the firm, myself included, will be assigned to a circle. Your circle will deal with problems, processes, and other matters that are under your supervision. It will meet bimonthly at 3 P.M. The first meeting is today, August 22.

The following persons have been assigned to your circle: Lon Landry (Maintenance Manager), Carmen Sils (Line Supervisor), Myra Holt (Tester), Bert Brial (Sales), Marel Cordova (Bookkeeper), Twyla Freed (Mixer), Tony Marcu (Mixer), Filo Fender (Market Analyst), Joel Shapiro (Product Developer), and, of course, yourself.

It is expected that the circles will reach recommendations by consensus. Input is expected from every member. I suggest you think of an agenda for your initial meeting. Include problems you face and procedures that can be improved. Later agendas can be established by the circle.

PLUSULTRA, INC.

MEMORANDUM

TO: Kilmer Gordon, Plant Manager
FROM: Allie Blauhut, Production Manager
DATE: August 22
RE: Production Schedule Report

The shipment of K-287 on which we are now working is due at the Southwestern Insecticide Company on August 27.

According to plan, processing of this K-287 order will be completed today August 22, at 3 P.M. Packing and shipping will be finished by 5 P.M. on August 24. This should give us plenty of time to meet the promised delivery date, using our usual commercial carrier.

Following the completion of this K-287 order, the mixing machines will have to be thoroughly cleaned (see notice below posted by Quality Control) so that work can begin on the ultralon order from Clayplay Inc. Cleaning is scheduled for August 25 and 26. Processing of ultralon can then begin promptly at 8 A.M. on Monday, August 27.

NOTICE FROM QUALITY CONTROL

TO AVOID PRODUCT CONTAMINATION, MIXING MACHINES MUST BE THOROUGHLY CLEANED BEFORE PROCESSING NEW COMPOUNDS.

EXHIBIT 5
Plusultra, Inc.
Memorandum

EXHIBIT 6
Plusultra, Inc.
Memorandum

PLUSULTRA, INC.

MEMORANDUM

TO: Allie Blauhut, Production Manager
FROM: Kilmer Gordon, Plant Manager
DATE: August 22
RE: New Order for K-287

We have just received a new order for K-287 from the Gamson Corporation. The order does not specify a delivery date, so I assume there is no pressure to get this out. However, we can save two days of downtime for cleaning of machines if we work on this immediately before starting on the ultralon order.

Delivery dates are not specified for ultralon either. We have been quite loose on ultralon deliveries possibly because of our close connection with Clayplay (As you know, Clayplay, in effect, is a marketing arm for ultralon.) Do what you think is best, but keep those cost factors in mind.

CLAYPLAY, INC.
ORANGE LANE
CITY

"Distributors of Creative Play Materials"

President, Jo Fendat

August 22

Dear Kilmer:

Our ultralon orders are delivered helter skelter, with no apparent attention to when they are placed. Under the circumstances, we find it hard to plan our own deliveries to our customers. We must do something about this situation.

When can we meet to discuss this?

Sincerely,

Jo Fendat

Jo Fendat
President

EXHIBIT 7
Clayplay, Inc.
Letter

EXHIBIT 8
Clayplay, Inc.
Letter

CLAYPLAY, INC.
ORANGE LANE
CITY

President, Jo Fendat

August 25

Ozzie Kliner, President
Plusultra, Inc.
149 Mayfair Place

Dear Ozzie:

I am sending this note by special courier to inform you that we are quadrupling our previous order for ultralon.

The United Hospital Group, which as you know operates 150 psychiatric hospitals throughout the country, has contracted with us to use ultralon in the occupational therapy programs of all of its facilities. The order not only is a substantial one but represents a major breakthrough to the health industry for Clayplay.

Our initial order will be used by United's new unit in Harnell and should be at Clayplay by 9/5 so we can package it and get it to Harnell in time for the unit's open house on 9/9.

Best Regards,

Jo Fendat

Jo Fendat, President,
Clayplay, Inc.

cc: Kilmer Gordon, Plant Manager, Plusultra, Inc.
         Allie Blauhut, Production Manager, Plusultra, Inc.

CLAYPLAY, INC.

MEMORANDUM

TO: All Managers
FROM: Jo Fendat, President
DATE: September 27
RE: Profit Margins

Rising prices for materials, utilities, etc., have cut into the company's profits. Therefore, I am asking each manager to review his or her area of responsibility to see where costs can be shaved.

As a general policy, overtime is to be discouraged because it requires premium pay. Also, you must do everything you can to reduce waste and spoilage. This involves, among other things, more efficient weighing of ultralon for packaging and more careful handling of the packaging materials and boxes. Too many boxes are damaged because of careless handling.

Remember, you can reduce the cost of operations by avoiding overtime and by eliminating waste. Both your performance ratings and your year-end bonuses will reflect your success in this endeavor.

EXHIBIT 9
Clayplay, Inc.
Memorandum

EXHIBIT 10
Clayplay, Inc.
Work Order

CLAYPLAY, INC.
WORK ORDER

DATE: October 2

COMPANY NAME: Zuyder Art Supplies, Inc.

COMPANY CLASSIFICATION: Wholesaler/jobber.
                                  Distributes to retail stores.

ORDER SIZE: 1000 cases art kit packaged ultralon
                                  (Small size, retail wrap).

WORK BEGINS: October 5, start of workday, 8 A.M.

COMPLETION DATE: October 17, close of workday, 5 P.M.

ORDER DUE DATE: To be received by Zuyder on
                                  October 19

TIME/HOUR ESTIMATE: Packaging: 360 hours
                                  Preparations for Shipping: 16 hours

ASSIGNED TO: Booth King, Packaging Supervisor

COMMENTS: Zuyder is using ultralon in a promo-
                                  tional deal with 500 retailers. Flyers
                                  which promote ultralon will be mailed
                                  on October 19. Sale begins October
                                  22. Zuyder says that ultralon pack-
                                  ages must be in retail stores as of that
                                  date. Arrange work schedule accord-
                                  ingly. Please remember that Jo Fendat
                                  does not want us to schedule overtime!

S/PP
     Petey Perrin, Packaging Manager
S/BK 6K
     Booth King, Packaging Supervisor

CLAYPLAY, INC.
ZUYDER ART SUPPLIES
HOURS WORK SHEET

Required packaging machine time:	360 hours
Number of machines:	5
Number of machine operators:	5
Scheduled hours per work day:	8
Total available work hours per scheduled work day:	40
Days required for packaging:	360 / 40 = 9
Required casing hours:	16 hours
Number of cases:	2
Scheduled hours per work day:	8
Total available work hours per scheduled work day:	16
Days required for casing:	16 / 16 = 1

SCHEDULE

Begin packaging:	October 5, start of business, 8 A.M.
Finish packaging:	October 15, close of business, 5 P.M.
Begin casing:	October 16, start of business, 8 A.M.
Finish easing:	October 16, close of business, 5 P.M.
Ship to Zuyder:	October 17
Received by Zuyder:	October 18 – October 19

s/
   Booth King, Packaging Supervisor
s/
   Zan Walters, Warehouse Manager

DATE: October 2

EXHIBIT 11
Clayplay, Inc.
Zuyder Art Supplies
Hours Work Sheet

EXHIBIT 12
Clayplay, Inc.
Memorandum

CLAYPLAY, INC.

MEMORANDUM

TO: Petey Perrin, Packaging Manager
FROM: Booth King, Packaging Supervisor
DATE: October 15
RE: Machine Repair

_____

Due to the breakdown of one of our packaging machines, we are two days behind schedule on the Zuyder order. We can make this up with overtime. Do we have your okay?

EXHIBIT 13
Clayplay, Inc.
Emergency Memorandum

CLAYPLAY, INC.

EMERGENCY   MEMORANDUM

DELIVER IMMEDIATELY!

TO: Ardie Morton, Vice President Operations
FROM: Jo Fendat, President
DATE: October 15
RE: Special Order

_____

Ardie, this is urgent. We need to ship three bulk-packaged cases of ultralon to Dexter University immediately. Dexter is using ultralon in an experimental study which will be worthless unless the order is sent at once.

Signed: _____

_____

ROUTE TO: Petey Perrin
FROM: Ardie Morton   REPLY IMMEDIATELY!
DATE: October 15

Petey,

Please take care of this.

Signed: _____

EXHIBIT 14
Profiles

PROFILES

Jo Fendat, President, Clayplay, Inc.

Fendat has a relaxed, easy manner; shows a personal interest in plant employees at all levels; greets them by first name; and asks about their families, their plans, and their problems.

Fendat believes firmly in participative management. She makes a point of seeking input from production line workers as well as from managers and supervisors. She is likely to ask your opinions on policy issues and to solicit suggestions for handling all types of problems. She is not likely to express her opinions until yours have been heard first. Fendat likes to consider all aspects of a problem and encourages individuality and independent judgment. She approaches proposals and comments analytically, using general principles and logic in evaluations. She is the chief executive officer of Clayplay and now owns 25 percent of its stock.

Ardie Morton, Vice President, Operations, Clayplay, Inc.

Ardie Morton regards selling as a game in which there are winners and losers. He has a strong need to win consistently and is competitive and persuasive. Morton believes that a good salesperson can sell anything to anyone. He expects maximum performance from sales and marketing staffs and is impatient with excuses. He can be charming and sympathetic when things look good, but abrasive when expectations are not met. His approach to problems is factual and concrete. Above all, Morton is a pragmatist. He believes what works is good and vice versa. Like Fendat, Morton owns 25 percent of Clayplay.

Ozzie Kliner, Executive Committee Chair, Clayplay, Inc.

Kliner's leadership style is directive and authoritarian. He accepts input from subordinates but rarely relinquishes decision-making authority. As principal owner of Plusultra and equal shareholder of Clayplay, he commands and enjoys great authority in the affairs of both of these firms. From Kliner's perspective, the sole purpose of Clayplay is to market ultralon. Although there is considerable overlap, his interests are not identical to those of the other Clayplay shareholders. Hence, Kliner may see things somewhat differently from Fendat and Morton.

EXHIBIT 15
Clayplay, Inc.
Memorandum

CLAYPLAY, INC.

MEMORANDUM

TO: Ardie Morton, Vice President
FROM: Glynne Bonney, Sales Manager
DATE: August 9
RE: Ultralon Sales

I am attaching two graphs which pertain to sales. From the line graph, you can see that, overall, we are maintaining last year's sales levels.

Since we are part of the toy and hobby industry I have also included industry sales on the graph. In making comparisons, bear in mind that we have only one product to sell, ultralon. Because of this, our sales movements will not necessarily parallel those of the industry as a whole.

In the attached histogram, sales shares of our sales staff are shown for this year and last. Reggie Cole is moving ahead of the others. Reggie says that he persuades his accounts to use prominent in-store displays. This seems to be an effective way to increase sales to the consumer.

Considering that we are a relatively young firm and marketing a relatively new product, I think we have done well. However, I believe that there are two steps we can take that will increase sales significantly. First we can market more aggressively, and second we can diversify our product lines.

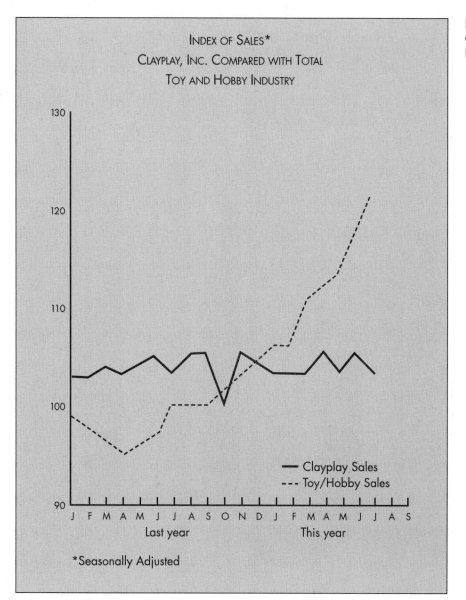

EXHIBIT 16
Clayplay, Inc.
Index of Sales

EXHIBIT 17
Clayplay, Inc.
Percent of Clayplay Dollar Sales
Generated by Sales Staff Members

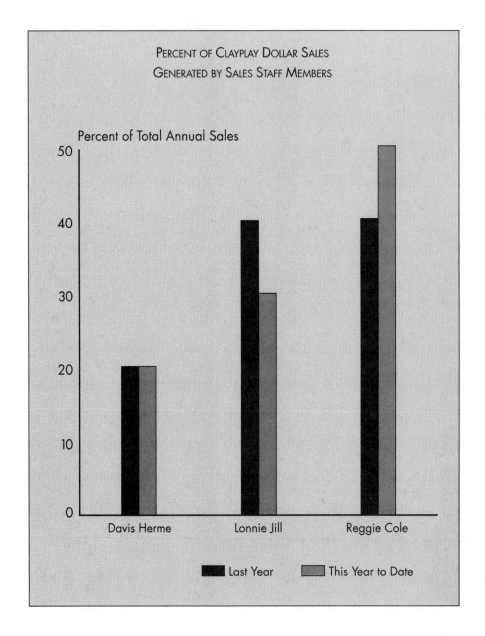

PERCENT OF CLAYPLAY DOLLAR SALES
GENERATED BY SALES STAFF MEMBERS

CLAYPLAY, INC.

MEMORANDUM

TO: Ardie Morton, Vice President
FROM: Jo Fendat, President
DATE: August 8
RE: Sales of Clayplay

Why are our sales moving sideways when the rest of the industry is moving up? Let's call in Glynne. I'll also get in touch with Ozzie and maybe together we can brainstorm our way out of this rut. We'll meet in my office on August 10th at 10 A.M.

FOLLOW-UP MEMORANDUM

TO: Glynne Bonney, Sales Manager
FROM: Ardie Morton, Vice President
DATE: August 9
RE: Sales Review Meeting

This is to remind you that you and I will be meeting with the Executive Committee Chair, Ozzie Kliner, and President Jo Fendat at 10 A.M. tomorrow to review sales. Fendat is particularly concerned about the fact that we are lagging behind the industry in gains over last year. Be prepared to discuss this matter.

EXHIBIT 18
Clayplay, Inc.
Memorandum

EXHIBIT 19
Plusultra, Inc.
Performance Appraisal Summary

PLUSULTRA, INC.

PERFORMANCE APPRAISAL SUMMARY

NAME: Kilmer Gordon

POSITION: Plant Manager

RATING SCALE

RATING	INTERPRETATION
1	Unsatisfactory
2	Needs Improvement .
3	Average
4	Above Average
5	Superior
6	Excellent

PERFORMANCE RATINGS

PERFORMANCE AREA	RATING
Planning	4
Coordination	4
Supervising	5
Staffing	5
Interpersonal sensitivity	6
Community representation	6
Overall average	5

COMMENTS:

Overall, this is a creditable rating. Improvement in planning and coordination would improve your performance. Specifically, there have been a few conflicts this past year in scheduling ultralon production and other compounds. As you know, we use the same machines for all compounds, so we can only mix one at a time. Better planning could have avoided situations in which ultralon and other orders apparently had to be filled at the same time. We could, for example, maintain a stock of ultralon rather than simply mix it on order. Also, maintenance operations should be scheduled more regularly to avoid machine breakdowns.

Other aspects of plant operations have been superior.

You are to be commended for your excellent rapport with the managers you supervise and for your ability to staff appropriately. Also, we have received excellent feedback from community organizations in which you serve. As a member of the mayor's Environmental Protection Committee, you have promoted an image of Plusultra as a responsible firm in the community.

We would like to see you become more active in the National Association of Plant Managers (NAPM). Contact with other plant managers will keep you in touch with the state of the art in your field.

Ozzie Kliner

Ozzie Kliner
President, Plusultra, Inc.

s/

EXHIBIT 20
Clayplay, Inc.
Memorandum

CLAYPLAY, INC.

MEMORANDUM

TO: Tully Justin, Marketing Manager
FROM: Glynne Bonney, Sales Manager
DATE: October 10
RE: Advertising Allowances

Tully, please review the attached letter. It is typical of many requests we have received recently.

This is the time that retailers plan their holiday promotions. We'd really boost sales if our accounts featured ultralon kits in their holiday ads. As you know, it is customary for suppliers to offer advertising promotional allowances to retailers for this purpose.

Promotional allowances are properly a marketing responsibility, so the decision is yours. It is customary to charge these allowances to the marketing budget. The sales department has no funds allocated for promotional purposes.

EXHIBIT 21
Modern Malleables
Letter

MODERN MALLEABLES
PURVEYORS OF ART AND HOBBY SUPPLIES
250 CACY ROAD

October 5

Glynne Bonney, Sales Manager
Clayplay
Orange Lane
City

Dear Glynne:

We are planning our advertising for the holiday and post-holiday sales. We would like to feature ultralon kits. The material is new and has unique qualities. We think it will catch on. Most of our suppliers offer advertising allowances for this purpose. Does your firm offer promotional advertising allowances?

Sincerely,

Mark Winer
President

EXHIBIT 22
Clayplay, Inc.
Memorandum

CLAYPLAY, INC.

MEMORANDUM

TO: Glynne Bonney, Sales Manager
FROM: Tully Justin, Marketing Manager
DATE: October 11
RE: Advertising Allowances

We have already planned our ad expenses for the remainder of the year. We have not included allowances for retailers. Since these allowances are directly connected to individual sales accounts, they should be charged to sales anyway. So, if you want them, you pay for them. They are a cost of sales item, in our view.

EXHIBIT 23
Excerpt from *The Merry Marketeer,*
October Issue

EXCERPT FROM *THE MERRY MARKETER,* OCTOBER ISSUE

Marketing is the flip side of sales and vice versa. Both divisions have the same goal, to increase sales. Interdivisional rivalry between these two departments makes no sense at all. One cannot succeed without the other. Studies show that marketing efforts are most successful when there is close cooperation with the sales division.

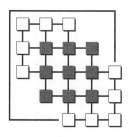

INDEX